1996

From Mouse
to Mermaid

From Mouse

The Politics of Film, Gender, and Culture

to Mermaid

Elizabeth Bell, Lynda Haas, Laura Sells

EDITORS

Indiana University Press

BLOOMINGTON AND INDIANAPOLIS

The paper used in this publication meets the minimum
requirements of American National Standard for
Information Sciences—Permanence of Paper for Printed
Library Materials, ANSI Z39.48-1984.

Manufactured in the United States of America

Library of Congress Cataloging-in-Publication Data

From mouse to mermaid : the politics of film, gender, and culture /
Elizabeth Bell, Lynda Haas, Laura Sells, editors.
p.   cm.
Includes bibliographical references and index.
ISBN 0-253-32905-1 (cl : alk. paper). — ISBN 0-253-20978-1 (pa :
alk. paper)
1. Walt Disney Company.   2. Disney, Walt, 1901–1966—Criticism and
interpretation.   3. Children's films—Political aspects.   I. Bell,
Elizabeth, date.   II. Haas, Lynda.   III. Sells, Laura.
PN1999.W27F76   1995
791.43′75′0973—dc20   94-49374

1 2 3 4 5   00 99 98 97 96 95

For the children in our lives
who showed us Disney again
(and again and again):
Miranda, Meredith, Will, Duncan, Bethan, Danny, and Willow

Contents

Contents

Acknowledgments

From the conception of this project three years ago, we frequently envisioned the task of acknowledging the people who helped shape this book. Now, finally, at its culmination, our words on paper in no way match the eloquence of our daydreams.

A number of people contributed to this project from the beginning with their support, encouragement, and inspiration. Constance Penley and Ava Collins gave us a place to start, pointing out the need for Disney film scholarship; David Bleich, Henry Giroux, and Jack Zipes lent us their prominent names and the courage to pursue the book; and Linda Lopez McAlister and Gary Olson showed us the way to publish.

Three organizations provided us with forums and receptive audiences for our initial analyses of Disney film: the International Association for the Fantastic in the Arts (IAFA), the Southeast Women's Studies Association (SEWSA), and the Southern States Communication Association (SSCA). Each conference bolstered our confidence in this project.

The people of the Department of Communication at the University of South Florida deserve our special acknowledgment. Terrence Albrecht and Kenneth Cissna created a graduate level course in analysis of Disney film—a space and place to "field test" many of the essays and ideas in this book. We are especially indebted to the students in this class; they always kept us honest. Sue Viens, Connie Hackworth, and T. J. Couch provided clerical and technical support, always graciously and always under deadlines.

Joan Catapano and LuAnne Holladay of Indiana University Press contributed, much more than they know, to making this book a reality.

Our friends and families come last, even though they have endured, more than anyone, the Disneyfication of our friendships and of our lives. Our thanks to June Casagrande for reminding us of our audience, to Mary Pharr for her wit and wisdom, to Tonja Olive for her joyful participation in the early stages of the project, and to Linda Forbes for her very presence. David Payne, Robert Haas, and Teresa Patriarco made room for Disney in their lives—and in ours.

And, of course, no acknowledgment would be complete without thanking our wives who typed the manuscript.

From Mouse
to Mermaid

Introduction
Walt's in the Movies

Elizabeth Bell, Lynda Haas, and Laura Sells

We just make the pictures, and let the professors tell us what they mean.
—Walt Disney

As you know, all of our valuable properties, characters, and marks are
protected under copyright and trademark law and any unauthorized use
of our protected material would constitute infringements of our rights
under said law.
—Editors' correspondence with the Walt Disney Company

The original animator of Mickey Mouse, Ub Iwerks, first met Walt Disney
in 1919 at the Kansas City Film Ad Company. Iwerks relates that the seventeen-year-old Disney was seated at a drawing board, practicing variations on
his signature (Schickel 1968, 59). For all the achievements—good or ill—at-
tributed to Walt Disney, perhaps none so well typifies the Disney empire's
cultural capital as this prophetic act of creating, coding, and owning the
Disney name. Indeed, this book treats Disney film as cultural capital—its
production, its semiotics, its audiences, its ideologies. But this book does not
bear the Disney name.

The working title for this book was *Doing Disney: Critical Dialogues in
Film, Gender, and Culture.* When we corresponded with Disney personnel
to gain access to the Disney archives in Buena Vista, California, we were
informed that Disney does not allow third-party books to use the name
"Disney" in their titles—this implies endorsement or sponsorship by the
Disney organization. Our authors responded to this news with academic
wrath and ideas for subversive publishing strategies.[1] Because we were denied
his patriarchal nomenclature, we considered following the Old Testament
Hebrew practice of referring to God by some other name. Our favorite sug-
gestion was made by Kenneth Payne (the Oklahoma native described in
David Payne's *Bambi* essay): "Well," he offered, "you just write them back.
Tell them every time you'd write 'Walt Disney' in the book, you'll write 'Ole
Chickenshit.' " *Doing Chickenshit, The Mousing of America, Call Me
Walt/Don't Call Me Walt, From Mickeywood to Minnie's World, Thoroughly
Postmodern Minnie, Critical Essays on the Films of You-Know-Who,* are all at-

Elizabeth Bell, Lynda Haas, and Laura Sells

tempts to *name* a collection of essays on the films of Walt Disney, while enjoying none of the symbolic and real power of ownership that Disney holds in its litigious grip.

Yet the authors in this volume all "own" the name Disney, despite the Disney Corporation's denial of permission for its use. And the Disney name is used in the essays collected here in a variety of ways. First, Disney is Walt: the seventeen-year-old who practiced his signature and subsequently wrote it on the title frame of each film his company created; the kindly "Uncle Walt" who addressed us on Sunday evenings as host of *The Wonderful World of Color*; the FBI informant who gave J. Edgar Hoover access to film scripts; the man who died on December 15, 1966, in St. Joseph's Hospital across the street from his Burbank studio; the cryogenically frozen body of urban legend that sleeps somewhere deep in the bowels of Disneyland. Second, Disney is a Studio: a production facility that grew from one camera in Disney's Uncle Bob's garage in 1923 to its 1990s multiple incarnations as Walt Disney Pictures, Touchstone, Hollywood, Caravan, the many subsidiaries of Buena Vista Television and the Disney Channel, as well as the recent studio acquisitions Miramax and Merchant/Ivory. Third, Disney is a canon of popular film. Between 1939 and 1992, the feature-length productions alone number 245, only seventy-seven of which were produced while Walt was alive. Fourth, Disney is a multinational corporation: in 1940, public stock in the Disney Company sold for $5 a share and today Disney is an entertainment and media conglomerate worth an estimated $4.7 billion. And fifth, Disney is an ideology: a sign whose mythology and cultural capital is dependent on and imbricated in all the above manifestations of the name "Disney."

Explicating Disney ideology through fifty-five years of feature films is an undercurrent of all the essays in this collection. The authors attempt to navigate the discourses of texts, audiences, and culture "as certain specific rhetorical and representation techniques which, when internalized, give rise to particular ways of constructing (perceiving and acting in) the social world" (Ryan and Kellner 1990, 15). The rhetoric in and of Disney film, however, requires a kind of critical self-reflexivity: an examination of the ways in which we as audience members internalize, construct, and, indeed, enjoy the "Disney magic." The title of Jack Zipes's essay, "Breaking the Disney Spell," offers an important challenge for all the authors here—only when we "break the spell" that places Disney in critically untouchable territory can we, as cultural critics of film, interrogate the "magic" there. "Breaking the Disney Spell" is a methodological entree that allows critics to develop vocabularies for the political in the seemingly apolitical world of Disney; to intervene in Disney's construction of gender, identity, and culture in the seemingly ahistorical world of Disney; and to enable oppositional readings—readings from the margins of the Disney text.

Interrogating the political stakes at the crossroads of Disney, Disney audiences, and Disney films is treacherous critical terrain: legal institutions, film theorists, cultural critics, and loyal audiences all guard the borders of Disney film as "off limits" to the critical enterprise, constructing Disney as metonym for "America"—clean, decent, industrious, "the happiest place on earth."[2]

The films and their concomitant "properties" made in this "happy" place are (self-)righteously protected by Disney within the U.S. legal system, even to the point of suing a Spring Hill, Florida, man for his "unauthorized use" of Disney characters as tattoos over 90 percent of his body.[3] Disney's "suit-happy" attitude is one of many mechanisms that constrain, if not censor and repress, the critical enterprise. Disney's main argument against so-called trademark-copyright infringement is loss of sales. When critical discourse about public (and political) texts is repressed because profits are threatened, Disney becomes anecdotal of the tensions between cultural critique and institutional containment of resistance. Having inserted itself into both the cultural register of common sense as well as the political, economic and ideological institutions of our society, Disney capitalizes on its status to the point where criticizing Disney is a kind of secular sacrilege.[4] Disney's overwhelming protectiveness of its cultural capital through the creation of a very deep "back stage" suggests that there is indeed something to protect. (Conspiracy theories aside, just where is Walt's frozen body stored?)

For film theorists, whether schooled in auteur theory of the 1960s or the gendered politics of spectatorship of the next two decades, this "happy place" of Disney film remains outside the critical landscape. Walt Disney as *auteur du cinema* strikes a dissonant, if not laughable, chord; male gaze so pertinent and insightful when explicated in Hollywood classic film turns absurd in *101 Dalmatians*; a Lacanian reading of Pinocchio's oedipal desires seems guilty of "stretching the point." The high theories of film as art not only ignore the Disney canon, but render suspect and expose the biases of their critical intervention. Not unlike certain relatives forcing their feet into Cinderella's shoe, Disney film is the ugly stepsister unfit for the glass slipper of high theory. With no conventional system or vocabulary for approaching Disney film, film theory ultimately protects and preserves the inviolability of the Disney canon and its status as American metonym. In this case, "American" Disney is below artistic and critical worth.

Those cultural critics who are attracted by "the popular" also absolve Disney film by omission.[5] Under critical surveillance by a barrage of ethnogra-

Elizabeth Bell, Lynda Haas, and Laura Sells

phers and cultural critics, Disney/Lands have become *de rigueur* sites for investigating cultural inscription. Against the "thick description" and somatic space of Disney/Lands, the flat space of film is decidedly unattractive, again the ugly stepsister of cultural critique. This critical exclusion of Disney film as political culture glosses over the fact that while middle-class families might vacation annually in Disney/Lands, broader audiences own Disney film again and again in the protected space of everyday filmic consumption.

Where cultural critics and film theorists omit Disney, popular critics and mass audiences valorize Disney as safe for children and a good investment for parents. In this space, Disney film is not beneath artistic attention, but above reproach. Even our own students, occupying a halfway house between film critics and mass audience, are extremely resistant to critique of Disney film. Assigned to read several essays from this collection for a class in cultural studies, our students commonly complained, "You're reading too much into this film!" and "You can't say that about Walt Disney!" These students consistently cite four easy pardons for their pleasurable participation in Disney film and its apolitical agendas: it's only for children, it's only fantasy, it's only a cartoon, and it's just good business. These four naturalizations create a Disney text exempt from material, historical, and political influences. The naturalized Disney text is "pure entertainment," somehow centrifuged from ideological forces; the naturalized Disney text is reducible to animated fairy-tale classics, even when only six feature films in the Disney canon fulfill this criterion; the naturalized Disney text is exemplary of successful American free enterprise, despite the corporation's lesser known financial failures and brushes with bankruptcy.

Our students' attitudes suggest that Disney successfully invites mass audiences to set aside critical faculties. Indeed, because we too are admiring fans who look forward to each new film release or theme park addition, the naturalized Disney text suggests that we as cultural critics should recognize and ask questions about our own pleasures and participation in Disney film. As Lawrence Grossberg suggests, "The fact that people cannot be treated as cultural dopes does not mean, however, that they are not often duped" (1993, 64, n8). Our own posture as cultural critics or organic intellectuals does not obviate our presence in the very ideology in which we hope to intervene.

U.S. legal institutions, film theorists, cultural critics, and faithful audiences all participate in Disney's self-proclaimed status as metonymic America; the bald eagle, however, is replaced by the equally iconic and symbolically loaded Mickey Mouse. The pleasures of participating in Disney film are necessarily tempered by the dangers of this metonymic construction.

If Disney film as *metonym* for America troubles both pleasure and critique, then a converse construction is equally troublesome: Disney as *monolith*. A monolithic Disney—a master trope for all the symbolic meanings of late-capitalist society—loads Disney with the dominant cultural myths of U.S. ideology. When all Disney texts are read as political, intentional, and hegemonic, cultural critics totalize and, ultimately, reify Disney's corporate acumen and ingenious ability to keep a finger on the pulse of America. This reification robs Disney texts of the very material relations and political realities of their production. Disney, too, contributes to the monolithic myth by hiding the immense industrial machinery of its cultural and symbolic production under the labels "the Disney magic," "pure Disney imagination," and "America's Best Loved Son." Disney film is an important place to begin to examine both metonymic and monolithic constructions of the Disney Corporation and its commercial products. As a production conglomerate releasing a staggering fifty films per year, Disney sends out too many "signals" to be policed from a center that cannot possibly remain fixed (Hartley 1983).

The ideological center that *does* hold, against both metonymic and monolithic constructions, is the "trademark" of Disney innocence that masks the personal, historical, and material relationship between Disney film and politics. Marc Eliot's 1993 biography reveals Disney's status as FBI informant, a role that is not surprising considering Disney's long-standing relationship with the federal government. Not only did the U.S. military commandeer the Disney studio as barracks in 1941, but the federal government underwrote Disney's production of military training films, educational projects, and blatantly propagandistic "cartoons" for popular indoctrination. In 1941 alone, government subsidies brought $2.6 million into the Disney Studio (Holliss and Sibley 1988, 47). During World War II Disney created the animated short, *Victory through Air Power*, explicitly designed to sway both government and public opinion in favor of large-scale strategic bombing (Jewett and Lawrence 1977, 137–38). The U.S. State Department recognized the potential for "direct propaganda films couched in the simplicity of the animation medium," and recruited Walt Disney as goodwill ambassador in South America to counter Nazi propaganda. Walt's South American tour resulted in a series of films designed to "show the truth about the American way [and] carry a message of democracy and friendship below the Rio Grande" (Burton 1992, 55). This project culminated in *The Three Caballeros* (1945), whose revenues saved Walt Disney Productions from impending bankruptcy caused, in part, by a very bitter labor strike. Walt, of course, was thoroughly convinced that the studio strike was "Communistically inspired" (Mosley 1985, 196). The trade-marked Disney innocence is not divorced from politics.

For conspiratorialists and political economists, the Disney story turns interesting again in the turbulent '60s and '70s when the Disney magic ran increasingly dry, whether explained as mismanagement or an inability to find America's entertainment pulse during volatile social and political times. The revitalization of the Disney imagination in the 1980s, under the leadership of Michael Eisner, Jeffrey Katzenberg, and the late Frank Wells, was the product of "a team of high-powered and successful executives unlike any a Hollywood company had ever put together. The team was eventually dubbed 'Team Disney' " (Grover 1991, 50). The rebirth of the "Disney magic" is an apt sequel to the original Disney-as-Horatio-Alger story. For once again, individual vision, imagination, and hard work are the ingredients of the American success story. From the fear of Communism of the 1940s to the celebration of late capitalism of the 1990s, the cloak of Disney's successful innocence hides the enormity of its political and economic reach:

> The Walt Disney company not only makes movies and runs the world's various Disneylands, it owns the Disney Channel and a TV station, it records music and publishes books, it buys books to make into movies that are shown on its cable channel and it licenses and produces songs and stories to publishers. Half a dozen other multinational media conglomerates do more or less the same thing: Time Warner, Times Mirror, Rupert Murdoch's News Corporation, Hearst, Bertelsmann. Their growing power to control the written word is bad news for readers, and for writers. (Weiner 1993, 743)

The $4.7 billion backdrop of the political economy of Disney films belies the naturalized Disney text, divorced from social and material influences.

Disney's innocence also masks a long-standing relationship between entertainment and pedagogy. When Disney's Hyperion Avenue Studio was financed in the early 1940s, bankers would not agree to the loan unless the building could be easily adapted to other, less financially risky, uses: "the building designated on the original ground plan as a school became, ignominiously enough, the headquarters for the publicity department" (Schickel 1968, 199). The Disney "blueprint" for education and enterprise continues. The 1965 Annual Report from the Disney company states that

> an estimated 55,000 different 16mm prints of Disney films (ranging from *Donald Duck in Mathmagic Land* . . . to *You the Human Animal.* . . .) are currently in circulation around the world. More than 2,000 clients rent or lease these films each year, including school systems [and] public libraries. (Qtd. in Holliss and Sibley 1988, 117)

The "sanitary happiness" of Disney film has long enjoyed the dubious distinction as the "finest example of educational entertainment" (Jewett and

Lawrence 1977, 140). In 1988 Disney purchased Childcraft, a successful maker of educational toys. In the 1990s, Disney sponsors "Teacher of the Year" awards and "Doer and Dreamer" scholarship awards to U.S. high school students, and offers free admission programs to Florida school children during the slow season in its Florida theme parks. Disney has so successfully blurred the border between entertainment and pedagogy that it has become, in Althusser's idiom, a "public school system":

> Althusser's claim that the school is the chief ideological state apparatus may hold for the production of the *symbolic* system, that constellation of signs and codes through which is construed the field of what counts as reliable knowledge. But the mass media construct the *social imaginary*, the place where kids situate themselves in their emotional life, where the future appears as a narration of possibilities as well as limits. (Aronowitz 1992, 195)

The situation of children and adults in a narratively constructed "social imaginary" finds Disney, not absolved for its fantasy and cartoon worlds, but directly accountable for them.

Mapping the ideological contours of economics, politics, and pedagogy by drawing Disney films as vehicles of cultural production is the project of this book. Despite Disney's innocent posture and open invitation ("We just make the pictures and let the professors tell us what they mean"), nothing in the Disney terrain is absent of border guards. The "professors" included in this book all cross the critical periphery of Disney's land and survey the complex intersections among texts, audiences, and the political and cultural economies of Disney film. Textual criticism is one place to begin to draw this map.

Disney's trademarked innocence operates on a systematic sanitization of violence, sexuality, and political struggle concomitant with an erasure or repression of difference. This collection, then, is organized into three sections: Sanitizations/Disney Film as Cultural Pedagogy; Contestations/Disney Film as Gender Construction; and Erasures/Disney Film as Identity Politics. Each phrase acknowledges Disney's hegemonic and capitalistic urge, as well as the critical possibilities for alternative, oppositional, and pleasurable appropriations of Disney film.

Disney is often described as the "Great Sanitizer," a label applied to both applaud and condemn his works. Situating Disney in the early days of Hollywood film and the Hayes Commission's morality codes, Jewett and Lawrence maintain that "Walt Disney needed no censor because he had internalized the values of the American public that had given the code its

Elizabeth Bell, Lynda Haas, and Laura Sells

distinctive shape. He operated happily within the limits of 'the Code' because it expressed his own sense of decency and artistic merit" (1977, 126).
The essays in Section One testify that Disney has raised sanitization to even
greater levels of sophistication. Disney film not only "cleans up" history and
political struggles, nature and culture, gender and sex/uality, but elevates
sanitization to pedagogy. The ways in which Disney instructs audiences in
what Henry Giroux calls "a politics of innocence" are lessons that locate
Disney film at the center of cultural ideology and its pedagogical urge.

Jack Zipes's essay places the work of Walt Disney in the material and cultural development of the European fairy tale. Zipes traces the functions,
themes, and mediums of fairy tales from communal, oral performances to
authorized, literary products of the seventeenth and eighteenth centuries.
The fairy tale on film represents a third violent shift in the uses and technologies of fairy tales. Zipes argues that Disney was a revolutionary
filmmaker, obfuscating the names of Charles Perrault, the Brothers Grimm,
and Hans Christian Andersen in the western fairy-tale canon. Disney's earliest cartoons evidence a technological "wizardry" that capture the fairy-tale
genre on film, creating images and ethos of democracy, technology, and
modernity that both usurp the *civilité* of the literary tale and replace the
emancipatory potential of the oral tale. For Zipes, Disney's *Snow White and
the Seven Dwarfs* (1937) becomes the definitive model for a new institutionalization of fairy tales in which technic, domestication, and diversion become
commodities that ultimately invite and instruct audiences to *still* the fairy
tale genre under the prominent signature of Walt Disney.

Henry A. Giroux also examines the ways in which Disney film teaches
audiences to "still" history, politics, and culture and participate in the legiti-
mation of Disney's aggressive rewriting of America's past in popular culture.
For Giroux, "innocence is not only about the discursive face of domination,
it also points to important pedagogical issues regarding how people as subjects learn to place themselves in particular historical narratives." The complexities of memory, pedagogy, and "the politics of innocence" are exemplified in Giroux's analysis of Touchstone's 1987 release *Good Morning,
Vietnam*. Placing the film amongst two decades of "celluloid history" that
rewrite the machismo, mythology, and outcome of the Vietnam War, Giroux
contributes to our understanding of Disney sanitization as pedagogy. Not
only does *Good Morning, Vietnam* readily dismiss, omit, and moralize the
politics and history of the U.S. involvement in Vietnam, but it teaches '90s
audiences to replace bombs with rock'n'roll music; the military-industrial
complex with yuppie upward mobility; atrocities with touristic spectacle;
and racist, sexist, and colonial representations with one-liner jokes. Disney's

"pedagogical politics of innocence" are laid bare when grafted onto the Vietnam War, so often used as a trope for "a country that had lost its innocence." For Giroux, the ways in which Disney repairs that loss suggest the need for cultural critics to situate pedagogy "far beyond the boundaries of schools" in the production of knowledge.

Pinocchio (1940), Disney's second full-length animated film, highlights pedagogy and innocence throughout. Indeed, Pinocchio's task throughout the movie is to "learn to be a real boy." Claudia Card compares the Disney film with Collodi's novel for the ways in which Disney not only excises the violence of the literary version, but erases the vehicles by which children acquire their humanity and conscience. The Disney version instructs children to prove themselves "brave, truthful, and unselfish," but the lessons reduce and transform bravery to "macho heroism," truthfulness to "avoiding humiliation," and selflessness to "learning to please others." The consequences of "becoming a real boy" are elided by the generic "good child," or to use Foucault's idiom, a docile body, prepared for the Disney ideology of consumption. For Card, Disney's ideal child demonstrates "good old American know-how," "innocence," and most importantly, "unquestioning obedience"—important lessons in 1940 for children and adults alike.

The parallels between Disney's ideal child in *Pinocchio* and the title character of E. L. Doctorow's novel, *Billy Bathgate*, are not obvious on the surface, but both boys are puppets in the Disney canon. Robert Haas, in "Disney Does Dutch: *Billy Bathgate* and the Disneyfication of the Gangster Genre" examines systematic Disney sanitization as it reaches into the violent world of gangster films. Film genre—whether science fiction, westerns, horror films, or gangster movies—is a rich site of pedagogy for audiences, teaching filmic conventions whose success can be measured at the box office and explored as ideology. But Touchstone's 1991 release ignored both the gangster audience and their expectations and excised the social, political, and economic critique of Doctorow's dark and multileveled story. The chiaroscuro of the Doctorow novel is not only incompatible with Disney but demonstrates how the invisible politics of Disneyfication become visible in this film.

Susan Miller and Greg Rode's essay, "The Movie You See, The Movie You Don't: How Disney Do's That Old Time Derision" explores the rhetorically constructed "protected space" of Disney memories. The "kid in me," for children and adults alike, is a constituted site of extracurricular identity formation, a place "to find *how* we are taught by so prominent and once apparently neutral a cultural teacher as the collective 'Walt Disney.' " The lessons in *Song of the South* (1946) and *Jungle Book* (1967) mark gender, race, and class not as simply stereotypes, but as persuasive strategies that *school* indi-

Elizabeth Bell, Lynda Haas, and Laura Sells

vidual and cultural immobility and resignation. For Miller and Rode, the interstitial space between "the movie you see" and "the movie you don't see" allows multiple discourses of identity alternately to bifurcate, mediate, and create "a space of exemption where 'individuals' can assert falsely private permission to sit out the hierarchies, prejudices, and seemingly temporary conflicts on which these films rely." Indeed, Disney films, according to Miller and Rode, prepare us with "elementary lessons in cultural authorship."

If the Disney corpus can be seen as peddling a pedagogy of innocence, perhaps one of the most telling lessons it sells us is that of gender—of bodies, sexuality, and desire. As Teresa de Lauretis points out, the technology of cinema constructs gender, controlling the field of social meaning, creating representations that we negotiate and inhabit (1987, 18). While an innocent view of Disney mythologizes Disney's *women* as the memorable icons, much of the Disney corpus of films memorializes masculinity, whether as Pinocchio's "real boy" or the "cardboard" princes who drive the earliest fairy-tale films. Section Two, "Contestations/Disney Film as Gender Construction," examines and contests the construction of gender in the Disney canon. These essays move beyond naturalized masculinity to explore the artifice of its normative technologies. As Brian Attebery maintains, "the heroes are male because that has been the considered choice, the norm, for American selfhood. Woman is the exception; man is the default setting."

The exceptional women treated in Elizabeth Bell's essay, "Somatexts at the Disney Shop: Constructing the Pentimentos of Women's Animated Bodies," are quintessential Disney—the heroines and villainesses of *Snow White* (1937), *Cinderella* (1950), *Sleeping Beauty* (1959), *The Little Mermaid* (1989) and *Beauty and the Beast* (1991). And yet behind those exceptional imaginary women are other women—real women—who applied paint to each individual "cel" of film, creating some 250,000 paintings for each animated film. Bell's analysis locates the construction of gender within the material production of animation. Where Zipes points out how Disney's filmic appropriations of fairy tales invite audiences to "fix" the genre of fairy tales, Bell shows how, like the oral tales from which they are drawn, Disney's animated films are multi-authored, as layers upon layers of retelling, and in particular, a retelling of women's bodies. Fairy-tale tropes are transformed into iconographies of dance, popular culture, and film that ultimately "crack" the painted Disney idealizations of feminine goodness and wickedness. The rich iconography of women's bodies is juxtaposed with the flat depictions of masculinity and the broad caricature of the "hollow crowns" of masculine power and authority.

In " 'The Whole Wide World Was Scrubbed Clean': The Androcentric

Animation of Denatured Disney," Patrick D. Murphy borrows Richard Schickel's important observation that Disney "always, and only, showed us a clean land." Murphy examines this landscape through the lens of ecofeminism, a critical agenda that articulates the "connections—historical, empirical, conceptual, theoretical, symbolic, and experiential—between the domination of women and the domination of nature" (Warren 1991, 1). The conflation and subjection of women and nature is especially apparent in six of Disney's best known animated feature films: *101 Dalmatians* (1961), *Jungle Book* (1967), the two *Rescuers* films (1977, 1990), *The Little Mermaid* (1989), and *Beauty and the Beast* (1991). For Murphy, Disney constructs gender and nature on "androcentric hierarchies and dichotomies, with women and nature objectified for the benefit of the male subject." In these animated worlds, good women are domesticators and resources; bad women are evil, greedy, individual perversions of natural orders; and men ultimately hold procreative and productive dominion as civilizing forces in these worlds. With children's audiences growing increasingly ecologically aware, Disney is reaching new generations of audiences whose ecological views—of gender and of nature—may suspect and reject denatured Disney.

David Payne also sees a gendered script written onto nature in the 1942 film *Bambi*. The story of Bambi's acculturation and maturation in this essay is told against two backdrops: the WWII years of its production and Payne's own coming-of-age story. In *Bambi*'s animation, the intense realism of the forest reaches heights unparalleled in the Disney canon and becomes the "technical psychosis" of its creators. The realism of nature, however, is overwritten with a scripted drama in which nature, and its conventional alignments with the feminine, is "reoccupied by a patriarchal social system that is the fullest perfection of Man's wish: a single male patriarch with absolute dominion and property ownership of all that transpires in the society." The iconic masculinity of *Bambi*, like the preparation for world war that interrupted the film's production and the hunters who invade Bambi's forest, are ways of seeing and telling the story of domination as the *natural* social order. Nature's story, rewritten in Man's language, becomes a story of contest, sexuality, and war.

In "Beyond Captain Nemo: Disney's Science Fiction," Brian Attebery denaturalizes the Disney canon of masculinity as rendered in the studio's surprising number of live-action films that can be classed as science fiction: "stories presenting a world that departs from our present consensus reality in ways that reflect science's techniques for observing, categorizing, and manipulating the physical universe." Attebery divides the Disney SF canon into two types: the "exploding gadget" of the Flubber movies creates "emotional

Elizabeth Bell, Lynda Haas, and Laura Sells

and social shock waves" through the white, American middle class of Disney inventors; and the "stranded ET" finds aliens aligning with Disney heroes to find their collective ways home. The second formula, apparent in three decades of Disney SF in *Moon Pilot* (1962), *The Cat from Outer Space* (1978), and *Flight of the Navigator* (1986), is evidence for a changing social script for masculine identity in American culture. The alien catalyst and the films' divergent resolutions of sexual maturation denaturalize the male adolescent passage to adulthood, ultimately fracturing the "ordinariness" of the American male.

Susan Jeffords's "The Curse of Masculinity: Disney's *Beauty and the Beast*" finds "extraordinariness" the center of the filmic portraits of hypermasculinity in live-action films of the 1980s; the next decade of films, however, corrects and repositions masculine heroism. The 1990 blockbuster *Kindergarten Cop* demonstrates the shift in masculine identity from "relentless, law-making, brutalizing" men to "nurturing, playful, and loving" fathers. This character conversion is dependent upon returning male heroes to their families, freeing them from their emotional straitjackets, and locating their motivations, not in "rescuing armies, corporations, and ancient artifacts," but in saving themselves. Disney's 1991 film, *Beauty and the Beast*, epitomizes the "curse" in which "masculinity is betrayed by its own cultural imagery: what men thought they were supposed to be—strong, protective, powerful, commanding—has somehow backfired and become their own evil curse." At the hands of Disney, *Beauty and the Beast* is not the story of Belle, but the story of the Beast and other 1990s film heroes who must be taught how to discover and recover themselves.

If feminist literary and film theorists are correct when they argue that cultural production tells the story of masculinity, then women—and other Others—are summarily erased in the Disney mythos. Section Three, "Erasures/Disney Film as Identity Politics," tells a different story of Disney feminine identities. Feminists, women of color, lesbians, even mothers find themselves in a "ghetto" not unlike "Toontown" of *Who Framed Roger Rabbit?* (1988) where the villainous judge threatens to erase them with the turpentine concoction "the dip." The traces of identity that remain in Disney films must be read against the grain, or as D. Soyini Madison phrases it, "with an oppositional gaze." For bell hooks, such opposition constructs "a theory of looking where cinematic visual delight is the pleasure of interrogation" (1991, 126).

Laura Sells finds much to interrogate in her oppositional reading of Disney's *The Little Mermaid* (1989), an important film that signals Disney's return, after a thirty-year hiatus, to the center of its filmic mythos—the literary fairy tale. Like many of Hans Christian Andersen's literary fairy tales, "The Little Mermaid" can be read as Andersen's painful class consciousness in his entrance to and patronage from aristocratic circles. Sells argues in her essay, "Where Do the Mermaids Stand? Voice and Body in *The Little Mermaid*," that the Disney version substitutes gender for class, and "embedded within this classic narrative about an adolescent girl's coming of age is a very contemporary story about the costs, pleasures, and dangers of women's access to the 'human world.' " On one level, Ariel's story is a parable of bourgeois feminist agendas, seeking upward mobility and access to a white male system from which she is excluded—a passage that costs Ariel her voice. On another level, the parable transcends the status quo and offers possibilities for recuperation and resistance, even as Ariel is passed from the arms of her father to the arms of her husband. For Sells, the undoing and the pleasures of *The Little Mermaid* are found in Ursula—a drag queen who destabilizes gender as she performs it, who is the "dark continent" of the feminine, who is *jouissance*—the multiplicity of woman's abundant pleasures.

Lynda Haas traces the Disney penchant for erasing mothers and takes her title, " 'Eighty-Six the Mother': Murder, Matricide, and Good Mothers," from Jeffrey Katzenberg's reported comment on early versions of *Aladdin* (1992). After writers scripted much of the action and a song around Aladdin's mother, Katzenberg is quoted as saying, "Eighty-six the mother. She's a zero" (Avins 1992, 111). The "zero" of Disney mothers—absent, murdered, or replaced—is a construction of "sexual difference and representation of the feminine in the imaginary and symbolic," an important place for examining cinematic visions of mothers. Haas examines three Disney films, Touchstone's *The Good Mother* (1988), *Stella* (1990), and Hollywood Pictures' *The Joy Luck Club* (1994), for the ways in which the politics of motherhood are culturally inscribed and cinematically portrayed. With Luce Irigaray's contention that western society installed a patriarchal story over the sacrifice of the mother and her daughters, Haas argues that *The Good Mother* and *Stella* continue the symbolic matricide: sexuality and pleasure are replaced with passivity and voicelessness; self-sacrifice and motherly devotion are sites of masochistic identification and an obverse narcissistic self-hatred. *The Joy Luck Club*, on the other hand, offers several different stories of mothers and daughters. With new metaphors of maternal strength and transformative strategies of resistance, the cultural register of the feminine and the maternal can reclaim the absent mother.

Chris Cuomo in "Spinsters in Sensible Shoes: *Mary Poppins* and *Bedknobs*

Elizabeth Bell, Lynda Haas, and Laura Sells

and Broomsticks" also examines Disney mothers—albeit reluctant, surrogate, witchy ones. Cuomo examines the "moral and sexual positioning" of Mary Poppins and Eglantine Price, both cast as magical nannies in troubled political and familial times. *Mary Poppins* (1964) is set in 1910 England, and the protagonist's "moral mission is to save a family run by a failed patriarch and an inattentive suffragette." *Bedknobs and Broomsticks* (1971) features a rural English village facing Nazi invasion during WWII. Both films hinge on the danger of the disintegrating family and the role of the spinster in recuperating the social order of familial and national bliss. Mary Poppins restores local order "by agitating but never truly upsetting prescribed gender roles and social configurations." While she escapes the domestication of family life, even while enacting antifeminisms, Mary Poppins teaches George that he "can save the family—the bedrock of the Empire." No such luck for Eglantine Price. Her independence, quirkiness, and her "secret" training for witchhood are ultimately undermined by the children in her care and the heroic magician love-interest. Cuomo argues that the stereotypic lesbian coding of Price, "drab, humorless, willing to sacrifice pleasure for the greater good, obsessively intellectual, private, and asexual," is so strong that the narrative must go to great lengths to domesticate her within the heterosexual family contract.

The 1990 Cinderella-story *Pretty Woman* is an important Touchstone release in the Disney canon, not just for its financial success but for its reflection of "changing attitudes and ambivalence concerning women's autonomy and sexuality, as well as values associated with class differences." D. Soyini Madison's "*Pretty Woman* through the Triple Lens of Black Feminist Spectatorship" maintains that these issues are ultimately resolved "by upholding traditional, hegemonic conceptions and practices regarding marriage, chivalry, and consumer capitalism," a resolution that is duplicitous for the black feminist spectator. Madison examines the beauty myth, as well as the marriage plot, for their race, class, and gender implications in *Pretty Woman*. Even while race is not explicitly implicated in the film, "it is fundamentally significant only because [Vivian] is a white woman, a 'pretty' white woman that the plot can unfold in the manner that it does." *Pretty Woman* trivializes race for the purposes of plot in the fairy-tale narrative, and ultimately erases it. Through a "lens of ambivalence and outsiderhood," the black feminist spectator knows "the adoration for the beauty, femininity, and sensuality displayed on film for white women is an adoration reserved for them, but at the same time [is] aware that it disempowers the very women it props up on its precarious pedestal."

Introduction

While Jack Zipes's essay begins "It was not once upon a time" in telling the story of Disney's filmic wizardry, Ramona Fernandez begins "There is a place. . . . " Both authors treat Disney as revolutionary in the development of literacy: for Zipes, Disney teaches audiences how to "read" fairy-tale films; for Fernandez, the films at EPCOT Center prepare us for a new literacy, a library of the future in which the shelf as storage system is *passé*. "Disney's currency at EPCOT is the simulacrum; its integrating medium is film and its pleasure is sensory. Film is folded into every experience at EPCOT." Fernandez explores three film texts at EPCOT Center: *Wonders of China*, *The American Adventure*, and Michael Jackson's 3D film, *Captain E/O*. Each film experience wraps the body in intoxicating sensual cues of sound, motion, touch, and smell as part of "increasingly addictive bodily pleasures." These somatic participations are central to "a library that relies on simulacra to create its narratives and soma to capture its audience while rigorously suppressing race, gender, and class." Disney's erasure of marginalized identities is problematized by the presence of Michael Jackson—an entertainer who is now a trope for constant transmogrification of race and gender. Jackson as trickster, not unlike the early Mickey, collides with Disney's "ideology and corporate structure [that] propagandizes our social selves, educate[s] our imaginations and appropriate[s] our bodies."

The films at EPCOT Center lead us to back to Disneyland. Organizational theorist and sociologist John van Maanen (1991) tells the story of his summer employment at Disneyland in the early 1960s. During working hours, word would travel fast that "Walt's in the park!" and Disneyland hosts and hostesses would jump to deliver their services with even greater friendliness and even bigger smiles. With Walt's death in 1966, Disney corporate trainers now intone, according to van Maanen, "Walt's *always* in the park." These essays explore the ways in which Walt Disney—as man and manager, as studio and canon, as corporation and ideology—is always in the movies.

Notes

1. Several titles in this collection reflect our authors' punning treatment of *Doing Disney*, especially Miller and Rode's "How Disney Do's that Old Time Derision," and Robert Haas's "Disney Does Dutch."

2. The dedication plaque at Anaheim, California's Disneyland reads: "To all who come to this happy place: Welcome. Disneyland is your land. Here age relives fond memories of the past . . . and here youth may savor the challenge and promise of the future" (qtd. in Gottdiener 1982, 139).

Elizabeth Bell, Lynda Haas, and Laura Sells

3. For a discussion of Disney's litigious nature and many examples of its legal actions, see Lawrence and Timberg (1980).

4. See Grossberg for a discussion of hegemony as it operates through the double articulation between the common sense of the people and the institutions of society (1993, 56).

5. Although the critical tide is beginning to shift, only a handful of cultural critics have undertaken the project of analyzing Disney films as worthy of interrogation. See, for instance, Burton (1992) on *The Three Caballeros*; Modleski's (1991) treatment of *Three Men and a Baby*; Willis (1987) on *Fantasia*; White (1993) on *The Little Mermaid*; Radner (1993) on *Pretty Woman*; and Giroux (1993) on *Dead Poets' Society*. See also Jewett and Lawrence (1977).

References

Aronowitz, Stanley. 1992. *The Politics of Identity*. New York: Routledge.

Avins, Mimi. 1992. "Aladdin." *Premiere*, December: 65–70, 111.

Burton, Julianne. 1992. "Don (Juanito) Duck and the Imperial-Patriarchal Unconscious: Disney Studios, the Good Neighbor Policy, and the Packaging of Latin America." In *Nationalisms and Sexualities*, ed. Andrew Parker, Mary Russo, Doris Sommer, and Patricia Yeager. New York: Routledge.

Collins, Jim, Hilary Radner, and Ava Preacher Collins, eds. 1993. *Film Theory Goes to the Movies*. New York: Routledge.

de Lauretis, Teresa. 1987. *Technologies of Gender*. Bloomington: Indiana University Press.

Eliot, Marc. 1993. *Walt Disney, Hollywood's Dark Prince: A Biography*. Secaucus, NJ: Carol/Birch Lane Press.

Giroux, Henry A. 1993. "Reclaiming the Social: Pedagogy, Resistance, and Politics in Celluloid Culture." See Collins, Radner, and Preacher Collins 1993.

Gottdiener M. 1982. "Disneyland: A Utopian Urban Space." *Urban Life* 11(2): 139–62.

Grossberg, Lawrence. 1993. *Relocating Cultural Studies*, ed. Valda Blundell, John Shepherd, and Ian Taylor. New York: Routledge.

Grover, Ron. 1991. *The Disney Touch*. Homewood, IL: Business One Irwin.

Hartley, John. 1983. "Encouraging Signs: Television and the Power of Dirt, Speech and Scandalous Categories." *Australian Journal of Cultural Studies* 1(2): 62–82.

Holliss, Richard, and Brian Sibley. 1988. *The Disney Studio Story*. New York: Crown.

hooks, bell. 1992. *Black Looks: Race and Representation*. Boston: South End Press.

Jewett, Robert, and John Shelton Lawrence. 1977. *The American Monomyth*. Garden City, NY: Anchor Press Doubleday.

Lawrence, John Shelton, and Bernard Timberg, eds. 1980. *Fair Use and Free Inquiry: Copyright Law and the New Media*. Norwood, NJ: Ablex.

Modleski, Tania. 1991. *Feminism without Women: Culture and Criticism in a "Postfeminist" Age*. New York: Routledge.

Mosley, Leonard. 1985. *Disney's World*. New York: Stein and Day.

Radner, Hilary. 1993. "Pretty Is as Pretty Does." In *Film Theory Goes to the Movies*. See Collins, Radner, and Preacher Collins 1993.

Ryan, Michael, and Douglas Kellner. 1990. *Camera Politica: The Politics and Ideology of Contemporary Hollywood Film*. Bloomington: Indiana University Press.

Introduction

Schickel, Richard. 1968. *The Disney Version: The Life, Times, Art, and Commerce of Walt Disney.* New York: Simon.

van Maanen, John. 1991. "The Smile Factory: Work at Disneyland." In *Reframing Organizational Culture*, ed. Peter J. Frost et al. Newbury Park, CA: Sage.

Warren, Karen. 1991. Introduction to Special Issue on Ecofeminism. *Hypatia* 6(1): 1–2.

Weiner, Jon. 1993. Murdered Ink. *The Nation*, 31 May, 743–50.

White, Susan. 1993. "Split Skins: Female Agency and Bodily Mutilation in *The Little Mermaid*." See Collins, Radner, and Preacher Collins 1993.

Willis, Susan. 1987. "Fantasia: Walt Disney's Los Angeles Suite." *Diacritics* 17: 83–96.

I.

Sanitizations/Disney Film as Cultural Pedagogy

One

Breaking the Disney Spell

Jack Zipes

It was not once upon a time, but at a certain time in history, before anyone knew what was happening, that Walt Disney cast a spell on the fairy tale, and he has held it captive ever since. He did not use a magic wand or demonic powers. On the contrary, Disney employed the most up-to-date technological means and used his own "American" grit and ingenuity to appropriate European fairy tales. His technical skills and ideological proclivities were so consummate that his signature has obfuscated the names of Charles Perrault, the Brothers Grimm, Hans Christian Andersen, and Carlo Collodi. If children or adults think of the great classical fairy tales today, be it *Snow White*, *Sleeping Beauty*, or *Cinderella*, they will think Walt Disney. Their first and perhaps lasting impressions of these tales and others will have emanated from a Disney film, book, or artifact. Though other filmmakers and animators produced remarkable fairy-tale films, Disney managed to gain a cultural stranglehold on the fairy tale, and this stranglehold has even tightened with the recent productions of *Beauty and the Beast* (1991) and *Aladdin* (1992). The man's spell over the fairy tale seems to live on even after his death.

But what does the Disney spell mean? Did Disney achieve a complete monopoly on the fairy tale during his lifetime? Did he imprint a particular *American* vision on the fairy tale through his animated films that dominates our perspective today? And, if he did manage to cast his mass-mediated spell on the fairy tale so that we see and read the classical tales through his lens, is that so terrible? Was Disney a nefarious wizard of some kind whose domination of the fairy tale should be lamented? Wasn't he just more inventive, more skillful, more in touch with the American spirit of the times than his competitors, who also sought to animate the classical fairy tale for the screen?

Of course, it would be a great exaggeration to maintain that Disney's spell totally divested the classical fairy tales of their meaning and invested them with his own. But it would not be an exaggeration to assert that Disney was a radical filmmaker who changed our way of viewing fairy tales, and that his revolutionary technical means capitalized on American innocence and utopianism to reinforce the social and political status quo. His radicalism was of the right and the righteous. The great "magic" of the Disney spell is that he animated the fairy tale only to transfix audiences and divert their potential utopian dreams and hopes through the false promises of the images he cast upon the screen. But before we come to a full understanding of this magical spell, we must try to understand what he did to the fairy tale that was so revolutionary and why he did it.

The Oral and Literary Fairy Tales

The evolution of the fairy tale as a literary genre is marked by dialectical appropriation that set the cultural conditions for its institutionalization and its expansion as a mass-mediated form through radio, film, and television. Fairy tales were first *told* by gifted tellers and were based on rituals intended to endow with meaning the daily lives of members of a tribe. As *oral folk tales*, they were intended to explain natural occurrences such as the change of the seasons and shifts in the weather or to celebrate the rites of harvesting, hunting, marriage, and conquest. The emphasis in most folk tales was on communal harmony. A narrator or narrators told tales to bring members of a group or tribe closer together and to provide them with a sense of mission, a *telos*. The tales themselves assumed a generic quality based on the function that they were to fulfill for the community or the incidents that they were to report, describe, and explain. Consequently, there were tales of initiation, worship, warning, and indoctrination. Whatever the type may have been, the voice of the narrator was known. The tales came directly from common experiences and beliefs. Told in person, directly, face-to-face, they were altered as the beliefs and behaviors of the members of a particular group changed.

With the rise of literacy and the invention of the printing press in the fifteenth century, the oral tradition of storytelling underwent an immense revolution. The oral tales were taken over by a different social class, and the form, themes, production, and reception of the tales were transformed. This change did not happen overnight, but it did foster discrimination among writers and their audiences almost immediately so that distinct genres were recognized and approved for certain occasions and functions within polite society or cultivated circles of readers. In the case of folk tales, they were gradually categorized as legends, myths, fables, comical anecdotes, and, of course, fairy tales. What we today consider fairy tales were actually just one type of the folk-tale tradition, namely the *Zaubermärchen* or the magic tale, which has many sub-genres. The French writers of the late seventeenth century called these tales *contes de fées* (fairy tales) to distinguish them from other kinds of *contes populaires* (popular tales), and what really distinguished a *conte de fée*, based on the oral *Zaubermärchen*, was its transformation into a literary tale that addressed the concerns, tastes, and functions of court society. The fairy tale had to fit into the French salons, parlors, and courts of the aristocracy and bourgeoisie if it was to establish itself as a genre. The writers, Mme D'Aulnoy, Charles Perrault, Mlle L'Héritier, Mlle de La Force, etc., knew and expanded upon oral and literary tales. They were not the initiators of the literary fairy-tale tradition in Europe (cf. Zipes 1989). Two Italian writers, Giovanni Francesco Straparola and Giambattista Basile, had already set an example for what the French were accomplishing.[1] But the French writers created an institution, that is, the genre of the literary fairy tale was institutionalized as an aesthetic and social means through which questions and issues of *civilité*, proper behavior and demeanor in all types of situations, were mapped out as narrative strategies for literary socialization, and in many cases, as symbolic gestures of subversion to question the ruling standards of taste and behavior.

While the literary fairy tale was being institutionalized at the end of the seventeenth and beginning of the eighteenth century in France, the oral tradition did not disappear, nor was it subsumed by the new literary genre. Rather, the oral tradition continued to feed the writers with material and was now also influenced by the literary tradition itself. The early chapbooks (cheap books), known as the *Bibliothèque Bleue,* that were carried by peddlers or *colporteurs* to the villages throughout France contained numerous abbreviated and truncated versions of the literary tales, and these were in turn told once again in these communities. In some cases, the literary tales presented new material that was transformed through the oral tradition and returned later to literature by a writer who remembered hearing a particular story.

By the beginning of the nineteenth century when the Brothers Grimm set about to celebrate German culture through their country's folk tales, the literary fairy tale had long since been institutionalized, and they, along with Hans Christian Andersen, Carlo Collodi, Ludwig Bechstein, and a host of Victorian writers from George MacDonald to Oscar Wilde, assumed different ideological and aesthetic positions within this institutionalization. These writers put the finishing touches on the fairy-tale genre at a time when nation-states were assuming their modern form and cultivating particular types of literature as commensurate expressions of national cultures.

What were the major prescriptions, expectations, and standards of the literary fairy tale by the end of the nineteenth century? Here it is important first to make some general remarks about the "violent" shift from the oral to the literary tradition and not just talk about the appropriation of the magic folk tale as a dialectical process. Appropriation does not occur without violence to the rhetorical text created in the oral tales (cf. Armstrong and Tennenhouse 1989). Such violation of oral storytelling was crucial and necessary for the establishment of the bourgeoisie because it concerned the control of desire and imagination within the symbolic order of western culture.

Unlike the oral tradition, the literary tale was written down to be read in private, although, in some cases, the fairy tales were read aloud in parlors. However, the book form enabled the reader to withdraw from his or her society and to be alone with a tale. This privatization violated the communal aspects of the folk tale, but the very printing of a fairy tale was already a violation since it was based on separation of social classes. Extremely few people could read, and the fairy tale in form and content furthered notions of elitism and separation. In fact, the French fairy tales heightened the aspect of the chosen aristocratic elite who were always placed at the center of the seventeenth- and eighteenth-century narratives. They were part and parcel of the class struggles in the discourses of that period. To a certain extent, the fairy tales were the outcome of violent "civilized" struggles, material representations, which represented struggles for hegemony. As Nancy Armstrong and Leonard Tennenhouse have suggested,

> a class of people cannot produce themselves as a ruling class without set-
> ting themselves off against certain Others. Their hegemony entails posses-
> sion of the key cultural terms determining what are the right and wrong
> ways to be a human being. (1989, 24)

No matter where the literary tale took root and established itself—France, Germany, England—it was written in a standard "high" language that the folk could not read, and it was written as a form of entertainment and education for members of the ruling classes. Indeed, only the well-to-do could purchase the books and read them. In short, by institutionalizing the literary fairy tale, writers and publishers violated the forms and concerns of non-literate, essentially peasant communities and set new standards of taste, production, and reception through the discourse of the fairy tale.

The literary fairy tales tended to exclude the majority of people who could not read, while the folk tales were open to everyone. Indeed, the literary narratives were individualistic and unique in form and exalted the power of those chosen to rule. In contrast, the oral tales had themes and characters that were readily recognizable and reflected common wish-fulfillments. Of course, one had to know the dialect in which they were told. From a philological standpoint, the literary fairy tale elevated the oral tale through the standard practice of printing and setting grammatical rules in "high French" or "high German." The process of violation is *not* one of total negation and should not be studied as one-dimensional, for the print culture enabled the tales to be preserved and cultivated, and the texts created a new realm of pleasurable reading that allowed for greater reflection on the part of the reader than could an oral performance of a tale. At the beginning, the literary fairy tales were written and published for adults, and though they were intended to reinforce the mores and values of French *civilité*, they were so symbolic and could be read on so many different levels that they were considered somewhat dangerous: social behavior could not be totally dictated, prescribed, and controlled through the fairy tale, and there were subversive features in language and theme. This is one of the reasons that fairy tales were not particularly approved for children. In most European countries it was not until the end of the eighteenth and early part of the nineteenth century that fairy tales were published for children, and even then begrudgingly, because their "vulgar" origins in the lower classes were suspect. Of course, the fairy tales for children were sanitized and expurgated versions of the fairy tales for adults, or they were new moralistic tales that were aimed at the domestication of the imagination, as Rüdiger Steinlein has demonstrated in his significant study.[2] The form and structure of the fairy tale for children were carefully regulated in the nineteenth century so that improper thoughts and ideas would not be stimulated in the minds of the young. If one looks carefully at the major writers of fairy tales for children who became classical and popular in the nineteenth century,[3] it is clear that they themselves exercised self-censorship and restraint in conceiving and writing down tales for children.

This is not to argue that the literary fairy tale as institution became one in which the imagination was totally domesticated. On the contrary, by the end of the nineteenth century the genre served different functions. As a whole, it formed a multi-vocal network of discourses through which writers used familiar motifs, topoi, protagonists, and plots symbolically to comment on the civilizing process and socialization in their respective countries. These tales did not represent communal values but rather the values of a particular writer. Therefore, if the writer subscribed to the hegemonic value system of his or her society and respected the canonical ideology of Perrault, the Grimms, and Andersen, he/she would write a conventional tale with conservative values, whether for adults or children. On the other hand, many writers would parody, mock, question, and undermine the classical literary tradition and produce original and subversive tales that were part and parcel of the institution itself.

The so-called original and subversive tales have kept the dynamic quality of the dialectical appropriation alive, for there has always been a danger that the written word, in contrast to the spoken word, will fix a structure, image, metaphor, plot, and value as sacrosanct. For instance, for some people the Grimms' fairy tales are holy, or fairy tales are considered holy and not to be touched. How did this notion emanate?

To a certain extent it was engendered by the Grimms and other folklorists who believed that the fairy tales arose from the spirit of the folk. Yet, worship of the fairy tale as holy scripture is a petrification of the fairy tale that is connected to the establishment of correct speech, values, and power more than anything else. This establishment through the violation of the oral practices was the great revolution and transformation of the fairy tale.

By the end of the nineteenth century the literary fairy tale had the following crucial functions as institution in middle-class society:

(1) It introduced notions of elitism and separatism through a select canon of tales geared to children who knew how to read.

(2) Though it was also told, the fact that the fairy tale was printed and in a book with pictures gave it more legitimacy and enduring value than an oral tale that disappeared soon after it was told.

(3) It was often read by a parent in a nursery, school, or bedroom to soothe a child's anxieties, for the fairy tales for children were optimistic and were constructed with the closure of the happy end.

(4) Although the plots varied and the themes and characters were altered, the classical fairy tale for children and adults reinforced the patriarchal symbolic order based on rigid notions of sexuality and gender.

(5) In printed form the fairy tale was property and could be taken by its owner and read by its owner at his or her leisure for escape, consolation, or inspiration.

(6) Along with its closure and reinforcement of patriarchy, the fairy tale also served to encourage notions of rags to riches, pulling yourself up by your bootstraps, dreaming, miracles, etc.

(7) There was always tension between the literary and oral traditions. The oral tales have continued to threaten the more conventional and classical tales because they can question, dislodge, and deconstruct the written tales. Moreover, within the literary tradition itself, there were numerous writers such as Charles Dickens, George MacDonald, Lewis Carroll, Oscar Wilde,

and Edith Nesbit who questioned the standardized model of what a fairy tale should be.

(8) It was through script by the end of the nineteenth century that there was a full-scale debate about what oral folk tales and literary fairy tales were and what their respective functions should be. By this time the fairy tale had expanded as a high art form (operas, ballets, dramas) and low art form (folk plays, vaudevilles, and parodies) as well as a form developed classically and experimentally for children and adults. The oral tales continued to be disseminated through communal gatherings of different kinds, but they were also broadcast by radio and gathered in books by folklorists. Most important in the late nineteenth century was the rise of folklore as an institution and of various schools of literary criticism that dealt with fairy tales and folk tales.

(9) Though many fairy-tale books and collections were illustrated (some lavishly) in the nineteenth century, the images were very much in conformity with the text. The illustrators were frequently anonymous and did not seem to count. Though the illustrations often enriched and deepened a tale, they were generally subservient to the text.

However, the domination of the word in the development of the fairy tale as genre was about to change. The next great revolution in the institutionalization of the genre was the film, for the images now imposed themselves on the text and formed their own text in violation of print but also with the help of the print culture. And here is where Walt Disney and other animators enter the scene.

Disney's Magical Rise

By the turn of the twentieth century there had already been a number of talented illustrators, such as Gustav Doré, George Cruikshank, Walter Crane, Charles Folkard, and Arthur Rackham, who had demonstrated great ingenuity in their interpretations of fairy tales though their images. In addition, the broadside, broadsheet, or *image d'Epinal* had spread in Europe and America during the latter part of the nineteenth century as a forerunner of the comic book, and these sheets with printed images and texts anticipated the first animated cartoons that were produced at the beginning of the twentieth century. Actually, the French filmmaker Georges Méliès began experimenting as early as 1896 with types of fantasy and fairy-tale motifs in his *féeries* or trick films (Jacobs 1979). He produced versions of *Cinderella*, *Bluebeard*, and *Little Red Riding Hood* among others. However, since the cinema industry itself was still in its early phase of development, it was difficult for Méliès to bring about a major change in the technological and cinematic institutionalization of the genre. As Lewis Jacobs has remarked,

> this effort of Méliès illustrated rather than re-created the fairy tale. Yet, primitive though it was, the order of the scenes did form a coherent, logical, and progressive continuity. A new way of making moving pictures had been invented. Scenes could now be staged and selected specially for the camera, and the movie maker could control both the material and its arrangement. (1979, 13)

During the early part of the twentieth century Walter Booth, Anson Dyer, Lotte Reiniger, Walter Lantz and others all used fairy tale plots in different ways in trick films and cartoons, but none of the early animators ever matched the intensity with which Disney occupied himself with the fairy tale. In fact, it is noteworthy that Disney's very first endeavors in animation (not considering the advertising commercials he made) were the fairy-tale adaptations that he produced with Ub Iwerks in Kansas City in 1922–23: *The Four Musicians of Bremen, Little Red Riding Hood, Puss in Boots, Jack and the Beanstalk, Goldie Locks and the Three Bears*, and *Cinderella*.[4] To a certain degree, Disney identified so closely with the fairy tales he appropriated that it is no wonder his name virtually became synonymous with the genre of the fairy tale itself.

However, before discussing Disney's particular relationship to the fairy-tale tradition, it is important to consider the conditions of early animation in America and role of the animator in general, for all this has a bearing on Disney's productive relationship with the fairy tale. In his important study, *Before Mickey: The Animated Film 1898–1928*, Donald Crafton remarks that

> the early animated film was the location of a process found elsewhere in cinema but nowhere else in such intense concentration: self-figuration, the tendency of the filmmaker to interject himself into his film. This can take several forms, it can be direct or indirect, and more or less camouflaged. . . . At first it was obvious and literal; at the end it was subtle and cloaked in metaphors and symbolic imagery designed to facilitate the process and yet to keep the idea gratifying for the artist and the audience. Part of the animation game consisted of developing mythologies that gave the animator some sort of special status. Usually these were very flattering, for he was pictured as (or implied to be) a demigod, a purveyor of life itself. (1982, 11)

As Crafton convincingly shows, the early animators before Disney literally drew themselves into the pictures and often appeared as characters in the films. One of the more interesting aspects of the early animated films is a psychically loaded tension between the artist and the characters he draws, one that is ripe for a Freudian or Lacanian reading, for the artist is always threatening to take away their "lives," while they, in turn, seek to deprive him of his pen (phallus) or creative inspiration so that they can control their own lives. (Almost all the early animators were men, and their pens and camera work assume a distinctive phallic function in early animation.) The hand with pen or pencil is featured in many animated films in the process of creation, and it is then transformed in many films into the tail of a cat or dog. This tail then acts as the productive force or artist's instrument throughout the film. For instance, Disney in his Alice films often employed a cat named Julius, who would take off his tail and use it as stick, weapon, rope, hook, question mark, etc. It was the phallic means to induce action and conceive a way out of a predicament.

The celebration of the pen/phallus as ruler of the symbolic order of the film was in keeping with the way that animated films were actually produced in the studios during the 1920s. That is, most of the studios, largely located in New York, had begun to be run on the Taylor system by men who joined together under the supervision of the head of the studio to produce the cartoons. After making his first fairy-tale films in close cooperation with Ub Iwerks in Kansas City, Disney moved to Hollywood, where he developed the taylorized studio to the point of perfection. Under his direction, the films were carefully scripted to project his story or vision of how a story should be related. The story-line was carried by hundreds of repetitious images created by the artists in his studios. Their contribution was in many respects like that of the dwarfs in *Snow White and the Seven Dwarfs*: they were to do the spadework, while the glorified prince was to come along and carry away the prize.

It might be considered somewhat one-dimensional to examine all of Disney's films as self-figurations, or embodiments of the chief designer's[5] wishes and beliefs. However, to understand Disney's importance as designer and director of fairy-tale films that set a particular pattern and model as the film industry developed, it does make sense to elaborate on Crafton's notion of self-figuration, for it provides an important clue for grasping the further development of the fairy tale as animated film or film in general.

We have already seen that one of the results stemming from the shift from the oral to the literary in the institutionalization of the fairy tale was a loss of live contact with the storyteller and a sense of community or commonality. This loss was a result of the social-industrial transformations at the end of the nineteenth century with the *Gemeinschaft* (community-based society) giving way to the *Gesellschaft* (contract-based society). However, it was not a total loss, for industrialization brought about greater comfort, sophistication, and literacy in addition to new kinds of communication in public institutions. Therefore, as I have demonstrated, the literary fairy tale's ascent corresponded to violent and progressive shifts in society and celebrated individualism, subjectivity, and reflection. It featured the narrative voice of the educated author and publisher over communal voices and set new guidelines for freedom of speech and expression. In addition, proprietary rights to a particular tale were established, and the literary tale became a commodity that paradoxically spoke out in the name of the unbridled imagination. Indeed, because it was born out of alienation, the literary fairy tale fostered a search for new "magical" means to overcome the instrumentalization of the imagination.

By 1900 literature began to be superseded by the mechanical means of reproduction that, Walter Benjamin declared, were revolutionary:

> the technique of reproduction detaches the reproduced object from the domain of tradition. By making many reproductions it substitutes a plurality of copies of a unique existence. And in permitting the reproduction to meet the beholder or listener in his own particular situation, it reactivates the object reproduced. These two processes lead to a tremendous shattering of tradition which is the obverse of the contemporary crisis and renewal of mankind. Both processes are intimately connected with the contemporary mass movements. Their most powerful agent is the film. Its social significance, particularly in its most positive form, is inconceivable without its destructive, cathartic aspect, that is, the liquidation of the traditional value of the cultural heritage. (1968, 223)

Benjamin analyzed how the revolutionary technological nature of the film could either bring about an aestheticization of politics leading to the violation of the masses through fascism, or a politicization of aesthetics that provides the necessary critical detachment for the masses to take charge of their own destiny.

In the case of the fairy-tale film at the beginning of the twentieth century, there are "revolutionary" aspects that we can note, and they prepared the way for progressive innovation that expanded the horizons of viewers and led to greater understanding of social conditions and culture. But there were also regressive uses of mechanical reproduction that brought about the cult of the personality and commodification of film narratives. For instance, the voice in fairy-tale films is at first effaced so that the image totally dominates the screen, and the words or narrative voice can only speak through the designs of the animator who, in the case of Walt Disney, has signed his name prominently on the screen. In fact, for a long time, Disney did not give credit to the artists and technicians who worked on his films. These images were intended both to smash the aura of heritage and to celebrate the ingenuity, inventiveness, and genius of the animator. In most of the early animated films, there were few original plots, and the story-lines did not count. Most important were the gags, or the technical inventions of the animators ranging from the introduction of live actors to interact with cartoon characters, to improving the movement of the characters so that they did not shimmer, to devising ludicrous and preposterous scenes for the sake of spectacle. It did not matter what story was projected just as long as the images astounded the audience, captured its imagination for a short period of time, and left the people laughing or staring in wonderment. The purpose of the early animated films was to make audiences awestruck and to celebrate the magical talents of the animator as demigod. As a result, the fairy tale as story was a vehicle for animators to express their artistic talents and develop their technology. The animators sought to impress audiences with their abilities to use pictures in such a way that they would forget the earlier fairy tales and remember the images that they, the new artists, were creating for them. Through these moving pictures, the animators appropriated literary and oral fairy tales to subsume the word, to have the final word, often through image and book, for Disney began publishing books during the 1930s to complement his films.

Of all the early animators, Disney was the one who truly revolutionized the fairy tale as institution through the cinema. One could almost say that he was obsessed by the fairy-tale genre, or, put another way, Disney felt drawn to fairy tales because they reflected his own struggles in life. After all, Disney came from a relatively poor family, suffered from the exploitative and stern treatment of an unaffectionate father, was spurned by his early sweetheart, and became a success due to his tenacity, cunning, courage, and his ability to gather around him talented artists and managers like his brother Roy.

One of his early films, *Puss in Boots* (1922), is crucial for grasping his approach to the literary fairy tale and understanding how he used it as self-figuration that would mark the genre for years to come. Disney did not especially care whether one knew the original Perrault text of *Puss in Boots* or some other popular version. It is also unclear which text he actually knew. However, what is clear is that Disney sought to replace all versions with his animated version and that his cartoon is astonishingly autobiographical.

If we recall, Perrault wrote his tale in 1697 to reflect upon a cunning cat whose life is threatened and who manages to survive by using his brains to trick a king and an ogre. On a symbolic level, the cat represented Perrault's conception of the role of the *haute bourgeoisie* (his own class), who comprised the administrative class of Louis the XIV's court and who were often the mediators between the peasantry and aristocracy. Of course, there are numerous ways to read Perrault's tale, but whatever approach one chooses, it is apparent that the major protagonist is the cat.

This is not the case in Disney's film. The hero is a young man, a commoner, who is in love with the king's daughter, and she fondly returns his affection. At the same time, the hero's black cat, a female, is having a romance with the royal white cat, who is the king's chauffeur. When the gigantic king discovers that the young man is wooing his daughter, he kicks him out of the palace, followed by Puss. At first, the hero does not want Puss's help, nor will he buy her the boots that she sees in a shop window. Then they go to the movies together and see a film with Rudolph Vaselino as a bullfighter, a reference to the famous Rudolph Valentino. This spurs the imagination of Puss. Consequently, she tells the hero that she now has an idea that will help him win the king's daughter, provided that he will buy her the boots. Of course, the hero will do anything to obtain the king's daughter, and he must disguise himself as a masked bullfighter. In the meantime Puss explains to him that she will use a hypnotic machine behind the scenes so he can defeat the bull and win the approval of the king. When the day of the bullfight arrives, the masked hero struggles but eventually manages to defeat the bull. The king is so overwhelmed by his performance that he offers his daughter's hand in marriage, but first he wants to know who the masked champion is. When the hero reveals himself, the king is enraged, but the hero grabs the princess and leads her to the king's chauffeur. The white cat jumps in front with Puss, and they speed off with the king vainly chasing after them.

Although Puss as cunning cat is crucial in this film, Disney focuses most of his attention on the young man who wants to succeed at all costs. In contrast to the traditional fairy tale, the hero is not a peasant, nor is he dumb. Read as a "parable" of Disney's life at that moment, the hero can be seen as young Disney wanting to break into the industry of animated films (the king) with the help of Ub Iwerks (Puss). The hero upsets the king and runs off with his prize possession, the virginal princess. Thus, the king is dispossessed, and the young man outraces him with the help of his friends.

But Disney's film is also an attack on the literary tradition of the fairy tale. He robs the literary tale of its voice and changes its form and meaning. Since the cinematic medium is a popular form of expression and accessible to the public at large, Disney actually returns the fairy tale to the majority of people. The images (scenes, frames, characters, gestures, jokes) are readily comprehensible by young and old alike from different social classes. In fact, the fairy tale is practically infantilized, just as the jokes are infantile. The plot records the deepest oedipal desire of every young boy: the son humiliates and undermines the father and runs off with his most valued object of love, the daughter/wife. By simplifying this oedipal complex semiotically in black-and-white drawings and making fun of it so that it had a common appeal, Disney also touched on other themes:

(1) Democracy—the film is very *American* in its attitude toward royalty. The monarchy is debunked, and a commoner causes a kind of revolution.

(2) Technology—it is through the new technological medium of the movies that Puss's mind is stimulated. Then she uses a hypnotic machine to defeat the bull and another fairly new invention, the automobile, to escape the king.

(3) Modernity—the setting is obviously the twentieth century, and the modern minds are replacing the ancient. The revolution takes place as the king is outpaced and will be replaced by a commoner who knows how to use the latest inventions.

But who is this commoner? Was Disney making a statement on behalf of the masses? Was Disney celebrating "everyone" or "every man"? Did Disney believe in revolution and socialism? The answer to all these questions is simple: no.

Casting the Commodity Spell with *Snow White*

Disney's hero is the enterprising young man, the entrepreneur, who uses technology to his advantage. He does nothing to help the people or the community. In fact, he deceives the masses and the king by creating the illusion that he is stronger than the bull. He has learned, with the help of Puss, that one can achieve glory through deception. It is through the artful use of images that one can sway audiences and gain their favor. Animation is trickery—trick films—for still images are made to seem as if they move through automatization. As long as one controls the images (and machines) one can reign supreme, just as the hero is safe as long as he is disguised. The pictures conceal the controls and machinery. They deprive the audience of viewing the production and manipulation, and in the end, audiences can no longer envision a fairy tale for themselves as they can when they read it. The pictures now deprive the audience of visualizing their own characters, roles, and desires. At the same time, Disney offsets the deprivation with the pleasure of scopophilia and inundates the viewer with delightful images, humorous figures, and erotic signs. In general, the animator, Disney, projects the enjoyable fairy tale of his life through his own images, and he realizes through animated stills his basic oedipal dream that he was to play out time and again in most of his fairy-tale films. It is the repetition of Disney's infantile quest—the core of American mythology—that enabled him to strike a chord in American viewers from the 1920s to the present.

However, it was not through *Puss in Boots* and his other early animated fairy tales that he was to captivate audiences and set the "classical" modern model for animated fairy-tale films. They were just the beginning. Rather, it was in *Snow White and the Seven Dwarfs* (1937) that Disney fully appropriated the literary fairy tale and made his signature into a trademark for the most acceptable type of fairy tale in the twentieth century. But before the making of *Snow White*, there were developments in his life and in the film industry that are important to mention in order to grasp why and how *Snow White* became the first definitive animated fairy-tale film—definitive in the sense that it was to define the way other animated films in the genre of the fairy tale were to be made.

After Disney had made several Laugh-O-Gram fairy-tale films, all ironic and modern interpretations of the classical versions, he moved to Hollywood in 1923 and was successful in producing fifty-six *Alice* films, which involved a young girl in different adventures with cartoon characters. By 1927 these films were no longer popular, so Disney and Iwerks soon developed Oswald the Lucky Rabbit cartoons that also found favor with audiences. However, in February of 1928, while Disney was in New York trying to renegotiate a contract with his distributor Charles Mintz, he learned that Mintz, who owned the copyright to Oswald, had lured some of Disney's best animators to work for another studio. Disney faced bankruptcy because he refused to capitulate to the exploitative conditions that Mintz set for the distribution and production of Disney's films (Mosley 1985, 85–140). This experience sobered Disney in his attitude to the cutthroat competition in the film industry, and when he returned to Hollywood, he vowed to maintain complete control over all his productions—a vow that he never broke.

In the meantime, Disney and Iwerks had to devise another character for their company if they were to survive, and they conceived the idea for films featuring a pert mouse named Mickey. By September of 1928, after making two Mickey Mouse shorts, Disney, similar to his masked champion in *Puss in Boots*, had devised a way to gain revenge on Mintz and other animation studios by producing the first animated cartoon with sound, *Steamboat Willie*, starring Mickey Mouse. From this point on, Disney became known for introducing new inventions and improving animation so that animated films became almost as realistic as films with live actors and natural settings. His next step after sound was color, and in 1932 he signed an exclusive contract with Technicolor and began producing his *Silly Symphony* cartoons in color. More important, Disney released *The Three Little Pigs* in 1933 and followed it with *The Big Bad Wolf* (1934) and *The Three Little Wolves* (1936), all of which involved fairy-tale characters and stories that touched on the lives of people during the Depression. As Bob Thomas has remarked, "*The Three Little Pigs* was acclaimed by the Nation. The wolf was on many American doorsteps, and 'Who's Afraid of the Big Bad Wolf?' became a rallying cry" (1991, 49). Not only were wolves on the doorsteps of Americans but also witches, and to a certain extent, Disney, with the help of his brother Roy and Iwerks, had been keeping "evil" connivers and competitors from the entrance to the Disney Studios throughout the 1920s. Therefore, it is not by chance that Disney's next major experiment would involve a banished princess, loved by a charming prince, who would triumph over deceit and regain the rights to her castle. *Snow White and the Seven Dwarfs* was to bring together all the personal strands of Disney's own story with the destinies of desperate Americans who sought hope and solidarity in their fight for survival during the Depression of the 1930s.

Of course, by 1934 Disney was, comparatively speaking, wealthy. He hired Don Graham, a professional artist, to train studio animators at the Disney Art School, founded in November 1932. He then embarked on ventures to stun moviegoers with his ingenuity and talents as organizer, storyteller, and filmmaker. Conceived some time in 1934, *Snow White* was to take three years to complete, and Disney did not leave one stone unturned in his preparations for the first full-length animated fairy-tale film ever made. Disney knew he was making history even before history had been made.

During the course of the next three years, Disney worked closely with all the animators and technicians assigned to the production of *Snow White*. By now, Disney had divided his studio into numerous departments, such as animation, layout, sound, music, storytelling, etc., and had placed certain animators in charge of developing the individual characters of Snow White, the prince, the dwarfs, and the queen/crone. Disney spent thousands of dollars on a multiplane camera to capture the live-action depictions that he desired, the depth of the scenes, and close-ups. In addition, he had his researchers experiment with colored gels, blurred focus, and filming through frosted glass, while he employed the latest inventions in sound and music to improve the synchronization with the characters on the screen. Throughout the entire production of this film, Disney had to be consulted and give his approval for each stage of development. After all, *Snow White* was his story that he had taken from the Grimm Brothers and changed completely to suit his tastes and beliefs. He cast a spell over this German tale and transformed it into something peculiarly American. Just what were the changes he induced?

(1) Snow White is an orphan. Neither her father nor her mother are alive, and she is at first depicted as a kind of "Cinderella," cleaning the castle as a maid in a patched dress. In the Grimms' version there is the sentimental death of her mother. Her father remains alive, and she is never forced to do the work of commoners such as wash the steps of the castle.

(2) The prince appears at the very beginning of the film on a white horse and sings a song of love and devotion to Snow White. He plays a negligible role in the Grimms' version.

(3) The queen is not only jealous that Snow White is more beautiful than she is, but she also sees the prince singing to Snow White and is envious because her stepdaughter has such a handsome suitor.

(4) Though the forest and the animals do not speak, they are anthropomorphized. In particular the animals befriend Snow White and become her protectors.

(5) The dwarfs are hardworking and rich miners. They all have names—Doc, Sleepy, Bashful, Happy, Sneezy, Grumpy, Dopey—representative of certain human characteristics and are fleshed out so that they become the star attractions of the film. Their actions are what counts in defeating evil. In the Grimms' tale, the dwarfs are anonymous and play a humble role.

(6) The queen only comes one time instead of three as in the Grimms' version, and she is killed while trying to destroy the dwarfs by rolling a huge stone down a mountain to crush them. The punishment in the Grimms' tale is more horrifying because she must dance in red-hot iron shoes at Snow White's wedding.

(7) Snow White does not return to life when a dwarf stumbles while carrying the glass coffin as in the Grimms' tale. She returns to life when the prince, who has searched far and wide for her, arrives and bestows a kiss on her lips. His kiss of love is the only antidote to the queen's poison.

At first glance, it would seem that the changes that Disney made were not momentous. If we recall Sandra Gilbert and Susan Gubar's stimulating analysis in their book, *The Madwoman in the Attic* (1979), the film follows the classic "sexist" narrative about the framing of women's lives through a male discourse. Such male framing drives women to frustration and some women to the point of madness. It also pits women against women in competition for male approval (the mirror) of their beauty that is short-lived. No matter what they may do, women cannot chart their own lives without male manipulation and intervention, and in the Disney film, the prince plays even more of a framing role since he is introduced at the beginning while

Breaking the Disney Spell

Snow White is singing, "I'm Wishing for the One I Love To Find Me To-day." He will also appear at the end as the fulfillment of her dreams.

There is no doubt that Disney retained key ideological features of the Grimms' fairy tale that reinforce nineteenth-century patriarchal notions that Disney shared with the Grimms. In some way, they can even be considered his ancestor, for he preserves and carries on many of their benevolent attitudes toward women. For instance, in the Grimms' tale, when Snow White arrives at the cabin, she pleads with the dwarfs to allow her to remain and promises that she will wash the dishes, mend their clothes, and clean the house. In Disney's film, she arrives and notices that the house is dirty. So, she convinces the animals to help her make the cottage tidy so that the dwarfs will perhaps let her stay there. Of course, the house for the Grimms and Disney was the place where good girls remained, and one shared aspect of the fairy tale and the film is about the domestication of women.

However, Disney went much further than the Grimms to make his film more memorable than the tale, for he does not celebrate the domestication of women so much as the triumph of the banished and the underdogs. That is, he celebrates his destiny, and insofar as he had shared marginal status with many Americans, he also celebrates an American myth of Horatio Alger: it is a male myth about perseverance, hard work, dedication, loyalty, and justice.

It may seem strange to argue that Disney perpetuated a male myth through his fairy-tale films when, with the exception of *Pinocchio* (1940), they all featured young women as "heroines": *Sleeping Beauty* (1959), *Cinderella* (1950), and *The Little Mermaid* (1989). However, despite their beauty and charm, these figures are pale and pathetic compared to the more active and demonic characters in the film. The witches are not only agents of evil but represent erotic and subversive forces that are more appealing both for the artists who drew them and the audiences.[6] The young women are helpless ornaments in need of protection, and when it comes to the action of the film, they are omitted. In *Snow White and the Seven Dwarfs*, the film does not really become lively until the dwarfs enter the narrative. They are the mysterious characters who inhabit a cottage, and it is through their hard work and solidarity that they are able to maintain a world of justice and restore harmony to the world. The dwarfs can be interpreted as the humble American workers, who pull together during a depression. They keep their spirits up by singing a song "Hi ho, it's home from work we go," or "Hi ho, it's off to work we go," and their determination is the determination of every worker, who will succeed just as long as he does his share while women stay at home and keep the house clean. Of course, it is also possible to see the workers as Disney's own employees, on whom he depended for the glorious outcome of his films. In this regard, the prince can be interpreted as Disney, who directed the love story from the beginning. If we recall, it is the prince who frames the narrative. He announces his great love at the beginning of the film, and Snow White cannot be fulfilled until he arrives to kiss her. During the major action of the film, he, like Disney, is lurking in the background and waiting for the proper time to make himself known. When he does arrive, he takes all the credit as champion of the disenfranchised, and he takes Snow White to his castle while the dwarfs are left as keepers of the forest.

But what has the prince actually done to deserve all the credit? What did Disney actually do to have his name flash on top of the title as "Walt Disney's Snow White and the Seven Dwarfs" in big letters and later credit his co-workers in small letters? As we know, Disney never liked to give credit to the animators who worked with him, and they had to fight for acknowledgment.[7] Disney always made it clear that he was the boss and owned total rights to his products. He had struggled for his independence against his greedy and unjust father and against fierce and ruthless competitors in the film industry. As producer of the fairy-tale films and major owner of the Disney studios, he wanted to figure in the films and sought, as Crafton has noted, to create a more indelible means of self-figuration. In *Snow White*, he accomplished this by stamping his signature as owner on the title frame of the film and then by having himself embodied in the figure of the prince. It is the prince Disney who made inanimate figures come to life through his animated films, and it is the prince who is to be glorified in *Snow White and the Seven Dwarfs* when he resuscitates Snow White with a magic kiss. Afterward he holds Snow White in his arms, and in the final frame, he leads her off on a white horse to his golden castle on a hill. His golden castle—every woman's dream—supersedes the dark, sinister castle of the queen. The prince becomes Snow White's reward, and his power and wealth are glorified in the end.

There are obviously mixed messages or multiple messages in *Snow White and the Seven Dwarfs*, but the overriding sign, in my estimation, is the signature of Disney's self-glorification in the name of justice. Disney wants the world *cleaned up*, and the pastel colors with their sharply drawn ink lines create images of cleanliness, just as each sequence reflects a clearly conceived and preordained destiny for all the characters in the film. For Disney, the Grimms' tale is not a vehicle to explore the deeper implications of the narrative and its history.[8] Rather, it is a vehicle to display what he can do as an animator with the latest technological and artistic developments in the industry. The story is secondary, and if there is a major change in the plot, it centers on the power of the prince, the only one who can save Snow White, and he becomes the focal point by the end of the story.

In Disney's early work with fairy tales in Kansas City, he had a wry and irreverent attitude toward the classical narratives. There was a strong suggestion, given the manner in which he and Iwerks rewrote and filmed the tales, that they were "revolutionaries," the new boys on the block, who were about to introduce innovative methods of animation into the film industry and speak for the outcasts. However, in 1934, Disney was already the kingpin of animation, and he used all that he had learned to reinforce his power and command of fairy-tale animation. The manner in which he copied the musical plays and films of his time, and his close adaptation of fairy tales with patriarchal codes, indicate that all the technical experiments would not be used to foster social change in America but to keep power in the hands of individuals like himself, who felt empowered to design and create new worlds. As Richard Schickel has perceptively remarked, Disney

> could make something his own, all right, but that process nearly always robbed the work at hand of its uniqueness, of its soul, if you will. In its place he put jokes and songs and fright effects, but he always seemed to diminish what he touched. He came always as a conqueror, never as a servant. It is a trait, as many have observed, that many Americans share when they venture into foreign lands hoping to do good but equipped only with knowhow instead of sympathy and respect for alien traditions. (1968, 227)

Disney always wanted to do something new and unique just as long as he had absolute control. He also knew that novelty would depend on the collective skills of his employees, whom he had to keep happy or indebted to him in some way. Therefore, from 1934 onward, about the time that he conceived his first feature-length fairy-tale film, Disney became the orchestrator of a corporate network that changed the function of the fairy-tale genre in America. The power of Disney's fairy-tale films does not reside in the uniqueness or novelty of the productions, but in Disney's great talent for holding antiquated views of society *still* through animation and his use of the latest technological developments in cinema to his advantage. His adaptation of the literary fairy tale for the screen led to the following changes in the institution of the genre:

(1) Technique takes precedence over the story, and the story is used to celebrate the technician and his means.

(2) The carefully arranged images narrate through seduction and imposition of the animator's hand and the camera.

(3) The images and sequences engender a sense of wholeness, seamless

totality, and harmony that is orchestrated by a savior/technician on and off the screen.

(4) Though the characters are fleshed out to become more realistic, they are also one-dimensional and are to serve functions in the film. There is no character development because the characters are stereotypes, arranged according to a credo of domestication of the imagination.

(5) The domestication is related to colonization insofar as the ideas and types are portrayed as models of behavior to be emulated. Exported through the screen as models, the "American" fairy tale colonizes other national audiences. What is good for Disney is good for the world, and what is good in a Disney fairy tale is good in the rest of the world.

(6) The thematic emphasis on cleanliness, control, and organized industry reinforces the technics of the film itself: the clean frames with attention paid to every detail; the precise drawing and manipulation of the characters as real people; the careful plotting of the events that focus on salvation through the male hero.

(7) Private reading pleasure is replaced by pleasurable viewing in an impersonal cinema. Here one is brought together with other viewers not for the development of community but to be diverted in the French sense of *divertissement* and American sense of diversion.

(8) The diversion of the Disney fairy tale is geared toward nonreflective viewing. Everything is on the surface, one-dimensional, and we are to delight in one-dimensional portrayal and thinking, for it is adorable, easy, and comforting in its simplicity.

Once Disney realized how successful he was with his formula for feature-length fairy tales, he never abandoned it, and in fact, if one regards the two most recent Disney Studio productions of *Beauty and the Beast* (1991) and *Aladdin* (1992), Disney's contemporary animators have continued in his footsteps. There is nothing but the "eternal return of the same" in *Beauty and the Beast* and *Aladdin* that makes for enjoyable viewing and delight in techniques of these films as commodities, but nothing new in the exploration of narration, animation, and signification.

There is something sad in the manner in which Disney "violated" the literary genre of the fairy tale and packaged his versions in his name through the merchandising of books, toys, clothing, and records. Instead of using technology to enhance the communal aspects of narrative and bring about major changes in viewing stories to stir and animate viewers, he employed animators and technology to stop thinking about change, to return to his films, and to long nostalgically for neatly ordered patriarchal realms. Fortunately, the animation of the literary fairy tale did not stop with Disney, but that is another tale to tell, a tale about breaking Disney's magic spell.

Notes

1. See Straparola's *Le piacevoli notti* (1550–53), translated as *The Facetious Nights* or *The Delectable Nights*, and Basile's *Lo Cunto de li Cunti* (*The Story of Stories*, 1634–36), better known as *The Pentamerone*. The reason that the Italians did not "institutionalize" the genre is that the literary culture in Italy was not prepared to introduce the tales as part of the civilizing process, nor were there groups of writers who made the fairy-tale genre part of their discourse.

2. Cf. *Die Domestizierte Phantasie: Studien zur Kinderliteratur, Kinderlektüre und Literaturpädagogik des 18. und frühen 19. Jahrhunderts* (Heidelberg: Carl Winter, 1987).

3. This list would include the Grimms, Wilhelm Hauff, Ludwig Bechstein, Hans Christian Andersen, and Madame De Ségur. In addition, numerous collections of expurgated folk tales from different countries became popular in primers by the end of the nineteenth century. Here one would have to mention the series of color fairy books edited by Andrew Lang in Great Britain.

4. Cf. Russell Merrit and J. B. Kaufman, *Walt in Wonderland: The Silent Films of Walt Disney*, for the most complete coverage of Disney's early development.

5. I am purposely using the word designer instead of animator because Disney was always designing things, made designs, and had designs. A designer is someone who indicates with a distinctive mark, and Disney put his mark on everything in his studios. A designing person is often a crafty person who manages to put his schemes into effect by hook or by crook. Once Disney stopped animating, he became a designer.

6. Solomon cites the famous quotation by Woody Allen in *Annie Hall*: "You know, even as a kid I always went for the wrong women. When my mother took me to see 'Snow White,' everyone fell in love with Snow White; I immediately fell for the Wicked Queen" (1980, 28).

7. Bill Peet, for example, an "in-betweener" in the early Disney studio, worked for a year and a half on *Pinocchio* (1940). Peet relates that, after watching the film in his neighborhood theatre, "I was dumbfounded when the long list of screen credits didn't include my name" (1989, 108).

8. Karen Merritt makes the interesting point that "Disney's *Snow White* is an adaptation of a 1912 children's play (Disney saw it as a silent movie during his adolescence) still much performed today, written by a male Broadway producer under a female pseudonym; this play was an adaptation of a play for immigrant children from the tenements of lower East Side New York; and that play, in turn, was a translation and adaptation of a German play for children by a prolific writer of children's comedies and fairy-tale drama. Behind these plays was the popularity of nineteenth- and early twentieth-century fairy-tale pantomimes at Christmas in England and fairy-tale plays in Germany and America. The imposition of childish behavior on the dwarfs, Snow White's resulting mothering, the age ambiguities in both Snow White and the dwarfs, the 'Cinderella' elements, and the suppression of any form of sexuality were transmitted by that theatrical tradition, which embodied a thoroughly developed philosophy of moral education in representations for children. . . . By reading Disney's *Snow White* by the light of overt didacticism of his sources, he no longer appears the moral reactionary disdained by contemporary critics. Rather, he is the entertainer who elevates the subtext of play found in his sources and dares once again to frighten children" (1994, 106). Though it may be true that Disney was more influenced by an American theatrical and film tradition, the source of all these productions, one acknowledged by Disney, was the Grimms' tale. And, as I have argued, Disney was not particularly interested in experimenting with the narrative to shock child-

ren or provide a new perspective on the traditional story. For all intents and purposes his film reinforces the didactic messages of the Grimms' tale, and it is only in the technical innovations and designs that he did something startlingly new. It is not the object of critique to "disdain" or "condemn" Disney for reappropriating the Grimms' tradition to glorify the great designer, but to understand those cultural and psychological forces that led him to map out his narrative strategies in fairy-tale animation.

References

Armstrong, Nancy, and Leonard Tennenhouse, eds. 1989. *The Violence of Representation: Literature and the History of Violence*. New York: Routledge.

Benjamin, Walter. 1968. "The Work of Art in the Age of Mechanical Reproduction." In *Illuminations,* trans. Harry Zohn. New York: Harcourt, Brace & World.

Crafton, Donald. 1982. *Before Mickey: The Animated Film 1898–1928*. Cambridge: MIT Press.

Gilbert, Sandra, and Susan Gubar. 1979. *The Madwoman in the Attic: The Woman Writer and the Nineteenth-Century Literary Imagination*. New Haven: Yale University Press.

Jacobs, Lewis. 1979. "George Méliès: Artificiality Arranged Scenes." In *The Emergence of Film Art: The Evolution and Development of the Motion Picture as an Art, from 1900 to the Present,* ed. Lewis Jacobs. 2nd ed. New York: Norton.

Merritt, Karen. 1988. "The Little Girl/Little Mother Transformation: The American Evolution of 'Snow White and the Seven Dwarfs.' " In *Storytelling in Animation: The Art of the Animated Image,* ed. John Canemaker. Los Angeles: American Film Institute.

Merritt, Russell, and J. B. Kaufman. 1994. *Walt in Wonderland: The Silent Films of Walt Disney*. Baltimore: Johns Hopkins University Press.

Mosley, Leonard. 1985. *Disney's World*. New York: Stein and Day.

Peet, Bill. 1989. *Bill Peet: An Autobiography*. Boston: Houghton Mifflin.

Schickel, Richard. 1968. *The Disney Version*. New York: Simon and Schuster.

Solomon, Charles. 1980. "Bad Girls Finish First in Memory of Disney Fans." *Milwaukee Journal,* 17 August.

Thomas, Bob. 1991. *Disney's Art of Animation: From Mickey Mouse to Beauty and the Beast*. New York: Hyperion.

Zipes, Jack. 1989. "The Rise of the French Fairy Tale and the Decline of France." In *Beauties, Beasts and Enchantment: Classic French Fairy Tales,* trans. Jack Zipes. New York: New American Library.

Two

Memory and Pedagogy in the "Wonderful World of Disney"

Beyond the Politics of Innocence

Henry A. Giroux

An alarming defensiveness has crept into America's official image of itself, especially in its representations of the national past. Every society and official tradition defends itself against interferences with its sanctioned narratives; over time these acquire an almost theological status, with founding heroes, cherished ideas and values, national allegories having an inestimable effect in cultural and political life. (Said 1993, 314)

Ideas, texts, even people can be made sacred . . . but even though such entities, once their sacredness is established, seek to proclaim and to preserve their own absoluteness, their inviolability, the act of making sacred is in truth an event of history. . . . And events in history must always be subject to questioning, deconstruction, even to declarations of their obsolescence. To respect the sacred is to be paralysed by it. (Rushdie 1991, 416)

Popular Culture and the Struggle for Memory

In different ways, Edward Said and Salman Rushdie address the complex relationship between memory and history on the one hand and culture and power on the other. By historicizing culture, and problematizing knowledge, both authors point to the necessity for a cultural politics that engages the relationship between knowledge and authority, how it is established, and what relationship it has to dominant regimes of representation. Today's "culture wars," largely organized around liberal and conservative arguments, each make claims about how the "past is remembered, understood, and linked to the present" (Simon 1993, 77). On one side conservatives invoke claims to national unity and world responsibility through an appeal to a nostalgic past written as an unchanging narrative, the loss of which marks a crisis of leadership and innocence. On the other side, various nationalists and progressives embrace collective memory as something to be merely recovered, an essentialized force that must be granted its place in the public arenas that define the parameters of cultural authority.

The many casualties produced by this debate over culture, authority, and memory include important theoretical insights regarding the relationship between culture and power that have developed during the 1980s and 1990s from the emerging discourses of cultural studies, postcolonialism, feminism and postmodernism. Diverse theorists in these fields have been generally united in their attempts to demonstrate that "the question of power has important cultural and ideological aspects" (Bailey and Hall 1992, 19). The focus on cultural resistance as a form of political resistance accompanied by critical attention to popular practices has made clear that the hybridized space of popular culture is where the conflicts over the related issues of memory, identity, and representation are being most intensely contested as part of a broader attempt on the part of dominant groups to secure cultural hegemony.[1] If the new cultural politics is to translate its theoretical insights into a viable strategy for political activism, it will be necessary for progressive cultural workers to understand more critically how the dynamics of culture and politics have changed given the emergence of the electronic media and its global capacity to create "new images of centrality." As Edward Said points out, it would be irresponsible politically for cultural workers to underestimate the profound effects the new media are having on the shaping of everyday life and global agendas. Unlike traditional cultural social forms, the new media constitute a unique moment in the expansion of cultural imperialism into the sphere of everyday life:

> The difference here is that the epic scale of the United States global
> power and the corresponding power of the national domestic consensus
> created by the electronic media have no precedents. Never has there been
> a consensus so difficult to oppose nor so easy and logical to capitulate to
> unconsciously. (Said 1993, 323)

The new shift toward culture as a terrain of struggle accentuates not only the emerging role of the media in securing cultural authority, it also requires that cultural workers become more attentive to the various pedagogical sites in which the politics of remembering and forgetting produce different narratives of a national past, present, and future. There is no escape from the politics of representation; moreover, issues of textuality, meaning, and identity cannot be limited to the academy or subordinated to the alleged more "serious" single issues related to low pay, poverty, child care, and other material concerns.[2]

I want to argue that the theoretical and political move toward culture must be simultaneously engaged in postcolonial terms as an inquiry into the formation of national identity, or a conjuring of what might be called "the American character." This suggests that, on one level, cultural workers in a variety of sites must focus on the pedagogy and politics of culture. That is, we need to be more critically attentive to how power is organized through the enormous number of cultural apparatuses that range from libraries, movie theaters, and schools, to high-tech media conglomerates that circulate signs and meanings through newspapers, magazines, advertisements, electronic programming, machines, films, and television programs. In this instance, the sphere of politics vastly broadens its potential both for cultural hegemony and political resistance. But the new cultural politics cannot be limited to expanding the range of sites in which politics, pedagogy, and power are made manifest as a space of contestation. A new cultural politics must also critically address those discourses outside of traditional domains of knowledge in order to extend the historical and relational definition of cultural texts while simultaneously redefining how "knowledge, however mundane and utilitarian, plays about in linguistic images and forms cultural practices" (Morrison 1992, 49–50). Under the rubric of fun, entertainment, and escape, massive public spheres are being produced through representations and social practices that appear too "innocent" to be worthy of political analyses. Such is the case with the Disney Company; its logo and characters have become almost synonymous with the very notion of American popular culture. In what follows, I want to engage the relationship between Disney's representation of itself and the politics of innocence through which it attempts to secure its moral and pedagogical legitimacy.

Disney and the Politics of Innocence

There are few cultural icons in the United States that can match the signifying power of the Disney Company. Relentless in its efforts to promote a happy, kindly, paternal image of its founder, Walt Disney, and an endless regime of representations and commodities that conjure up a nostalgic view of America as the "magic kingdom," the Disney Company has become synonymous with a notion of innocence that aggressively rewrites the historical and collective identity of the American past. Behind the ideological appeal to nostalgia, wholesome times, and the land that is "the happiest place on earth," there is the institutional and ideological power of a $4.7 billion multinational conglomerate that wields enormous influence pedagogically and politically in a variety of public spheres.

When corporate politics is cloaked in the image of innocence, there is more at stake than the danger of simple deception. There is the issue of cultural power and how it works to make claims on our understanding of the past, national coherence, and popular memory as a site of injustice, criticism, and renewal.[3] Innocence in Disney's world becomes the ideological vehicle through which history is both rewritten and purged of its seamy side. In this case, innocence becomes important as an ideological construct less through its appeal to nostalgia, stylized consumption, or a unified notion of national identity than as a marker for recognizing the past as a terrain of pedagogical and ideological struggle. The Disney Company is not ignorant of history, it reinvents it as a pedagogical and political tool to secure its own interests, authority, and power.

Innocence is not only about the discursive face of domination, it also points to important pedagogical issues regarding how people as subjects learn to place themselves in particular historical narratives. As a pedagogical construct that promotes a particular view of history in Disney's diverse public cultures, innocence, when coupled with a mythic rendering of the past, offers people the opportunity to envision themselves as agents of history, as part of a community longing for security and redemption in a world that often seems hostile to such desires.

Through its ordering and structuring of popular representations, Disney mobilizes a notion of memory that parades under the longing for childlike innocence, wholesome adventure, and frontier courage. Organized through affective and ideological forms of address, such representations make particular claims upon the present and serve to define how we "come to know how we are constituted and who we are" (Hall 1992, 30). What is so important about the "wonderful world of Disney" as an "historical-cultural theater of memory" (Clifford 1990, 164) is that it powerfully represents the degree to which

> popular culture has historically become the dominant form of global culture . . . the scene, par excellence, of commodification, of the industries where culture enters directly into the circuits of . . . power and capital. It is the space of homogenization where stereotyping and the formulaic mercilessly process the material and experiences it draws into its web, where control over narratives and representations passes into the hands of established cultural bureaucracies, sometimes without a murmur. (Hall 1992, 26)

The "Wonderful World of Disney" is more than a logo; it signifies how the terrain of popular culture has become central to commodifying memory and rewriting narratives of national identity and global expansion. Disney's power and reach into popular culture combine an insouciant playfulness and the fantastic possibility of making childhood dreams come true with strict gender roles, an unexamined nationalism, and a notion of choice that is attached to the proliferation of commodities.

The strategies of entertaining escapism, historical forgetting, and repressive pedagogy in Disney's books, records, theme parks, movies, and TV programs produce a series of identifications that relentlessly define America as white and middle class. Pedagogy in Disney's texts functions as a history lesson that excludes the subversive elements of memory. Reduced to vignettes of childhood innocence, adventure, and chivalry, memory is removed from the historical, social, and political context that defines it as a process of cultural production that opens rather than closes down history. It is precisely this pedagogical policing of memory that undercuts its possibility as a form of critical remembrance that positions human agency against the restrictions and boundaries set by the historical past. For Disney, memory has nothing to do with remembering differently, nor is it a compelling force for arousing "dormant emancipatory energies. . . . [and] intellectually satisfying and emotionally compelling political images" (Adamson 1984, 238). On the contrary, narrating the past becomes a vehicle for rationalizing the authoritarian, normalizing tendencies of the dominant culture that carry through to the present. Hence, Disney's pretense to innocence is shattered under the weight of a promotional culture predicated on the virtues of fun, innocence, and, most importantly, consumption.[4] In the past year, with the bankruptcy of EuroDisney and the appearance of a number of unflattering revelations concerning Walt's life, the mythology of a clean consumerism and an unproblematic innocence has been gradually demystified. According to Herbert Mitgang of the *New York Times*, "from 1940 until his death in 1966 . . . [Disney served] as a secret informer for the Los Angeles office of the Federal Bureau of Investigation" (1993, B1). It seems that Walt Disney was not only an agent dedicated to rooting out communist agitators in the film industry, but he also allowed the FBI access to the Disneyland facilities for "use in connection with official matters and for recreational purposes" (Mitgang 1993, B4). Most disturbingly, Disney allowed J. Edgar Hoover, then Director of the FBI, to censor and modify the scripts of Disney films such as *That Darn Cat* (1965) and *Moon Pilot* (1962) so as to portray Bureau agents in a favorable light.

Behind the pretense to innocence and its appeal to a childlike state in which forgetting the past becomes more important than engaging it, the policing function of memory erases its emancipatory possibilities. This is illuminated, in part, through recent public revelations indicating that the

Henry A. Giroux

Disney Company has, on occasion, exceeded the moral bounds of its promotional enthusiasm by preventing the publication of books critical of Walt Disney and the Disney Company's image.[5] It appears that beneath the promotion of the magical name of Disney and the public spaces it represents as "the happiest place on earth" lurks the power of a multinational conglomerate that has little regard for free speech and public criticism.

As an ideological construct that mobilizes particular cultural practices in diverse regimes of representations, whether they be theme parks, comics, or movies, Disney's appeal to pristine innocence and high adventure is profoundly pedagogical in its attempt to produce specific knowledge, values, and desires. It is precisely this intersection of the political and pedagogical as a hegemonic practice that necessitates making Disney's world of representations the object of critical analysis. Moreover, such an analysis is not warranted simply through its claim to welding deconstructive skills; it is also important because it offers possibilities for educators and other cultural workers to understand more clearly how politics and pedagogy intersect in the production, circulation, and reception of popular culture and the formation of national identity.

As part of a broader attempt to make the political more pedagogical, I want to analyze a popular cultural text that demonstrates the link between the related issues of memory, politics, and pedagogy. More specifically, I want to analyze the film, *Good Morning, Vietnam* (1987) as an exemplary text for engaging the terrain of popular culture as it is constructed within the discourse of innocence and "fun" that lies at the heart of the Disney company's worldview. I want to demonstrate how the discourse of colonialism is couched in the language and representations of innocence, and how such representations mobilize popular memory to incorporate not only a particular view of what Renato Rosaldo calls "nostalgic imperialism" but also a politics of forgetting in producing a particular view of history, racial identity, and nationalism.

The War of Laughter and Forgetting

It has become commonplace that the Vietnam War represents a watershed in American history. Marked by widespread popular protest against American colonialism, the war demythologized the role of the United States as a world leader; it mobilized diverse movements of resistance and revealed a deep-seated racism that structured policies both toward minorities at home and people of color outside our national boundaries. Moreover, this was a postmodern war, a media event that signaled the limits of conventional warfare and the power of American militarism and imperialism while simultaneously transforming the horror and violence of the Vietnam War into a television spectacle. The postmodern spectacle of the Vietnam conflict signaled not simply the death of "truth" but also what Theodor Adorno has called, in another context, the withering of experience and hence, the displacement of the imperatives of moral responsibility and human agency.

> The total obliteration of the war by information, propaganda, commentaries, with cameramen in their first tanks and war reporters dying heroic deaths, the mishmash of an enlightened manipulation of public opinion and oblivious activity: all this is another expression for the withering of experience, the vacuum between men and their fate, in which their real fate lies. It is as if the reified, hardened plaster-cast of events takes the place of events themselves. Men are reduced to walk-on parts in a monster documentary-film. (Adorno 1974, 55)

In the 1970s and 1980s, the rewriting of the United States' intervention in Vietnam became the focus of celluloid history. Vietnam as a spectacle provided the impetus for a series of Hollywood films engaged in the process of organized forgetting, a process that substituted myths for reality, redemption for truth, and collective self-pity for social justice. Vietnam became a trope used to illuminate the angst, despair, and rage of the United States as a country that had lost its innocence and responded by attempting to purge its collective conscience of any moral responsibilities for its actions there.

The legacy of historical amnesia and the construction of popular memory in Hollywood Vietnam films is well known and need not be repeated in depth.[6] Hollywood blockbusters such as *Rolling Thunder* (1977), *Coming Home* (1978), *The Deer Hunter* (1978), *First Blood* (1982), and *Born on the Fourth of July* (1990) focused on the plight of returning veterans, their personal reactions to the war, and their readjustment to a society that appeared to reject them. In these films, the war was brought home while subverting any substantive political and moral commentary on the war itself. In this filmic instance, the legacy of the Vietnam conflict is either displaced through a focus on the subjective experiences of veterans or, as in the case of the Rambo films, viewed as an expression of individual corruption and political ineptness on the part of U.S. government officials.

In the 1980s, films such as *Platoon* (1986), *Gardens of Stone* (1987), and *Hamburger Hill* (1987) initiated another round of mythologizing. Reduced to the existential struggles and narratives of actual combat troops, the Vietnam War was rewritten as a coming-of-age tale. The war in these scenarios is viewed as a dehumanizing and apocryphal affair, but it is framed through a liberal and narrowly defined humanist focus on individual suffering that serves in the end to dehistoricize and decontextualize the American military presence in Vietnam. Angst, guilt, revenge, and personal suffering combine with Hollywood therapy to reduce the war to a soul-searching, celluloid narrative that erases the demands of an ethical and political discourse. Soothing to the collective conscience, these films betray any sense of social justice.

At the height of the Reagan era, Hollywood rewrote the Vietnam War in the image of an unbridled and arrogant national machismo. Films such as *Uncommon Valor* (1983), *Missing in Action* (1984), *Missing in Action 2: The Beginning* (1985), *Rambo: First Blood Part II* (1985), and *The Hanoi Hilton* (1987) used Vietnam as a backdrop to celebrate the tale of endless, heroic rescues. At stake in this version of popular memory was not the expurgation of collective guilt, but the construction of a vision of masculinity that resonated with the conservative image of national identity and patriotism that informed the Reagan years. After all, this was the decade in which the United States needed to reassert itself as the leader of the "new world order" by exorcising the critical legacy of the 1960s and reversing the public humiliation it suffered during the Iran hostage crisis. At the same time, the United States was actively obscuring and erasing its own legacy of military intervention and terrorism in world affairs by constructing third world peoples as either terrorists or religious fundamentalists.

It is impossible to separate the critical acclaim and popular success of *Good Morning, Vietnam* from the context and content of Vietnam films that preceded it. Directed by Barry Levinson, written by Mitch Markowitz, and the eighteenth film produced by Touchstone Pictures, *Good Morning, Vietnam* appeals to a generation of youth whose knowledge of the Vietnam War comes from the electronic media. This is a generation twice removed from the exacting moral and political issues that surrounded the Vietnam conflict. In fact, David Butler, the author of *The Fall of Saigon*, revealed in a *New York Times* article that one of the key elements in making the film was "the coming [of age] of a younger audience for whom the war is less controversial." According to Butler, "Vietnam intrigues the yuppie generation but it doesn't torture them" (quoted in Mydans 1987, 19). Barry Levinson, the director of the film, supports this position through his own experience of the Vietnam conflict. While working at a television station in the late 1960s, Levinson claims he learned about Vietnam by watching daily footage come in over the CBS feed. It is hard to discern what he learned, however, since he claims that he didn't understand what the war was about (Reese 1985).

In addition to the emergence of a new generation of movie watchers and a director who had no political and personal commitment with regard to the Vietnam War, the third major factor structuring the context of this film was the role it provided for Robin Williams to exercise the full range of his comic, manic improvisations. This is borne out not simply by the endless reviews that focus almost exclusively on Williams's comic improvisations in the film, but by Jeffrey Katzenberg, chairman of Walt Disney Studios, who claimed that *Good Morning, Vietnam* appealed to him because it gave Williams a chance to enact the full range of his improvisations (Culhane 1986, 34).

What separates Touchstone's *Good Morning, Vietnam* from other Vietnam films is its unabashed refusal to engage the Vietnam conflict through the traditional dominant tropes of homelessness, revenge, and patriotism. Instead, *Good Morning, Vietnam* willfully expunges the discourses of history, politics, and ethics from its narrative in order to appeal to a generation of youth raised on the affective energies of high-tech rock, 1980s yuppie buffoonery, and a narcissistic assertion of whiteness as the singular referent for intelligence, manhood, and sensuality. In this instance, a Reagan era–inspired slapstick conception of the world functions to license a reactionary view of the war that substitutes spectacle for critical engagement. It is precisely because of its facile dismissal of politics and history that *Good Morning, Vietnam* unwittingly lays bare, through its omissions and self-righteous moralism, the ideological components at work in its representational politics and its wider articulation of the broader discourse of Western colonialism.

Good Morning, Vietnam takes place in Saigon in 1965. The film is a partly fictionalized comedy drama about an army disc jockey, Adrian Cronauer, played by Robin Williams, who is sent to Vietnam to beef up the morale of the troops at a point when the military conflict is beginning its steep escalation. Cronauer arrives with two weapons in his personal arsenal. Deeply iconoclastic in style and wit, he combines his sense of irreverence with a manic wit that immediately breathes new life into the American Armed Forces radio station. Cronauer's short-lived sojourn in Saigon constitutes the heart of the film and parallels that period of the Vietnam conflict marked by increased conflict over the war at home and the escalation of military aggression against the Vietnamese people.

Cronauer first appears in Saigon as an irrepressible motor mouth who combines the style of the 1960s counterculture with the comic wit of an irreverent Bob Hope. Waiting to meet Cronauer at the Saigon military airport is Edward Garlick, an African American soldier played by Forest Whitaker. Garlick is one of the few blacks to appear in the film, and is immediately cast as a shuffling, clumsy grunt whose only mission in life appears to be laughing indiscriminately at all of Cronauer's jokes as his dutiful servant. Within the first minute of the film, Cronauer rattles off five jokes, insulting Garlick by telling him to get a new name and learn how to drive a jeep. Removing any doubt about his role as the colonial master, Cronauer proceeds to treat Garlick as his "domestic" tour guide, and orders him to follow various Vietnamese women about whom he makes sexist remarks while being driven to the military base. In many ways, Cronauer's arrival and his drive to the base sets up one of the primary structuring principles of the film. Not only does humor serve to position the identity of Vietnamese women as merely Western sexual commodities, it also links the objectification of the Vietnamese to the internal colonialism that Cronauer reproduces in his relationship with Garlick. Put another way, Cronauer's irreverence is far from free-floating. In fact, it is fueled, in part, by the sexism and racism that deeply scarred American actions in Vietnam. But Cronauer's racism, sexism, and unquestioned belief in the moral righteousness of the war are neither framed nor tempered in the scorching realism of earlier Vietnam films. Instead, they are couched in daily routines and actions that appear simply to provide fodder for the incessant delivery of one-liner jokes. Grounded in comic routines, Cronauer's reference to the Vietnamese as "little people," his claim that the Vietnamese women have "behinds designed by a Jewish scientist in Switzerland," and his portrayal of "dykes" as "big women standing near a river" position the audience to indulge their own complicity with such racism and sexism without having to be morally responsible for it.

Cronauer personifies all of the "sweetness and goodness" typical of Disney characters. Besieged on all fronts, he moves between the irreverence of Donald Duck and the gritty humanism of Dick Tracy. The first display of Cronauer's resistance appears early in the film over the choice of music to be aired on the army radio station. Confronted by his immediate army superiors, whose musical taste was shaped in the 1940s and is totally out of touch with the musical interests of the troops, Cronauer ditches the Mantovani, Percy Faith–style programming and unleashes a barrage of rock'n'roll music along with accompanying satirical skits. To the dismay of his commanding officer, Cronauer's radio show becomes a big hit among the troops and Cronauer begins to emerge as a popular, controversial figure in Saigon. By stressing the subversive qualities of rock'n'roll and popular culture, the film constructs one of the three major conflicts that will serve to define the Touchstone view of the war.

In the first instance, the struggle over popular music suggests that the war was primarily a generational conflict between teenaged soldiers reared on the rock'n'roll of James Brown, Martha and the Vandellas, and Wayne Fontana and the antiquated, middle-brow taste of an insensitive, out-of-touch military leadership. But the use of rock'n'roll music in this film also serves to rearticulate the politics of the war into a stylized aesthetics that renders the presence of the American troops in terms fashioned out of a tourist magazine. With few exceptions, the voice-over music is played against images of American soldiers playing volleyball, lounging casually on boats, hanging out in cafes, and walking in the streets of Saigon. One gets the impression, reproduced by the images that accompany the musical soundtrack of the film, that the soldiers in Vietnam are tourists flooding the local economy with their good will and buying power, or that they mostly hang around when on duty listening to the radio. As the champion of popular culture, Cronauer combines a touch of MTV hipness with a traditional dose of up-beat patriotism. Iconoclasm links in this case a depoliticized form of resistance with the highly political task of attempting to boost the morale of army soldiers intent on "exterminating the enemy."

The second major conflict that Cronauer faces concerns the military censorship of news. After a terrorist bombing of Jimmy Wha's, a popular Saigon nightclub, Cronauer defies his commanding officer and reports the incident in his radio news broadcast. What in fact might have emerged as an illuminating insight into the role of the media, government, and army in distorting the information given to the public about the war emerges instead as a narrative of personal anguish and self-pitying disillusionment. Suspended from his job, Cronauer offers neither critical insight into the broader reasons behind his dismissal nor any resistance to his fate. Instead, he soothes his wounded ego by hanging out in Saigon bars, fraternizing with Vietnamese nationals, and telling jokes to anyone who will listen. By privatizing the issue of media censorship, Touchstone erases any reference to the historical conditions that necessitated such censorship in the first place, shifting the terrain of anguish and suffering away from the massive devastation being waged on the Vietnamese people. In the end the audience is positioned to sympathize with the problems of a disgruntled, middle-class white man who also happens to be actively complicitous with a military machine "that dropped the greatest tonnage of bombs [in Vietnam] in the history of warfare—half a ton of explosives for every man, woman, and child" in Vietnam (Pilger 1990, 23).

The third major conflict that structures the film concerns Cronauer's relationship with "Otherness," that is, those Vietnamese men and women who inhabit the landscape outside of Cronauer's radio station. Soon after Cronauer arrives in Vietnam, he accosts and then follows a Vietnamese woman to an English class for Vietnamese civilians. He bribes the army officer teaching the class and takes it over in order to make contact with the woman he had followed. Using the class as the vehicle for a comedy routine, Cronauer attempts to teach English by focusing on the nuances of street corner American slang. This is a significant moment in the film not merely because of its unabashed celebration of portraying Vietnamese women as simply objects of a white, American male's sexual lust, but also because it further denies the cultural specificity of the linguistic and historical setting that Cronauer inhabits. After all, why should Vietnamese nationals be learning English? And why should they be learning American slang taught by a white man talking as if he were a working-class black? More importantly, the film's refusal to recognize that the Vietnamese have their own rich culture and history is at the heart of this scene. English has a long tradition of being the linguistic face of colonialism and that tradition is reinforced rather than disrupted in this film.

At the end of the class, Cronauer is confronted by the Vietnamese woman's brother, Tran, who tells him to keep away from his sister. Tran is quite clear about Cronauer's motives and describes him as simply another colonialist trying to buy his way into the culture. Cronauer ignores the comment and attempts to befriend him by taking him to a local nightclub. While at Jimmy Wha's club, Tran is confronted by some racist GIs who insult him and try to throw him out of the bar. Cronauer, once again, occupies the center stage and, in attempting to defend Tran, initiates a full-fledged brawl. Amazingly, Tran then becomes his Vietnamese friend and sidekick. Functioning as a devoted guide, Tran saves Cronauer from Jimmy Wha's nightclub minutes before it is blown up by the Vietcong. He arranges for Cronauer to visit his village, and he eventually saves Cronauer's life by rescuing him from a Vietcong patrol that has blown up his jeep and is searching for him in the jungles outside of Saigon. What is startling about Tran's character is that near the end of *Good Morning, Vietnam* it is revealed that he is a Vietcong terrorist!

Tran's character is significant because it combines a dual reading and interpretation, one that is both racist and colonial. In the first instance, Tran embodies the long history of racial stereotypes that permeate hegemonic versions of popular culture in the United States.[7] More specifically, Tran's character and relationship to Cronauer exemplify the use of racial representations to designate "Otherness" as an embodiment of infantilism, as a signifier for excluding those who do not belong to the national community. In this representation, Tran is denied any significant human presence. Instead, he is presented through a dominant fantasy which reduces the Other to an object of pleasure and servility. In terms closer to home, Tran is the

Vietnamese version of Tonto serving his colonial master obediently and generously. Within such representations, Tran is denied any sense of agency that would problematize the American military presence in Vietnam. Within this "racially saturated field of visibility" (Butler 1993, 15), Tran becomes simply another "gook" who is both marginal and irrelevant to the viewer's understanding of the political and historical nature of the Vietnamese war. Commenting on the use of such representations in American literature, Toni Morrison puts it well: "cooperative or sullen," she writes, "they are Tontos all, whose role is to do everything possible to serve the Lone Ranger without disturbing his indulgent delusion that he is indeed alone" (1992, 82).

But Tran is doubly represented in this film. Not only is he presented as the Hollywood version of Tonto, he is also portrayed at the end of the film as a Vietcong terrorist. Shocked by the revelation that his trusted friend is a member of the Vietnamese resistance, Cronauer searches Tran out and castigates him for betraying their friendship and trust. Embodying both the myth of the solitary hero and the righteous, puritanical American, Cronauer employs the language of humanism to highlight his own angst and to position Tran (and all Vietnamese resistance fighters) as criminal and terrorist. Mobilizing all of the courtroom drama that was recently played out in the public press over the Los Angeles riots, *Good Morning, Vietnam* presents criminality and lawlessness as a racial category. In this instance, Tran symbolizes all those "Others" who jeopardize American national unity and threaten Western culture and civility.

If Tran is the colonial Other, Tran's sister is nearly invisible except as an object of lust and desire. Though she refuses to date Cronauer, her identity is completely constructed within his patriarchal gaze. Her refusal is not expressed as a form of resistance to American imperialism or to the relentless assaults of Cronauer's sexism, but as the Vietnamese custom of civility. Tuan refuses to become romantically involved with him because her family and community frown on such behavior by Vietnamese women. When Cronauer is about to leave Saigon, he meets with her and his class of students one last time. As a parting gesture, he engages in a game of American baseball with the students and appears forlorn that he could not consummate his romantic fantasies. Tuan also smiles, indicating that if it weren't for the war, they would be able to indulge their repressed passions. In this instance, Tuan is portrayed as a tragic character who has to repress her desires because of the inconvenience of the war. Tuan becomes nothing more than a stick figure, a Barbie doll who merely testifies to the frustration, heterosexuality, and virility of the lonely, American hero. At the conclusion of the film, an extraordinary spectacle of Disney sentimentality is displayed when Cronauer's English class thanks him for teaching them English and Tuan in turn thanks him for being so kind!

There are two related but important scenes that frame the conclusion of *Good Morning, Vietnam*. As Cronauer is being driven to the airfield, the camera focuses on the new recruits entering Saigon. On one level, this is an obvious comment on the increasing escalation of the war that took place in 1965. On another less obvious level, it expresses the deeply racist nature of this film. Almost all of the recruits are white and middle class. This is an amazing representation given that a disproportionate number of soldiers who fought in Vietnam were poor, high school dropouts, black, and Hispanic. As Cronauer is about to catch his plane, he says to Garlick, his black aide, "Carry on, Montesque." True to the colonial character of the film, Garlick replies "I like that, it makes me feel British."

Good Morning, Vietnam does more than produce a series of racial and colonial representations. It also constructs all of the comfortable myths at work in the dominant rewriting of the war itself. Specifically, the film substitutes psychological, existential, and subjective narratives for a historical and political analysis of American involvement in the war. It erases any sense of collective agency or responsibility and builds its narrative structure around the emotional and "heart-rending" experiences of the isolated, alienated, American resister. Moreover, it redefines resistance in terms that are apolitical and ahistorical. Completely missing from this film is any indication that there was a massive anti-war movement and an enormous number of soldiers who opposed the war, or any examination of the nature of the colonial and racist policies that produced such resistance in the first place.

Pedagogies of Power and the Imperative of Pedagogy

Good Morning, Vietnam is an exemplary cultural text because it offers the potential for a critical reading of how the politics of innocence works to conceal the ideological principles used to legitimate a racist conception of the Vietnam War, a nostalgic sense of history, and a narrow view of the imperatives of the nation-state. As a popular culture text, *Good Morning, Vietnam* functions through a series of discursive and ideological practices that are both pedagogical and political. As part of a larger cultural apparatus, it signifies the importance of film as a central medium of popular culture that must be addressed not simply as a pedagogical apparatus actively involved in diverse identity formations, but also for the crucial role it plays in the construction of national identities in the service of global expansion and colonialism. What I am suggesting here is the need for social movements and cultural workers to redefine the parameters of the relationship between the political and the pedagogical and to recognize the need to produce alternative pedagogical approaches to popular culture. These alternatives would disrupt dominant cultural attempts to mobilize popular memory that enable "cultural institutions and cultural arbiters to present their histories as seamless, disinterested, and authoritative, and their hierarchies of value as universally valid, ecumenical, and effectively consensual" (Solomon-Godeau 1991, xxii).

In recognizing that cultural texts such as *Good Morning, Vietnam* mobilize social memories to legitimate particular versions of the past, it becomes imperative for left cultural workers to expand their understanding of the various sites in which a pedagogy of power is used to produce particular narratives, representations, and stories about who is authorized to speak, under what conditions, and in whose interest. If we live in an age that borders on a crisis of forgetting, it is all the more imperative that we expand the boundaries of the political to encompass not merely formerly marginalized cultural practices, but also a new politics of representation.[8] At the very least such a politics would require, as Roger Simon has pointed out, a consideration of all those various pedagogical sites in which the past is being constructed as crucial locations of struggle. This suggests extending the meaning and practice of pedagogy far beyond the boundaries of schools. Furthermore, it suggests redefining how cultural politics can be understood beyond the often highly guarded boundaries of single-issue considerations and identity politics. This is both a call for a hybridized politics and the recognition that questions concerning the relationship between authority and power must address the issue of who has control over the conditions necessary for the production of knowledge. At stake here are questions of access, political economy, and a representational politics that lays bare its own practices in relation to the dominant relations of cultural, material, and social production.

By erasing the political and ethical considerations that make history a site of struggle, Disney has produced a filmic version of popular culture through a pedagogy that rewrites history as inheritance and human agency as a condition for adapting to existing sites of injustice. Electronically mediated images, especially television and film, represent one of the most potent arms of cultural hegemony in the twenty-first century. Constituted as a public sphere with an enormous global reach, the power of the electronic media reinforces

Henry A. Giroux

Stuart Hall's claim that there is no politics outside of representation. But if progressive cultural workers are to take such a politics seriously they must use pedagogy as an articulating category to unravel how they might actively share in developing alternative conditions for giving people ownership over the control and production of knowledge and authority in the service of a radical democratic politics. The influential pedagogues of the twentieth century are not simply the hard-working teachers of the public school system, they are the hegemonic cultural workers who wield a pedagogy of power through the representations that structure the public cultures of advertising, radio talk shows, the malls, and the cinema duplexes. It is in these public cultures, fashioned through powerful forms of address, that the intersection of unmet needs and the mundane desires of daily life are made concrete. Within these public cultures, people both identify and lose themselves differently in representations that bring them the promise of hope or, more likely, the swindle of fulfillment.

The challenge of a new cultural politics, one that takes popular and media culture seriously, is as much a pedagogical challenge as it is a political one. The issue for cultural workers is not merely to recognize the importance of cultural texts such as *Good Morning, Vietnam* in shaping social identities, but to address how representations are constructed and taken up through social memories that are taught, learned, mediated, and appropriated within particular institutional and discursive formations of power. Any social movement that ignores this issue, regardless of how theoretically enlightened it may be, runs the risk of reproducing a politics that is silent about its own pedagogical formation and thus unresponsive to how it silences or terrorizes in the name of a self-serving appeal to social justice. Central to the formation of a new cultural politics are both the need for a renewed interest in the relationship between material determinations and the arousal of dormant emancipatory memories, and the construction of social movements that are as deeply pedagogical as they are political in their attempts to revitalize the institutional and ideological conditions necessary for diverse forms of political activism aimed at sustaining democratic public life.

Notes

1. This issue is taken up in Giroux (1992); Aronowitz (1993); Gilroy (1991); Trinh (1991); hooks (1992); and Grossberg (1993).
2. For a critique of theoretical positions that argue that the "real" issues in left politics

are undermined by discourses around identity, representations, agency, and culture, see Butler (1991) and Barrett (1992).

3. For example, Jane Kuenz (1993) and Susan Willis (1993) have analyzed how in Disney's theme parks intimacy, imagination, and spontaneity are replaced by the expertise of the well-placed park attendants, the picture perfect photo sites, and the endless spectacles in which fun becomes consumption and memory is reduced to the purchase of souvenirs. Similarly, theorists such as Dorfman and Matellart (1975) have indicated how Disney's comics serve to reproduce sexist, racist, and colonial ideologies. (Editor's note: see also Ramona Fernandez's "Pachuco Mickey" [1995].)

4. On the issue of memory and politics, I am indebted to the writings of Simon (1993); Kaye (1991); Adamson (1984); Tiderman (1985); Yerushalmi (1989); and Young (1990).

5. For example, see Weiner's (1993) comments on the Disney company's involvement in preventing Marc Eliot's book, *Walt Disney: Hollywood's Dark Prince*, from being published by Bantam in 1991.

6. A superb anthology on Hollywood films and the Vietnam War can be found in Dittmar and Michard (1990). For two exceptional critiques of Vietnam War films, see Pilger (1990) and Hoberman (1989).

7. For an interesting analysis of this issue, see the various essays in Gooding-Williams (1993); see also Pieterse (1992) and Gilman (1985).

8. On the politics of pedagogy and representation, see Aronowitz and Giroux (1991) and Trend (1992).

References

Adamson, Walter. 1984. *Marx and the Disillusionment of Marxism*. Berkeley: University of California Press.

Adorno, Theodor. 1974. *Minima Moralia: Reflections from a Damaged Life*. Trans. E. F. N. Jephcott. London: New Left Books.

Aronowitz, Stanley. 1993. *Roll Over Beethoven: The Return of Cultural Strife*. Hanover, NH: Wesleyan University Press.

Aronowitz, Stanley, and Henry A. Giroux. 1991. *Postmodern Education*. Minneapolis: University of Minnesota Press.

Bailey, David, and Stuart Hall. 1992. "The Vertigo of Displacement." *Ten.8* 2(3): 15–23.

Barrett, Michele. 1992. "Words and Things: Materialism and Method in Contemporary Feminist Analysis." In *Destabilizing Theory*, ed. Michele Barrett and Anne Phillips. Stanford: Stanford University Press.

Butler, Judith. 1991. "Contingent Foundations: Feminism and the Question of Postmodernism." In *Feminists Theorize the Political*, ed. Judith Butler and Joan W. Scott. New York: Routledge.

———. 1993. "Endangered/Endangering: Schematic Racism and White Paranoia." In *Reading Rodney King, Reading Urban Uprising*, ed. Robert Gooding-Williams. New York: Routledge.

Clifford, John. 1990. "On Collecting Art and Culture." In *Out There: Marginalization and Contemporary Cultures*, ed. Russell Ferguson, Martha Gever, Trinh T. Minh-ha, and Cornel West. Cambridge: MIT Press.

Henry A. Giroux

Corrigan, Timothy. 1991. *A Cinema without Walls: Movies and Culture after Vietnam.* New Brunswick: Rutgers University Press.

Culhane, John. 1986. "Robin Williams Belts Out Verbal Jazz in *Vietnam.*" *New York Times,* 20 December.

Dittmar, Linda, and Gene Michard, eds. 1990. *From Hanoi to Hollywood: The Vietnam War in American Film.* New Brunswick: Rutgers University Press.

Dorfman, A., and A. Mattelart. 1975. *How to Read Donald Duck: Imperialist Ideology in the Disney Comic.* New York: International General Editions.

Eliot, Marc. 1994. *Walt Disney: Hollywood's Dark Prince.* New York: Bantam.

Fernandez, Ramona. 1995. "Pachuco Mickey." In *From Mouse to Mermaid: The Politics of Film, Gender, and Culture,* ed. Elizabeth Bell, Lynda Haas, and Laura Sells. Bloomington: Indiana University Press.

Gilman, Sander L. 1985. *Difference and Pathology: Stereotypes of Sexuality, Race, and Madness.* Ithaca: Cornell University Press.

Gilroy, Paul. 1991. *There Ain't No Black in the Union Jack.* Chicago: University of Chicago Press.

Giroux, Henry A. 1992. *Border Crossings: Cultural Workers and the Politics of Education.* New York: Routledge.

Giroux, Henry A., and Peter McLaren, eds. 1993. *Between Borders: Pedagogy and the Politics of Cultural Studies.* New York: Routledge.

Gooding-Williams, Robert, ed. 1993. *Reading Rodney King, Reading Urban Uprising.* New York: Routledge.

Grossberg, Lawrence. 1993. *We Gotta Get Out of This Place: Popular Conservatism and Postmodern Culture.* New York: Routledge.

Hall, Stuart. 1992. "What Is This 'Black' in Popular Culture?" In *Black Popular Culture,* ed. Gina Dent. Seattle: Bay Press.

Hoberman, J. 1989. "Vietnam: The Remake." In *Remaking History,* ed. Barbara Kruger and Phil Mariani. Seattle: Bay Press.

hooks, bell. 1992. *Black Looks: Race and Representation.* Boston: South End Press.

Kaye, Harvey. 1991. *The Powers of the Past.* Minneapolis: University of Minnesota Press.

Kuenz, Jane. 1993. "It's a Small World After All: Disney and the Pleasures of Identification." *The South Atlantic Quarterly* 92(1): 63–88.

Mercer, Kobena. 1992. "Back to My Routes: A Postscript on the 80s." *Ten.8* 2(3): 32–39.

Mitgang, Herbert. 1993. "Disney Link to the F.B.I. and Hoover Is Disclosed." *New York Times,* 6 May, B1, B4.

Morrison, Toni. 1992. *Playing in the Dark: Whiteness and the Literary Imagination.* Cambridge: Harvard University Press.

Mydans, Seth. 1987. "Made in Thailand: New Films about Vietnam." *New York Times,* 4 June, A19.

Pieterse, Jane. 1992. *White on Black: Images of Africa and Blacks in Western Popular Culture.* New Haven: Yale University Press.

Pilger, John. 1990. "Vietnam, Another Hollywood Fairy Story." *The Guardian,* 10 March, 22–23.

Reese, Michael. 1985. "Black Humor Goes to War." *Newsweek,* 4 January, 50–51.

Rushdie, Salman. 1991. *Imaginary Homelands: Essays and Criticism 1981–1991.* London: Penguin Books.

Said, Edward. 1993. *Culture and Imperialism.* New York: Alfred A. Knopf.

Simon, Roger I. 1993. "Forms of Insurgency in the Production of Popular Memories: The

Columbus Quincentenary and the Pedagogy of Counter-Commemoration." *Cultural Studies* 7(1): 73–88.

Solomon-Godeau, Abigail. 1991. *Photography at the Dock: Essays on Photographic History, Institutions, and Practices.* Minneapolis: University of Minnesota Press.

Tiderman, Richard. 1985. *Discourse/Counter-Discourse.* Ithaca: Cornell University Press.

Trend, David. 1992. *Cultural Pedagogy: Art/Education/Politics.* New York: Bergin and Garvey.

Trinh T. Minh-ha. 1991. *When the Moon Waxes Red.* New York: Routledge.

Weiner, Jon. 1993. "Murdered Ink." *The Nation,* 256(21): 743–50.

Willis, Susan. 1993. "Disney World: Public Use/Private Space." *South Atlantic Quarterly* 92(1): 119–37.

Yerushalmi, Yosef Hayim. 1989. *Zakhor: Jewish History and Jewish Memory.* New York: Schocken Books.

Young, James E. 1990. *Writing and Rewriting the Holocaust: Narrative and the Consequences of Interpretation.* Bloomington: Indiana University Press.

Three

Pinocchio

Claudia Card

TO L.S.B. FOR WINTER SOLSTICE

In 1978 I bought a red and green Italian Pinocchio doll in a Solstice shopping spree with feminist friends in Syracuse. The doll triggered these reflections on honesty, childhood, moral education, and Walt Disney. These reflections also bear the influence of Susan Griffin's *Woman and Nature: The Roaring Inside Her* (1978) and Mary Daly's *Gyn/Ecology: The Metaethics of Radical Feminism* (1978), both then new texts for my course on feminism and sexual politics. I wrote most of this essay, and the poem following, between terms in Hanover, New Hampshire, while I was a visiting professor at Dartmouth.[1]

This season's holiday toy offerings feature an Italian-made wooden doll with two noses—a long one and a short one—that can be screwed onto his face. He comes in at least two sizes. There is a life-sized version for $200 and a smaller one for $35. I bought the one for $35, which seemed right enough for the shortest day of the year. He does not look like Walt Disney's Pinocchio. But he is unmistakable. I then bought a copy each of Carlo Collodi's *Adventures of Pinocchio* (1882; 1988) and *Walt Disney's Version of Pinocchio* (1939; 1989), and I read them both in one afternoon.[2] Honesty, lying, and fantasy had been on my mind. I had recently taught an honors course in philosophy on the topic of honor, reading Sissela Bok's *Lying: Moral Choice in Public and Private Choice* (1978) and Adrienne Rich's "Women and Honor: Some Notes on Lying" (1977). It was a good time to reread the Pinocchio tales. When I began, I could not recall the differences between the original and the Walt Disney version, apart from the looks of the Disney animated characters.

Mother read me both Pinocchios when I was five. Someone had given me the Walt Disney book. We went to the library to find the original story, which Mother remembered from her childhood. Pinocchio was a symbol for her.

Pinocchio

She had among her mementos a miniature wooden figure with a long nose, which I now have among mine, along with a Jiminy Cricket pin that she gave me when I was nine. Mother immortalized Pinocchio for family and friends in the first of her unpublished "Poems to Pinocchio" from the mid 1930s, composed after an affair of unrequited love. Mother's poem reverses a certain direction of the Pinocchio tale: she finds that someone she had thought was a human being is really made of wood. He has no feeling, no empathy. He is unreliable. He is a fake. She could not have written that poem had she not been familiar with the original story. Yet she decided in the 1940s that Disney's version was more suitable for me; his was the version that I heard over and over. That decision tells a tale of my early moral training.

It was the violence in the original story that led Mother to favor the Disney version for me. As I reread Collodi's *Adventures*, I remembered Mother telling me that Pinocchio didn't *really* kill Jiminy Cricket, who is only a nameless cricket in the original work. The violence appalled me as I read on. I was looking forward to revisiting Disney for a more humane version of this otherwise moving tale. Then I read the Disney version and found that the moral substance of the stories had been excised with the violence. Violence in the Italian fantasy of the 1880s is not gratuitous but serves as a vehicle of the knowledge and sensitivity required for the transition from puppet to person. *Pinocchio* tells a story of the acquisition of humanity, to which an appreciation of inhumanity is essential. By 1940, inhumanity was moving toward such dimensions that it is perhaps no wonder if Walt Disney was tempted to deny certain basic forms of it. And yet, the result is a moral distortion of what it means to grow up. Growing up, in the Disney version, is not only becoming tamed but also learning to please others and learning to follow orders. Growing up, in Collodi's original tale, requires not only learning self-discipline but also learning to discriminate whom to trust and whom not to, learning to reciprocate others' caring, and discovering when and why truth-telling is important.

In Collodi's *Adventures* Pinocchio acquires a conscience as he acquires the capacity to empathize and to reciprocate others' care. When he is in trouble and needs help, the ghost of the cricket (whom he *did* kill) appears and reminds him how he has treated those who were good to him. Disney's Jiminy Cricket, however, is a conscience in name only. Presented comically, not expecting to be taken seriously (and he is not), Jiminy Cricket is a reluctant surrogate parent, mouthing instructions to Pinocchio and tagging along to scold when they are disobeyed. No reason is given why Pinocchio should obey these instructions. Disney's Blue Fairy gives Pinocchio the potentiality to become a Real Boy as a reward *to Geppetto* for bringing pleasure to children as a toymaker. Pinocchio, it seems, is to be Geppetto's own special toy. But why should *Pinocchio* want to *be* a Real Boy? Why should he want to please Geppetto or the Blue Fairy? Apparently, it does not matter. Disney makes Jiminy Cricket a tolerant conscience who causes Pinocchio no real pain.

In Carlo Collodi's fantasy Pinocchio is formed by his "Papa," Geppetto, from a piece of wood given him by the carpenter, Mr. Antonio, also known as Mr. Cherry (because of the look of his nose). The matter from which Pinocchio is formed—the piece of wood—is already alive. It is organic, hostile, mischievous, and magical. Magic has a history as the knowledge possessed by witches—herbal healers, midwives, abortionists—who have been misogynistically viewed in popular culture as evil (as is matter itself, with which women have been identified). None of the evil characters in Collodi's story is explicitly female. But the symbolism is there in the hostile, wild, magical matter from which the puppet is formed. It is also there in the animals. Most of the evil characters are animals. Not only are they not human, they are inhumane. Although they are given masculine genders, they personify myths of feminine evil stereotypically in the form of deception and manipulation: the fox (vixen) who feigns lameness, the cat who feigns blindness, the serpent who laughs. There is also the great fish with a womb-like belly from which an escape must be made. All but the fish suffer or die because of their character traits. However, nothing bad happens to evil men in the story. All the humans in the story are male. The only good female is a Fairy with blue hair. She appears first as a beautiful child, and Pinocchio falls in love with her. Later, grown up while Pinocchio is still a child, she is seductive, unattainable, immaterial. The deep structure of this tale appears to present becoming human as a triumph of masculine order, responsibility, and honor over earthly feminine wildness and evil. Nothing is so blatant in Carlo Collodi's chapters, however, as the sexual politics Walt Disney introduced with Geppetto's male cat, Figaro, who *eats fish* and carries on flirtation with Geppetto's female goldfish, Cleo, who lives in a glass bowl. Such a flirtation with an intended item of consumption introduces the child viewer, however inadvertently, to the pleasures of pornography, the erotic joys of males preying upon females. Neither Figaro nor Cleo were among Collodi's characters.

Despite the thinly veiled sexuo-political message about who can become a person and what that requires, Carlo Collodi's conception of what it means to be a person has a moral depth that the Walt Disney conception lacks. In Collodi's story both the Fairy and Geppetto care for Pinocchio. What it means to care varies according to the gender of Collodi's carer. For males it means magnanimous sacrifice for another's needs. Geppetto sells his coat to buy Pinocchio a spelling book. By the end of the tale, Pinocchio is working hard to buy Geppetto a new coat and to pay for care for the Fairy in the hospital. For the Fairy, caring means service—physical and moral nurturing. She nurses Pinocchio back to health when he is dying, getting him to take the bad-tasting medicine. (She is a good witch.) She also embarrasses him by making his nose grow when he lies to try to conceal his betrayal of her trust. (She is exposing him. The nose looks like a grotesque phallus.) She is explicitly in charge of his moral development in a way that Geppetto is not. Through her care, Pinocchio comes to appreciate Geppetto's as well. Her suffering over Pinocchio consists in her mourning his absence when he does not return to her after he is well. Unlike Geppetto, she does not go out to search for him. Pinocchio also mourns her when he thinks she has died. But he searches for Geppetto. Although they do it differently, Geppetto and the Fairy each care for him for his own sake. This is what he gradually discovers and learns to do for them in return.

Collodi's Pinocchio starts out impulsive, hostile, disobedient, selfish, and lazy. His moral development is presented not simply, or even basically, as learning obedience but, basically, as learning to discriminate regarding whom to trust, which requires his discovering what it means to be cared about for himself. As he learns this, he learns to live up to the trust of those who care for him and to trust and care for them as well. A work ethic is part of these lessons. An episode near the end reminds contemporary readers of the story of the little red hen, with the Fairy playing the part of the hen (disguised as an old woman). It has finally fallen to the Fairy even to teach Pinocchio the value of work.

Carlo Collodi treated the topic of lying in terms of trust, reciprocity, and caring. In the beginning, Geppetto tells a magnanimous lie: "Why did you sell your coat, Papa?" "Because I was too warm." (The reader is told that Pinocchio understood this instantly.) Near the end, the Fairy—less admirably—deceives Pinocchio to test his character by pretending to have died to see whether he will mourn her, too. Then she pretends to be an old woman to see whether he will help her even though she is not beautiful and to give him a chance to work for his keep. The fox and cat, on the other hand, pretend misfortune in order to swindle Pinocchio and then actually suffer the misfortunes they have pretended. Pinocchio's nose grows when he betrays the trust of the Fairy who is caring for him. (He promises to take the medicine if she will give him sugar first and then tries to back out after the sugar.)

But Pinocchio must also learn to lie in self-defense against tyrants. This emerges in an adventure containing a piece of social criticism, reproduced nowhere by Walt Disney. After being swindled by the fox and cat, Pinocchio is imprisoned for being the *victim* of a crime. He is released only when a new ruler comes to power. However, in order to be released, he must identify himself *falsely* as a criminal. (His nose does not grow this time.)

Walt Disney preserves only three of the dozen or so adventures between the separation and reunion of Pinocchio and Geppetto: the episodes of the puppeteer, Pleasure Island, and the rescue from the belly of the great fish (who has become a whale, a mammal). The meanings of these episodes, however, are not preserved. A new tone is set in the beginning. The Italian carpenter has been transformed into a kindly, but none-too-bright, well-fed toymaker who resembles Santa Claus and lives in a cool climate. (Frequent scenes of peaceful village rooftops under moonlight suggest a sleigh and reindeer, contributing a Christmas-like atmosphere.) To reward Geppetto for pleasing children, the Fairy gives life to one of his toys, and she tells this lucky toy that he can become a Real Boy if he learns to be good, brave, and true, but that it is totally up to him. And she is right. It is. Nobody teaches him what these things mean, and the only one he clearly figures out for himself is bravery. But he becomes a Real Boy, anyway (because in America there is always a happy ending). The Fairy does not nurture him, although she reappears at one point to punish him (by making his nose grow).

The story begins with Geppetto singing and dancing with him, which is exactly what Pinocchio sets out to do in the world at large when Geppetto sends him off to school. It seems entirely a matter of gratuitous misfortune that this attitude gets Pinocchio into trouble. Pinocchio's badness is reduced to his hedonism, disobedience, and a kind of cheerful capriciousness. He is not hostile, nor even particularly selfish or mischievous. He is an adorable child. Eventually he is led into smoking, drinking, and vandalism, which are presented as fun until it becomes ridiculous. Being bad has finally boiled down to making an ass of oneself. A donkey in Collodi's day was someone who was used by others and discarded when no longer useful. A Walt Disney donkey is someone who is absurd, someone who is not adorable or cute.

A Disney ideal of being good is conveyed in the tale's climax, a macho exercise in heroism, supplemented by good old American know-how. Papa Geppetto comes off as fairly stupid. (This will help sell the movie to children.) If all that were necessary to escape from the whale were to make the beast sneeze, why did Geppetto not think of it? In Collodi's adventure, Pinocchio was able to save Geppetto because he could swim so well (he floats better because he is made of wood), and even this was not sufficient: he received help from a tuna fish whom he had helped on a previous occasion. (He has joined the Old Boy network.) It was not even necessary to make the great fish (a shark, not a mammal) sneeze. They waited until he was asleep and swam out together. Pinocchio is thus not made to appear cleverer than his Papa but is presented as reciprocating Geppetto's braving of dangers in order to be reunited and as reaping the benefits of his previous goodwill.

Pinocchio's bad lies in the Disney version (unlike in Collodi's tale, there are no good lies) are clumsy attempts to cover disobedience. He lies about why he did not go to school, but not about why he has not kept a bargain with someone who cares for him. One wonders why he bothers to lie. Is he afraid? But he has suffered already. Apparently, he lies to cover his embarrassment for having been made a fool (by the puppeteer and the fox and cat). This lie, not presented as a betrayal of trust, is merely a poor cover for having disobeyed orders and got himself into a ridiculous position. (He is in a cage.) He is made even more ridiculous when his nose grows. The message conveyed is altogether different from that of the original story: one must tell the truth to one's superiors (those in power), contrary to Carlo Collodi's social criticism of that very idea. Telling the truth no longer has any connection with reciprocity, trust, or caring. Obedience becomes unhinged from these things as well. The penalty for dishonesty and disobedience is that *one makes a fool of oneself*—or one is made a fool. It is not that one ceases to be loved for oneself. The Walt Disney Pinocchio has no such thing to lose. The worst that befalls him is losing his good looks, ceasing to be adorable.

The Walt Disney objective, one suspects, was to *sell* Pinocchio to children rather than to *teach* them. The Disney version erased not only the physical cruelty and violence of the original story but also the pain of betrayal, and substituted the pain of humiliation at the hands of the powerful. Becoming a person is presented as learning to avoid humiliation by pleasing one's father (and making up for disobedience with heroism), to whom one is a reward conferred by the Good Fairy for having provided pleasure. Ironically, becoming a person in the Disney version is, in some ways, becoming more of a puppet than Geppetto's toy was in Carlo Collodi's tale.

Pinocchia (1978)

She was a child of Disneyland, much like Pinocchio—
    A reward to her father, his favorite toy
    (Left to his Fairy to train and subdue).
    She tried very hard to become a Real Boy.
    She was told she must learn to be Good, Brave, and True.
After years in the School of Humiliation
    She learned to please the Powerful.
She suffered the cruelty and the violence
    That Disney's Land denies.

She learned in this Land to deny her own pain
    (She denied that of others as well).
She was finally seduced by another mad Fairy,
    Who laughed at the stuff she was made of.
She stopped being a Disney child.
She stopped being a puppet.
Who is she becoming NOW?
A Midwife? A Witch? An Amazon Spinster?
She never became a Real Boy,
But at last she's a Wild piece of Matter.

Postscript (1992)

Maurice Sendak, in his introduction to the beautiful Abrams edition of *The Walt Disney Version of Pinocchio* (1989), presents an interpretation that is diametrically opposed to mine, in contrasting the Walt Disney version with Carlo Collodi's original tale. Like my mother, he, too, is stopped by the violence in the original. It seems to him, as it did to her, cruel and frightening. However, his main objection to Collodi's *Adventures*, which he confesses to never having liked even as a child, is what he finds to be its premise about the nature of the child. As Mr. Sendak sees it, "Children, Collodi appears to be saying, are inherently bad, and the world itself is a ruthless, joyless place, filled with hypocrites, liars, and cheats. Poor Pinocchio is *born* bad."[3] The solution he sees Collodi offering is for Pinocchio "to yield up his own self entirely, unquestioningly, to his father" and later, likewise, to the Fairy, whom he promises to obey. Mr. Sendak's basis for this view is the Fairy's sermon to Pinocchio late in the story about the value of work and how laziness is "a serious illness." The Walt Disney version, by contrast, presents Pinocchio as "innocent," "both lovable and loved," and "therein lies Disney's triumph . . . a reassuring sense that Pinocchio is loved for himself—and not for what he should or shouldn't be." Thus, Mr. Sendak finds, "Disney has corrected a terrible wrong. Pinocchio, he says, is good; his 'badness' is only a matter of inexperience."

It would be hard to find an interpretation more opposed to mine. The keys to our differences may lie in our understandings of good and bad character and of what it means to be loved for oneself. In Mr. Sendak's view, as perhaps in the Walt Disney view, a child's "goodness" appears to be a combination of attractiveness, absence of hostility ("innocence"), and malleability. And it is surely true that the Walt Disney Pinocchio is a beautiful child, free of hostility, and utterly pliable. The child's "badness," in Mr. Sendak's

Pinocchio

words, "is only a matter of inexperience." Collodi's Pinocchio, by contrast, is not beautiful; he is funny-looking. (He is not yet attractive, not yet lovable.) And he is bad in ways that romanticists of childhood may like to forget. Not only does he not yet know how to take another's point of view—nor, therefore, how to empathize—but also he takes a certain pleasure in cruelty (as in killing the cricket), which he needs to learn empathy to overcome. Children's pleasures in cruelty need not be construed as malicious in order to be acknowledged as bad. The sense of power or agency experienced in behavior that evidently hurts others can be as much fun to a child as any other evidently effective behavior. Yet, enjoyment in deliberately harming others is bad. Nor is Pinocchio totally innocent. He has incurred obligations to benefactors, obligations he neither recognizes nor knows how to fulfill. Indifference to the sufferings of benefactors is one meaning of ingratitude. Pinocchio at first experiences both cruel enjoyment and the indifference of ingratitude. This is not just incidental to who he is, thus far. To be loved for himself at this stage is to be loved for the sake of potentialities not yet realized.

Through his adventures, Collodi's Pinocchio learns empathy. He is not simply molded, passively affected, however. His faculty of judgment develops, and he changes himself. In learning to take others' viewpoints, he learns about reciprocity and how to discriminate regarding whom to trust. He is developing character, becoming good, at the same time as he learns to recognize goodness in others. Unfortunately, the world *is* full of "hypocrites, liars, and cheats." Collodi had faith that one could learn to distinguish between the many who are and the few who are not. The goodness that Pinocchio acquires in Collodi's *Adventures* is neither the "lovableness" with which Pinocchio is born in the Walt Disney version nor the simple-minded obedience that Mr. Sendak rightly deplores. Rather, it is the ability and desire to reciprocate caring, thereby becoming worthy of being cared for. Perhaps only in America (or in some segments of American popular culture) are children not expected to become, eventually, worthy of the freely bestowed love of their care-takers. And perhaps only in American popular culture is heroism widely thought an adequate substitute for having a sense of justice.

My mother's "Pinocchio," dated December 1935, was addressed to a man who remained a child, in Collodi's sense. It says, in part:

I thought beneath that crisply
    gleaming shell
There was a human man to love or
    hate—

And so I strove to reach the man,
Futilely hoping, soon or late,
To touch him.

And when at last I broke the
    shining case,
I found a mockery, a cheat,
    a foe—
Only a little man of wood was
    there,
Pinocchio.

Notes

1. Editors' note: Disney's animated version of *Pinocchio* (1940) is widely regarded as one of the best animated films ever made. As one of the most technologically sophisticated and financially risky films of its time, *Pinocccchio* is a central piece in the Disney corpus. Readers interested in the technological and financial origins of the film are directed to the entry on *Pinocchio* in John Grant (1993). An excellent analysis of plot and character changes Disney made in Collodi's novel, which supports much of the present essay and postscript, is available in Street (1983). Carlo Collodi, pseudonym of Carlo Lorenzini (1826–1890), was an Italian journalist and government official. *The Adventures of Pinocchio*, originally written as a serial, was released as a book in 1883 and translated to English in 1892.

2. I no longer have the editions that I had in 1978. See references for 1988 and 1989 editions. I recently viewed once again the 1940 Walt Disney animated film, *Pinocchio*. The Disney book follows the film closely.

3. All quotations in this Postscript are from Maurice Sendak, "Walt Disney's Triumph: The Art of *Pinocchio*," a four-page introduction to *Walt Disney's Version of Pinocchio* (1989). The pages in this book are not numbered.

References

Bok, Sissela. 1978. *Lying: Moral Choice in Public and Private Life*. New York: Pantheon.

Collodi, Carlo. (1882) (1988) 1944. *The Adventures of Pinocchio,* trans. E. Harden. Illustrated by Roberto Innocenti. New York: Knopf.

Daly, Mary. 1978. *Gyn/Ecology: The Metaethics of Radical Feminism*. Boston: Beacon.

Disney, Walt. (1939) 1989. *Walt Disney's Version of Pinocchio*. New York: Random House Abrams.

Grant, John. 1993. *Encyclopedia of Walt Disney's Animated Characters*. New York: Hyperion.

Griffin, Susan. 1978. *Woman and Nature: The Roaring Inside Her*. New York: Harper and Row.

Rich, Adrienne. 1977. "Women and Honor: Some Notes on Lying." *Heresies* 1(1): 23–27.

Pinocchio

Pamphlet by Motherroot Publications, Pittsburgh, 1978. Rpt. in *On Lies, Secrets, and Silence: Selected Prose 1966–1978*. New York: Norton, 1979.

Sendak, Maurice. 1989. "Walt Disney's Triumph: The Art of *Pinocchio*." Introduction to *Walt Disney's Version of Pinocchio*. New York: Random House Abrams.

Street, Douglas. 1983. "*Pinocchio*—From Picaro to Pipsqueak." In *Children's Novels and the Movies*, ed. Douglas Street. New York: Frederick Ungar.

Four

Disney Does Dutch
Billy Bathgate and the Disneyfication
of the Gangster Genre

Robert Haas

> Traditionally, Hollywood studios subdivided their annual production into
> specific genre films that, if nothing else, served as a useful way of strik-
> ing a balance between product standardization and differentiation. Main-
> taining certain formulas that would stabilize audience expectations and,
> by extension, stabilize those audiences, was obviously in Hollywood's
> best interests. But how does the category of genre "work" today when
> popular entertainment is undergoing such a massive recategorization
> brought on by the ever-increasing number of entertainment options and
> the fragmentation of what was once thought to be a mass audience into a
> cluster of "target" audiences? (Collins 1993, 243)

Film genre criticism is enjoying a renaissance through the intervention of
cultural critics and their attention to popular film. Carol J. Clover's *Men,
Women, and Chainsaws* (1992), for example, examines gender issues in the
modern horror film; Jane Tompkins explores the cultural, aesthetic, and gender codes of the western in *West of Everything* (1992); and William Paul's
Laughing Screaming: Modern Hollywood Horror and Comedy (1994) treats the
extremely popular and lucrative "gross out" movie. These new studies attempt to interrogate and rearticulate formalistic approaches to narrative
cinema. Classifying films by genre in the 1990s, as either a conscious or unconscious act, allows critics to examine the complexities of audience/enun-
ciation/identification, sociocultural values and their historical significance,
and constructions of gender/sexuality. Genre theory sets these issues within
a recognizable framework of filmic conventions by which meaning is interpreted in and through accepted patterns and expectations of particular films.

To that end, genre conventions have, over the years, remained fairly constant. Westerns, horror, science fiction, and gangster films have maintained
culturally accepted and constructed conventions that promote, through box
office revenue, a profitable enterprise for the producers and distributors of
the film. Even films classified as "postmodern" maintain generic conven-

tions: the panoramic vistas, saloon shootouts, and enigmatic protagonist of *Stagecoach* (1939) are equally evident in Clint Eastwood's "revisionist" Western, *Unforgiven* (1992), but the power of these conventions is disputable. The gangster genre, for example, has remained relatively unchanged since the 1930,s[1] and John G. Cawelti claims it "may have reached a point of creative exhaustion" (1985, 519). Even use of the phrase "genre" may have reached a similar point. In a postmodern society, genre boundaries are routinely blurred, and critics often prefer to examine films in terms, not of generic expectations, but of audience expectations.

Despite a postmodern erosion of genre as a critical category, gangster films are as inseparable from their fulfillment of generic conventions as they are from their loyal audiences. Typically, the formulaic gangster film fulfills three essential characteristics: (1) secularized Puritanism, especially a person's relationship to good and evil; (2) social Darwinism, which insists that a person is very often a product of environment; and (3) perversion of the Horatio Alger myth, in which the "hero" must "rise from his status as urban waif to a position of monetary security and respectability" (Mitchell 1986, 160). This last pattern is especially important in terms of the visual conventions of gangster films, the trappings that fill the shot and influence the *mise-en-scène*—the urban streets, fedoras, double-breasted suits, limousines, running boards, and tommy guns. These indelible and formulaic images leave their impressions on audiences—and writers.

During press release interviews, E. L. Doctorow recalled that the image of a gangster in a tuxedo with his feet in a tub of cement motivated him to write *Billy Bathgate* (1989). From this familiar gangster-film convention of the 1930s, Doctorow created a novel that resonates across decades into the 1990s. Examining issues of history, gender, race, sexuality, and individuality, Doctorow remains faithful to and transcends the limitations of generic gangster conventions. Jim Collins could easily be referring to Doctorow's *Billy Bathgate* when he claims that

> the genre texts of the late 1980s–early 1990s demonstrate a . . . sophisticated hyperconsciousness concerning not just narrative formulae, but the conditions of their own circulation and reception in the present, which has a massive impact on the nature of popular entertainment. (1993, 248)

Audiences of the 1990s, with their vast stored knowledge of media-influenced trivia, can easily relate to a text that both applies and criticizes the patterns of any particular genre, especially one as readily identifiable as the gangster genre.

In 1991, Touchstone Pictures, a division of the Walt Disney Corporation, released its film version of *Billy Bathgate*. The film was a critical and financial failure, due in large part to its rejection of ideological and visual conventions of gangster films and the culture that made them relevant to Doctorow's *fin de siècle* readers. Disney replaced the generic conventions with its own series of equally successful but incongruous conventions and conspicuously ignored the social, political, or economic overtones of the novel. While Disney can be, and is, highly successful at predicting cultural reception, *Billy Bathgate* ventured into a generic world incompatible with the company's own ideological perspective. In simpler terms, they "Disneyfied" it. Culturally trained to judge a gangster film based on its predecessors, the "gangster" audience rejected this sanitized product as meaningless and uninteresting.

The Emergence of the Two Cinemas

In 1928, compelled by the enormous box office earnings of *The Jazz Singer* (1927), the major Hollywood studios converted to sound film production. The success of this new technology had an immediate effect on two distinct genres of motion pictures: the gangster film and the animated musical. While most studios considered sound a passing fad with the public and were slow to change their production facilities, two companies were able to forecast the lasting popular appeal and financial benefits of the "talkies," securing a powerful economic position in the film industry that they maintain today.

Warner Brothers, the producers of *The Jazz Singer*, was one of several minor studios formed after World War I, but was no threat to the five major companies before 1927. After the development of sound on film, however, Warners quickly overshadowed its competitors and the focus of its success rested on a series of violent and realistic gangster films that included William Wellman's *The Public Enemy* (1931), Howard Hawk's *Scarface* (1932), and *The Roaring Twenties* (1938).[2] The new realism permitted by the use of sound allowed this cycle of tersely directed urban gangster films to exploit armed violence and tough vernacular speech in a context of social alienation. Suddenly, Warner Brothers was a major player in "Tinsel Town" politics.

At the other end of the Hollywood spectrum was the fledgling Walt Disney Studio. Beginning with its first musical cartoon, "Steamboat Willie" (1928), which introduced Mickey Mouse to the world, and the "Silly Symphony" shorts, in which all of the action is set to music, Disney's success in sound/image synchronization was aimed squarely at the audience Warners ignored—the family. In fact, Disney's "Silly Symphony" series, begun in 1929 with "The Skeleton Dance" and culminating in 1933 with the immensely popular all-color hit, "The Three Little Pigs," pioneered the "animated musical" that today has attained feature length and critical status.

Unhampered by the restrictions of early sound-filming procedures that often required actors to assume unnatural positions and cameras to remain stationary behind soundproof glass, Disney combined sound and image in an expressive manner impossible for live-action narrative cinema. Because Disney could fit visual action to dialogue and music, achieving perfect frame-by-frame synchronization, the product was immensely appealing to audiences of the late 1920s and early 1930s.[3] The success of the cartoon shorts ultimately provided Disney with the recognition necessary to create *Snow White and the Seven Dwarfs* (1937), *Pinocchio* (1940), and *Fantasia* (1940) before the onset of World War II.

The cinema of Warners' gangster genre and Disney's family animation both filled a necessary niche in the search for audience and ticket sales. And although Warners ultimately self-censored its films due to pressure from the Hays Office and the League of Decency, which insisted that gangsterism be displayed as an odious and offensive lifestyle, both companies managed to survive and flourish throughout the next several decades and become two of the very few companies to withstand corporate takeover in the 1970s and '80s.

The Merging of the Two Cinemas

In the fall of 1991, sixty years after Warners initiated the first successful crime talkies, Touchstone Pictures released its first "gangster film": *Billy Bathgate*.[4] Directed by Robert Benton (*Kramer vs. Kramer* [1979] and *Places in the Heart* [1983]) and written by acclaimed playwright Tom Stoppard, this $50 million film was expected to be an enormous critical and commercial success, one of the jewels in Disney's 1991 season. Instead, the film was critically slammed and a commercial box office failure, prompting many critics to dub Benton's film "Billy-Gate" (after Michael Cimino's 1980 failure, *Heaven's Gate*).[5]

Since the 1960s, when big business conglomerates absorbed Hollywood, studio executives (who have more in common with CPA's than film artists) have attempted to plan strategies for every contingency in the filmmaking process and allow no project the "green light" unless it can prove itself risk free. It seems especially strange that Disney—known for its savvy in the business of making movies since its revitalization by Michael Eisner (CEO of the Walt Disney Corporation) and Jeffrey Katzenberg (chairman of Walt Disney Studios)—could blunder with such a seemingly foolproof commodity as *Billy Bathgate*. And yet, tracing the cause of the film's failure isn't necessarily difficult; the problem was the imposition of the Disney corporate philosophy, which emphasizes a high financial return on its family-oriented product, onto a generic framework antithetical to family. Yet box-office receipts from the early 1990s showed only that gangster films sold well, as evidenced by the success of *Goodfellas* (1990) and *The Godfather III* (1989). Their only drawback, as far as the Disney Corporation was concerned, was their high above-the-line costs.

In a press-leaked 1990 interoffice memo (known as the "Dick Tracy Memo"), Jeffrey Katzenberg railed against extravagant "above-the-line" spending costs that have become the norm in the 1990s.[6] He advocated low-cost, warm-hearted films that yield a high return on investment, such as *Pretty Woman* (1990), *Sister Act* (1992), and *The Mighty Ducks* (1992).[7] Additionally, a 1984 press release announcing the formation of Touchstone Pictures states:

> All across America, moviegoers want mature entertainment. But they
> don't want violence. They don't want exploitation. They don't want taste-
> less themes. They want quality. They want standards. And that is what we
> want at Disney's Touchstone Films.

With their stated credo of nonviolent, tasteful, low-cost production, a "green light" for the ultraviolent, sexy, high-cost *Billy Bathgate* would seem inconsistent with Disney's corporate philosophy and public image. In all fairness to Disney, this may only be obvious in retrospect. The studio executives were presented with a highly appealing property, combining top talent with a successful bestseller. And they were armed with the knowledge that they could employ the Disney formula, which had worked lucrative magic on other novels, to film.

In order to succeed as Disney's first gangster film, *Billy Bathgate* had to bridge the gap, which had existed for sixty years, between Warners' gangster genre audience and Disney's family audience. All genre films "provide a sense of repetition and familiarity. But the close tie between genre films and social ideology means as well that genre films are among the most fragile forms" (Ryan and Kellner 1988, 76). The creative team overlooked this fragility when they tied the Disney formula for success to an ideologically incompatible genre, audience, and powerful Doctorow novel. If the narrative were too racy and too violent, then it could easily be molded to the Disney conventions of innocent protagonists, male-oriented mentoring, patronized and objectified women, and the incorporation of luck mixed with destiny—standards that had always worked successfully in their animated work. Unable to rearticulate the gangster form in Disney's own idiom, *Billy Bathgate* instead unmasks Disney's own narrative and filmic ideologies. In spite of its fragility, the gangster genre, as the dark side of the Horatio Alger myth, was fundamentally at odds with Disney.

A Capable Boy

> I was a street kid from the Bronx living in the country like Little Lord Fauntleroy. None of these things made sense except as I was contingent to a situation. And when the situation changed, would I change with it? Yes, the answer was yes. And that gave me an idea that maybe all identification is temporary because you went through a life of changing situations. I found this a very satisfying idea to consider. I decided it was my license-plate theory of identification.—*Billy Bathgate*

Identification in Doctorow's novel is vastly important. Likewise, the notion of changing situations is relevant in the "text to film" experience that most successful novels undergo. In the novel *Billy Bathgate*, the character of Billy consistently expresses contradictory values, emotions, and symbolic references, often voicing the opposition between capitalist and Marxist ideology. Doctorow's Billy is a highly intertextual character who

> demonstrate[s] cultural continuity, which surfaces because Billy is parodically reminiscent of other "good" American Billies—the comic book Billy Batson and Melville's Billy Budd—all boys who are very "capable," a term used repeatedly to describe Billy Bathgate's talents. (Wagner-Martin 1990, 6)

But unlike these others, Billy the "good," despite his apparent desire to be ethical, is also a conscious accomplice to evil: "I could be a Bible student, and I could shoot a gun" (Doctorow 1989, 187). Billy successfully negotiates the moral oppositions in his life, solidifying both the problems and the solutions to identification throughout the novel, and engaging the reader on multiple levels of meaning.

The transformation of Billy's multifaceted personality from written text to film narrative presented an insurmountable challenge. Rooted firmly in melodramatic conventions, the Disney philosophy (or the Hollywood philosophy, for that matter) insisted that the characterization of young Billy could not be maintained on multiple generic levels. If Billy were to follow his cinematic peer-heroes at Disney, then his motives had to be pure and honorable, any character flaws recognized and corrected by film's end. And, most important economically, he had to represent Disney's audience: the family, especially young white males, who not only had to recognize themselves within the character, but conversely, accept Billy as one of their own. First, then, the filmmakers had to overcome Billy Bathgate's background.

Billy is a first generation, ethnic street kid, born and raised in the Bronx. His mother is Irish Catholic and his father is Jewish. However, Disney's choice of Loren Dean to play Billy in the film elides the Jewish ethnicity of Doctorow's character; with his boyish good looks, high cheekbones, washed hair, and clean face, Disney's Billy might have come from any one of a slew of Disney films.[8] His role became homogenized, interchangeable with Kurt Russell in *The Computer Wore Tennis Shoes* (1971) or Tommy Kirk in *The Shaggy D.A.* (1964). Dean's wholesome appearance contradicts the notion that this boy has been raised on the streets and in poverty. Likewise, his cinematic persona, based on actions and reactions, does not suggest Doctorow's agenda of streetwise proletarian unrest but, instead, middle-class bourgeois complacency.

Perhaps even more important than the actor playing the part was the decision to remove (or at least deemphasize) a vital element from the character's persona: intelligence. In Doctorow's novel, Billy lives by his wits; he learns to see the angles, calculate the odds. However, Benton's film, in classic Disney style, manipulates Billy by fate and luck. To emphasize this reliance on fate, Benton and Stoppard have Otto Berman (Steven Hill) explicitly state this theme when Billy blunders his way into Dutch Schultz's (Dustin Hoffman) numbers room masquerading as a bag man. The bag should contain money but instead contains chocolate cupcakes. As Billy is about to be thrown out, Schultz enters, distractedly picks up one of the cupcakes, and starts to eat it. Luckily for Billy, these cupcakes are Schultz's favorite and he says so. When Schultz spots Billy, he asks, "Who are you?" Berman, who has observed the entire scene, replies, "A kid with luck." From this point on, Billy is accepted in the gang.

Otto's last line blatantly reinforces the idea of destiny in the film. Sensing danger, that the end is near, he benignly forces Billy out of the gang's hiding place. As young Billy exits the Palace Chop House, Berman sits inside, gazing wistfully at the youth, and says, "Now there goes a kid with luck." Moments later, members of Luciano's gang enter the Chop House and assassinate Schultz and his henchmen. Abducted by Luciano's gang on the street, Billy, who is now a witness to the murders, should be killed by Luciano—he knows too much. Luckily, before Billy can be killed, he spots Schultz's lawyer, Dixie, and provides information to Luciano. He accuses the lawyer of stealing all of Schultz's money for himself, and uses $17,000 (money Berman has provided for him) to prove that Schultz had millions at the time of his death.

Luciano has Dixie taken away, returns Billy's money to him, tells him that they'll be keeping an eye on him, and lets him go. Billy walks out into the street, $17,000 richer and a lot wiser—but still just an innocent boy.

Removing the maturity that adds to the complexity of the character transforms *Billy Bathgate* from socially reflective art into monogeneric product. Mature themes are often viewed as unnecessary and subversive elements by conservative economic corporations like Walt Disney; the first of these mature elements that Disney is bound to tone down (or completely excise) in any text is sexuality. Doctorow's Billy is sexually active before the novel begins. He has sexual relationships no fewer than five times, pays for sex, and exhibits expertise in his sexual relationship with Rebecca, a fourteen-year-old girl.

Benton's Billy, however, is a sexual innocent. There is a vague suggestion that Billy and Rebecca have some sort of liaison on their tenement rooftop early in the film. Shot with a wide angle lens from a distance to "flatten" the scene, Billy fiddles with his belt as Rebecca looks at a dollar bill he has given her. On the surface, they don't look like they've had sex. As the shots cut to close-ups, both characters are clean and dry; they don't talk about sex, they talk about Dutch Schultz, they stand and then sit apart until the final shot of the scene where they benignly share a cigarette in classic film tableau that fades to black.

Sex for Doctorow's Billy is often a primal experience, literalized in the novel when Billy and Drew Preston rout in a hidden swamp; slime and scum cover their bodies as their physical passion forces them deeper into the mud. Not only is this scene not in the film, but Billy's filmic relationship with Drew is tentative and sweet: they hold hands, at one point he kisses her as she sleeps, and when they finally consummate their relationship, it's in a sumptuous suite in a Saratoga hotel on linen sheets. Soft blue lighting, fluid camera pans of their gracefully intertwined bodies, and lush strings soaring on the soundtrack help color the scene romantic for the audience. Disneyfication creates a *Billy Bathgate* that is clean and civilized. Characters consistently dress in tuxedos and evening gowns, the streets are all swept, the hotel rooms are luxurious, even the tenement children are scrubbed and well dressed. Nestor Almendros's burnished cinematography, the characteristic use of natural light notwithstanding, is overdramatic, even stagy, and Mark Isham's score sounds like a series of coronation fanfares.

Despite the romanticism, many media reviewers and critics mention a Disney first: *Billy Bathgate* is the first Disney film to present full female frontal nudity. In a full shot, a nude Drew Preston exits a spring, approaches wide-eyed Billy (and the camera), and then is quickly draped with a white dress.

Robert Haas

Disney's idea of progressive, "mature entertainment" is conventional Hollywood objectification of the female body. But even nudity must take a back seat to the even more stunning, although implicit, admission from the Disney studios: the existence of homosexuality.

After Bo Weinberg has been "ceremonially drowned, [with] his feet in a bucket of setting cement," Drew and Billy return to the penthouse apartment. As they enter, they spot two pairs of legs protruding from an oversized sofa. Harvey Preston, Drew's husband, stands and follows her into their bedroom and then a young man stands up, his clothes disheveled, and stares at Billy. What is missing is the complicity of the camera's gaze that exists when it objectifies Drew's body.[9] Perhaps even more important in this scene is the decision to omit Billy's recognition of similarities between himself and the young man on the sofa:

> With thumb and forefinger the fellow on the couch removed an antimacassar from the sofa and dropped it over himself. He looked up and laughed in a way that suggested we were complicitors, and I realized he was working-class, like me. I had not, at first glance, understood this. (Doctorow 1989, 43)

Since Billy is the protagonist, his actions must comply with the target audience's expectations. Therefore, according to the Disney philosophy, any identification, however abstract, with homosexuality—and with the working classes—is erased. Billy's alteration from text to film—from an ethnic, sexual, cunning, multidimensional character to a bland, naive, lucky kid—serves a specific purpose: economic necessity. He must profitably appeal to young, white, heterosexual males. Ironically, when Disney erased Billy's "capable boy" characteristics, they also erased his appeal and their profit.

Someone's Daughter or Someone's Mother

> Drew escapes her killers by flying off from a secluded airfield in her husband's private plane. As the woman, whose one positive act has been Billy's deflowering, soars off to celestial strains, one cannot forget we're saying goodbye to a moneyed thrillseeker, not a vaulting spirit. (Sheehan 1992, 39)

The character of Drew Preston is *Billy Bathgate*'s opportunity to provide resistance to Disney homogenization because she has the potential to manifest qualities that the typical Disney genre female character cannot. Her sexuality, independence, non-maternal attitude, and lust for adventure in the dangerous world of the gangster are, however, subverted as Disney again relies on economically proven, formulaic patterns to produce audience recognition of conventional Disney beauty mixed with naivete. Two scenes are key to recognizing the visibility of Disney conventions and their incompatibility with the gangster genre.

First, in an early scene on the tugboat taking Bo Weinberg (Bruce Willis) to his death, Drew is escorted by Dutch below deck to a private room. The graphic sexual conventions of the modern gangster genre (both cinematic and textual) have become so firmly planted in the psyche of the audience, especially based on a similar sequence in *The Godfather* (1972), that audiences respond with jarring disbelief to the paternal scene enacted in the cabin. Dutch, instead of using violence and tyranny to diminish Drew, seems to comfort her with calming words and actions. And with great rapidity, she seems to respond to this patriarchal pose, forsaking her doomed lover in an instant and transferring her attentions to Dutch.[10]

This unlikely response from Drew is typical of the Disney convention that maintains the overriding power of patriarchal relationships found in many other Disney films. These relationships are usually naturalized, and therefore generally go unquestioned or unnoticed; this is not usually true, however, for the gangster genre.[11] This paternal protection is reinforced by its apparent reversal in the film.

After the gang relocates their operations to the small upstate New York town of Onondaga, Drew begins to assume a more dominant role in her relationship with Dutch—she starts to act like Dutch's mother; she corrects his grammar, his manners, and his malapropisms. An odd change midway through the film, this seems to be motivated by the absence of the other mother of the narrative, Billy's mother. A major character in the novel, Billy's mother barely exists in the film. She is cut down to one single line: "Billy, look at you. You're the richest man on Bathgate Avenue." Her emotionless reading registers neither approval, disapproval, awareness, or nonawareness of the situation. This lack of affect contrasts sharply with her novelistic excess: she is the distracted, distraught, possibly insane mother straight out of gothic tradition, the madwoman in the tenement. She spends her nonworking hours sitting at her kitchen table, lighting candles in jelly glasses, or strolling a baby doll in an old, decrepit baby carriage on Bathgate Avenue. Doctorow's agenda is clear: with no one to nurture, she is nonexistent or hysterical. The new baby at the end of the novel (a product of Billy and Drew's swamp fest) brings her back to society as a functioning person.

The second notable scene, nearing the end of the film, reencodes Drew as a Disney innocent, in need of protection and rescue. At Saratoga, Drew is completely oblivious to the danger that surrounds her. As Irving, one of

Schultz's hit men, moves in to kill her, she is saved by Billy, who has designed barriers between them and Irving. Moreover, Billy has made an opportune phone call to Drew's husband, who rescues her in the nick of time, flying her off to safety. Here we observe the other side of patriarchy: the innocent daughter. The mother/daughter dichotomy severely limits the choices afforded Drew's character. She does have points of resistance to this dichotomy, but only as oddly inconsistent lip service. Statements like "I'm not his girl, he's my gangster" and "It's strange that Bo didn't think I could take care of myself" contradict the strictly imposed and enacted codes of dependence written by the Disney representation of (good) women: women are daughters or mothers. Drew's active and death-defying affair with Billy is ultimately rewritten. Of pivotal importance to the dramatic tension and resolution of the novel, their relationship is transformed by Disney into young and wacky love.

Gangsterland

Billy Bathgate looks like a new Disney attraction—Gangsterland. (Sheehan 1992, 39)

Billy Bathgate cum Gangsterland is a transformation from the gritty social commentary of Doctorow's novel into a film that adheres closely to the mission statement of Touchstone's originators—mature entertainment without violence or exploitation. The Disney Studio, the writer, and the director accomplish this homogenization of the violent and sexual through a formulaic approach to the text. On screen, Billy is a cipher who mostly watches. With no strong anchor or point of view, the movie drifts episodically in ways that are often compelling, but ultimately pointless. By removing those elements vital to the character of the novel, Touchstone's *Billy Bathgate* undercuts Doctorow's fictional analysis of 1930s social and economic necessities and critique of capitalist and Marxist dogma. It dissolves any resonance to other texts and reflexivity to contemporary society; instead, Touchstone creates a conventional *bildungsroman*.

The lack of violence in *Billy Bathgate* is typical of almost all Disney films. However, unlike other Disney films, there is a conscious attempt to reverse the company's usual methodology that provides its proven hits. The usual reliance on wholesome, middle-class, white, safe story lines that have been "spiced up" with mild violence and suggested (hetero)sexuality is reversed with a highly ethnic, highly violent, highly sexual narrative that erases these subversive elements that may offend its largely profitable target audience.

Disney Does Dutch

Unlike other films from the gangster genre (both early Warner Brothers and contemporary examples), images of violence are subverted through the use of extreme close-ups of angered faces, quick cuts away from the victims, little blood, and a deemphasis on violence as a motivator for the narrative. Two scenes in particular deemphasize the violence in the original *Billy Bathgate*. The first is the fire inspector's death, a scene that Benton has admitted to recutting at the behest of Disney executives. Having just killed a man, Schultz immediately begins reflecting on his financial troubles and the defection of Bo Weinberg. No camera time is devoted to the dead man. The second is the death of Julie Martin, President of the Restaurant and Cafeteria Owners' Association. He is shot through the mouth at point-blank range and falls backward. Again, little camera time is devoted to him, and a single spot of blood is the only clue to his death. Compare these two scenes with the death of Joe Pesci in Martin Scorcese's *Goodfellas* or the death of Al Capone's henchman on the train station steps in *The Untouchables* (1987).

Unlike *Goodfellas* or *The Untouchables*, *Billy Bathgate* ignores its generic past, its literary genesis, and the dialectics between them. In an interview with Larry McCafferty (1983), E. L. Doctorow recognizes the "undeniable importance" of film in how we read literature today. His reliance on cinematic conventions and associations is often apparent in his writing. In *Billy Bathgate*, John Trenner has noted, Doctorow "appropriates Sergei Eisenstein's famous baby carriage motif which symbolized innocence and victimization in the massacre scene on the Odessa Steps from the film *Battleship Potemkin* (1925)" (1989, 40).[12] As an intertextual homage to Eisenstein's cinematic montage and to more than sixty years of film technology, the novel's baby carriage is used as a narrative leitmotif, as well as a parody of vast systems of narrative discourse that see innocence and evil in black and white terms. Such pervasive practices in contemporary fiction are designed "to make the reader aware of the distinction between the events of the past and the facts by which we give meaning to the past, by which we assume to know it" (Hutcheon 1988, 223). Doctorow's parodies and his thematic and technical treatment of history, popular culture, politics, and innovation, often reflecting postmodernist heroics and ethics, are incomprehensible—not to gangsters—but to Disney.

Notes

1. For an examination of gangster-film conventions, see Mitchell (1986). A few variations of the gangster conventions are evident, especially in *The Godfather* trilogy directed

by Francis Ford Coppola that successfully incorporated spectacle and myth into the genre, and in the work of Joel and Ethan Coen, whose *Miller's Crossing* (1989) is ultimately a reflexive (and self-reflexive) examination of gangster-film conventions.

2. There were a handful of silent antecedents including Lewis Milestone's *The Racket* (1928) and Josef Von Sternberg's *Underworld* (1927), but sound films like Mervyn LeRoy's *Little Caesar* (1930), *The Public Enemy* (1931), and *Scarface* (1932) forged a new generic tradition.

3. The precise coordination of sound and image in animation is still called "Mickey Mousing."

4. Disney has produced several films in which gangsters are prominent, most notably *Who Framed Roger Rabbit* (1986), which was coproduced by Warner Brothers, *Dick Tracy* (1990), *The Rocketeer* (1991), and *Sister Act* (1992). However, none of these films frame their narratives around gangsterism nor are their main characters gangsters as in *Billy Bathgate*. Additionally, in the films mentioned, the gangsters that do appear are generally played as broad caricatures: cartoons, goons, and buffoons.

5. The film has also been popularly dubbed "Benton Gate."

6. Above-the-line costs in films are generally for the artistic talent as opposed to the technical and support services, which are classified as below-the-line. Above-the-line costs include salaries for actors, writers, and directors, and in the 1990s have caused (with special effects budgets) the greatest increase in total film budgets.

7. For instance, based on its low cost, *Sister Act* made a higher profit than *Terminator 2* (1992); even though the latter film made more money at the box office, its $90 million price tag and Arnold Schwarzenegger's and James Cameron's percentages of the gross box office receipts barely allowed the film to break even.

8. Dean was reportedly hired to play Billy Bathgate because of his strong resemblance to the boy appearing on the dustjacket of the hardcover edition of the novel.

9. Benton does acknowledge the homosexual nature of the scene through implication.

10. In Doctorow's novel, Dutch announces to Bo that he will rape Drew so that Bo will have a reason to want to die. He then drags her to the cabin, slapping her along the way.

11. A possible exception to this would be Joel and Ethan Coen's *Miller's Crossing* (1989), which hinges on the patriarchal relationship between crime boss Leo (Albert Finney) and Tom Reagan (Gabriel Byrne), his advisor. Ultimately, however, the film rejects the notion of patriarchal alliances (and all other familial alliances) as incompatible with gangster genre conventions.

12. The inclusion of a vulnerable baby carriage also evokes the one caught in the crossfire between the violent gangsters and the valiant police in Brian DePalma's recent film, *The Untouchables* (1987), and thereby enriches Doctorow's transference of this motif to his view of a corrupt American scene of cops and robbers (Trenner 1989, 40).

References

Cawelti, John G. 1985. "*Chinatown* and Generic Transformation in Recent American Films." In *Film Theory and Criticism*, ed. Gerald Mast and Marshall Cohen. New York: Oxford University Press.

Clover, Carol J. 1992. *Men, Women, and Chainsaws: Gender and the Modern Horror Film*. Princeton: Princeton University Press.

Collins, Jim. 1993. "Genericity in the Nineties: Eclectic Irony and the New Sincerity." In *Film Theory Goes to the Movies*, ed. Jim Collins, Hilary Radner, and Ava Preacher Collins. New York: Routledge.

Doctorow, E. L. 1989. *Billy Bathgate*. New York: Random House.

Hutcheon, Linda. 1988. *A Poetics of Postmodernism: History, Theory, Fiction*. New York: Routledge.

McCafferty, Larry. 1983. "Spirit of Transgression." In *E. L. Doctorow: Essays and Conversations*, ed. John Trenner. Princeton: Ontario Review Press.

Mitchell, Edward. 1986. "Apes and Essences: Some Sources of Significance in American Gangster Films." In *The Film Genre Reader*, ed. Barry Keith Grant. Austin: University of Texas Press.

Paul, William. 1994. *Laughing Screaming: Modern Hollywood Horror and Comedy*. New York: Columbia University Press.

Ryan, Michael, and Douglas Kellner. 1988. *Camera Politica*. Bloomington: Indiana University Press.

Sheehan, Henry. 1992. Review of *Billy Bathgate*. *Sight and Sound* 1(9): 39.

Tompkins, Jane. 1992. *West of Everything*. Oxford: Oxford University Press.

Trenner, John. 1989. *E. L. Doctorow: Essays and Conversations*. Princeton: Ontario Review Press.

Vieira, Nelson H. 1991. " 'Evil Be Thou My Good': Postmodern Heroics and Ethics in *Billy Bathgate* and *Bufo & Spallanzani*." *Comparative Literature Studies* 28(4): 356–78.

Wagner-Martin, Linda. 1990. "*Billy Bathgate* and *Billy Budd*: Some Recognitions." *Notes on Contemporary Literature* 20(1): 4–7.

Five

The Movie You See, The Movie You Don't

How Disney Do's That Old Time Derision

Susan Miller and Greg Rode

When I got to Atlanta I assumed he was going to be there. When I asked why he wasn't, there didn't seem to be an answer. Finally I found out it was because the hotel wouldn't accept him and he was told he would have to stay with some family in a certain part of town. It spoiled the whole occasion for me. I was outraged. *But of course there wasn't anything I could do about it.* It was already a fact. (Ruth Warrick, recalling her response to the absence of James Baskett [Uncle Remus] from the gala Atlanta premiere of *Song of the South*. Emphasis added. [Thompson 1986, 19])

Patriarchalism, the uncritical forms of the modern family, the patterns of sexual dominance, the disciplining of pleasure, the reinforcement of the habits of social conformity are some of the key ways in which the political movements of the left have remained deeply conservative and traditionalist at their culture core. *The tiny "family man" is still hiding away in the heads of many of our most illustrious "street-fighting" militants.* (Emphasis added. Hall 1988, 250)

Walt Disney was always, for some of us, a name to conjure with—protected space, the one for "the kid in me." Even when Disney movies scared us as youngsters, they were "ours"; the beauty, adventure, surprise, and spontaneity (if slapstick spontaneity) belonged to us, and in times of wondering we still reinvent when we watch them. Your memories, like ours, probably include the relentless brooms in *Fantasia* (1940), opening flowers on *The Living Desert* (1953), Cinderella's dropped shoe on the palace stairs, and the split subjects who comprise the One Dwarf who saves the pure from fearsome female authority. As we will point out, these cartoon visions, like many other films for children, make crucial contributions to our most important discourses of the self. The nebulous happiness in which we encase them is a membrane assuring their coherence as vital organs of cultural continuity.

The Movie You See, The Movie You Don't

Now, thinking ourselves adults, we may alertly equate such images with Disney the "Dark Prince" of Marc Eliot's new biography (1993), and with the conglomerate "Disney World(s)" whose financial status regularly receives more interpretive pressure than their cinematic authority. It is obvious, or appears to be obvious, that the movies we saw as children, which younger home video viewers now see as many as 100 times over, were products of a story about their celebrated supposed origin that we didn't see—the one about Walt's status as a Special Correspondent for the FBI (Eliot 1993) and his exclusive right to commodify various Western myths, including Joel Chandler Harris's Ovidian Uncle Remus tales and Kipling's colonialist *The Jungle Books*.[1] These material considerations suggest that we can no longer protect from critique these charmed images or the hazy space in which we easily remember them. But this new story does not entirely plot the complex cultural space of teaching and learning comprised by Disney films and the discourses around them. In this space, many aesthetic, social, economic, technical and political pressures converge; from it, these pressures direct simultaneously adult and child-like desires toward and from a screen, the blank that may be loaded from either right or left with political claims about the "realities" of Disney's purposes or results.

We want to suspend consideration of those purposes for now, for the sake of grounding this look at *Song of the South* (1946) and *Jungle Book* (1967) in a rhetorical analysis that sets aside Disney and their "authorship," and that avoids interpretation of these films as self-contained representations of purposefully distorted "realities." An alternative, culturally oriented rhetorical analytic allows us to focus on plausible results for the overlapping audiences that these films persuade. Their viewers are multiple and split—neither "adult" nor "child," but a simultaneously original and maintained "kid in me" who desires happy resolutions that Disney films create and exploit, to our benefit and detriment. The particular mode of self-teaching fostered by the films ideologically constitutes an "adult child," such as the one now often described as the result of retardation of one or another site for emotional growth over the course of maturation. Specifically, this "character in us" imagines its own inability to affect troubling circumstances.

A rhetorical critique of these films also allows us to explore how their audiences are constituted not psychologically, but as sites of extracurricular cultural formation. Culture is actual people, who have collectively been shown some, but not other, images. They consequently have some, but not other, ways of organizing, of valuing, and of making and understanding language about their solitary and shared experiences. Remembered images like those that we have described are seeds of cultural formation that high-

Susan Miller and Greg Rode

light gender, value energetic work, privilege a tamed nature, and verify the value of loose authority and its psychological "permission." The persistence of such images suggests how important it is to explore this site of persuasion to find *how* we are taught by so prominent and once apparently neutral a cultural teacher as the collective "Walt Disney."

To expose this extracurricular pedagogy, especially in the two commonplace, stereo-topical productions that interest us here, we consequently need to highlight specific questions that include the audiences of these films: what do we "see" or think we have seen, as children and adults who watch, and how do we learn, especially about prejudices of any kind, when we see it? How might we connect images deeply embedded in each of us to the important cultural pedagogy that produced Ruth Warrick's reaction to the exclusion of the actor James Baskett, Uncle Remus himself, from the premier of *Song of the South*, just as it produces others' too typical responses to the "fact" of racial, sexual, and class conflicts? In Althusser's idiom, how does Disney "hail" us into subject positions from which we *freely* reproduce a certain sort of discriminatory culture? How does this call to identity require us to answer, not as well-rehearsed speakers for the substantial messages in these movies' biased social scripting, but as the *kind of people* who—no matter what our conscious politics—continue to reproduce deep cultural structures of discrimination? In sum, how does this complex cultural pedagogy teach us how "to be"? As we will argue, it assures the reproduction of a cultural identity that we can figure not only as "middle class" but as always in middles and muddles like those that trapped Warrick into a self-deconstructing "outrage" at the premiere of *Song of the South*.

The Movies We Do See

Obviously, possible answers to such questions are not in the often-invoked "messages" of these films, although both their content and choices about production values clearly verify criticisms directed at their overt racism, sexism, and classism. The movies we see and can summarize each operate through a plethora of prejudicial tropes. *Song of the South*, for instance, where we learned that frogs say "RIBBETT" and more, is paradoxically but literally a "movie you do not see," a film that Disney World regretfully tells us is only distributed now in Japan where, according to them, it is a howling success. Released in Atlanta four years after *Gone With the Wind*, surely riding that blockbuster's breeze, it was publicized as a cultural retrieval of important American "folk literature," the late nineteenth-century stories of Joel Chandler Harris. Its opening scene shows a small family—mother, father, and son—in a carriage riding to visit Grandmother, somewhere near Atlanta. Father is teaching the sounds of frogs, and the joy of listening to Uncle Remus's stories, which Son will soon be hearing. But there is clearly tension between Mother and Father, who evidently is in trouble for writing about cotton mills and other political issues in the Atlanta paper.

This "evidently" is important. We cannot, that is, exactly hear the garbled interplay between Mother and Father, presented *sotto voce* to keep it from son Johnny, but simultaneously to mystify and distance adults' troubles from us all. And we never will understand it fully—Father and Mother are simply having trouble, despite their responding to Johnny's "are you mad at each other?" with the "of course not's" that were the middle-class norm before family therapy informed such scenes. When it turns out that Father is leaving Johnny and Mother with Grandmother and returning immediately to the city over their and Grandmother's objections, which for Johnny become hysterical protestations that "I won't stay here!" without Father, we don't exactly know why Father goes. And when he reappears in the film's last frames, declaring that he has realized that his place is "here," in the country with his family, we still do not know what is at stake in this choice for the couple (or for his "public," "business" life) in the context of a crisis precipitated by Johnny's coma after being chased by a bull. (If like us you grew up in cities, you also may have learned to fear bulls in fields from this movie, just as you learned how to imitate frogs.)

It becomes obvious immediately that Hattie McDaniel's Mammy (here the housekeeper Tempy) has merely lingered at the set for Tara, awaiting another domestically disarranged family. If now less obviously slave-owning, and now with a healthy and vocal Miss Ellen figure of comfort replacing Scarlett's fretful mother in the character of Grandmother, this family is nonetheless equally surrounded by African American retainers of now indeterminate status. They periodically enter stage right and left to surround the facade that portrays this Big House when its white residents gather on the front porch to enact significant moments. But they appear more at home out in the surrounding woods, gathered around a communal fire to sing after equally theatrical coming-in-from-the-fields scenes. The African Americans in *Song of the South* are, precisely, "happy campers."

The NAACP objected strenuously to these representations before the film was first released in 1946 and at every one of its re-releases in 1956, 1972 (two years after Disney claimed it would never release the film again [Kantrowitz 1986, 63], 1980, and 1986). Kind accounts merely say that Disney paid little attention to these objections (Thompson 1986, 19); he responded only by claiming that the importance of this retrieval and preservation of important

American folktales outweighed these concerns. Worry about portraying African Americans as happy on the plantation, singing their work and toil away, turbaned and playful rather than achieving and serious, are all obviously and accurately aimed at this Disney stereotyping. But such objections also obviously support the bourgeois consciousness and work ethic that Disney himself was defending as a Special Correspondent of the FBI. *Song of the South* itself, in all its cultural "messages," is a far more problematic way of teaching about race than these objections reveal.

But we don't want to leave Johnny in tears indefinitely. He is assigned a "boy" his own age, Toby, to "keep him out of trouble," which is, in fact, where he is going to be throughout the movie. Johnny attempts to run away to Atlanta and is intercepted by Uncle Remus. After he cautiously overhears the first telling of the cartoon portrayal of Brer Rabbit stories, Uncle Remus determines to go with him, packing up but then unpacking his carpet bag, ruminating pro and con about the distance to Atlanta and the possibility of food along the way. Immediately, Johnny is in trouble—mother can't find him, and neither can Toby, to whom the woods and the retainers' camp is open. The first gathering on the porch of the Big House occurs, with the roles of the adults clearly demarcated: Uncle Remus has "tried to help," primarily by telling a story, but has been misguided in Mother's view and is misunderstood; Grandmother "wisely" hears everyone out and puts everyone to bed; Hattie McDaniel's Tempy is equally "wise" but silent—like Faulkner's Dilsey, but we can imagine also like Hattie McDaniel, she "endures." And Mother, who is simultaneously the daughter Sally in a similar vein, is almost entirely witless as well as at her wit's end, early and late in the game.

That game involves her repeated attempts to control Johnny's dress (she produces a lace collar he must wear), his relationships (she gives him a party and tells him not to invite his lower-class tenant playmate *cum* girlfriend, Ginny), his initiation to the ways of men (she punishes Uncle Remus for telling a story that leads to his fight with Ginny's trashy brothers), and finally his recourse to Uncle Remus himself and the play of imagination, which are banned from his company. The movie alternates its representations between the stories that Uncle Remus and the Disney artists portray and the "trouble" repeatedly caused by Johnny's desire to escape Mother's apparently misguided strictures. Most accounts of the film have bitterly complained about its frame tale. As Peggy Russo puts it, "critical opinion split in a clear pattern: praise for the animation and rejection of the rest" (Russo 1992, 26). Russo's account argues that *Song of the South* should be faulted for tampering with "the Harris text" (19) and its less subservient Remus, for "robbing us of a folk hero" (32) who conveys "the inherent wisdom of the folktales . . . a teacher" (24). She also complains that "Disney eliminates the possibility of tragedy [in Harris's tales], . . . their beauty, wonder, and terror" (25).

Russo's claim that Disney has ruined Uncle Remus stories may make us think that the film is, as her summarized reviews say of the images we do see, divided between the quality of the animated tales and the flatness of the frame tale, a seeming "excuse" for their telling. But to examine briefly yet another aspect of its overt content, it is equally possible to argue that *Song of the South* is a decisively *unified* representation of racist, sexist, and classist agendas. We can easily connect the cartoon and human worlds as a story that is harmoniously joined by the person of Uncle Remus, the passage of time, and other devices that can argue for its seamless narrative "sense." Clues for such a reading abound, in parallels between Johnny's early attempt to run away and Brer Rabbit's first story of deciding to leave the briar patch to get out of "trouble," between Father's abandonment of Son and Sally for a conflicted world of "work" and the violent attempts of Brer Bear and Brer Fox to "acquire" and eat Brer Rabbit, and even in the structural repetition between the animated musical chorus of bees and birds and the repeated choral renditions of the African American supernumeraries who reappear off and on like a Greek chorus. We might figure this unifying reading as the film "we" see, who are skilled readers and "authors" of interpretation, authorities by virtue of both our formal schooling and our extracurricular experience. This interpretation would accept "many meanings" within a unified aesthetic and insist on remembering that the Realism of the acted scenes is only a trope. It would have us misrecognize Disney as the consciousness of a unified *auteur*, the single agency and source of both the man's recently revealed political agendas and their supposed opposites, the "beauty" and "play" of "his" kingdom, a magic world that still (precisely) interpenetrates the world we must live in when we are neither children nor at a movie.

Such an enclosed, aesthetically oriented interpretation could also be applied to *Jungle Book*. But this later, entirely animated production seems on this method to argue instead that the "real" world we must live in may be postponed, in fact should be postponed, as long as possible. In *Jungle Book*, the young Mowgli's journey, like Johnny's in *Song of the South*, is a return to family, "the man-village," to which Mowgli is guided by a surrogate father, Bagheera, who allows the buffoon bear, Baloo, to travel with him. Here, lessons about difference are more emphatically represented, in encounter after encounter with species and "types" whose adventures always depend on making distinctions, and at least tacitly define "distinction" as racist and sexist discrimination.

Faithful to Kipling's stories in plot if not its tone, Disney's *Jungle Book* suggests mythic fragments from a long tradition of Western rite-of-passage stories. Mowgli is discovered as an abandoned infant whose vague origin and ensuing adventures are reminiscent of the story of the discovery and elevation of Moses. He is raised by a family of wolves, much like Romulus and Remus. This sense of destiny for his roundabout progress is further reinforced by his victory in the climactic showdown with wickedness incarnate, the despotic tiger, Shere Khan. In that encounter, Mowgli recalls Shakespeare's Prince Hal and Falstaff's guilty insistence that the "lion will not touch the true prince" (*Henry IV, Pt.I*, II, iv).

Such allusiveness undergirds the deceptively playful aspiration of the film's plot to get its hero where he belongs, to get Mowgli home. But in its series of encounters with various manifestations of the other, *Jungle Book* also overtly invokes negative stereotypes rarely noted in commentary on the film. Racial stereotypes in particular organize certain key characters, including Baloo, the scat-singing, bebop-inflected bear with whom Mowgli forms his deepest attachment, and King Louie, the potentate ape who desires, in vain, to be human. This racial stereotyping, even at a remove from the two-dimensional African Americans in *Song of the South*, finds its fullest expression in a scene in King Louie's jungle kingdom, the decaying, abandoned remains of some now extinct, supposedly "primitive" culture. Mowgli is captured by King Louie's subjects and brought to this "other" world, where monkeys speak in jazz vocalese and everybody "swings." Baloo, infected by the "crazy" beat, disguises himself as an ape in an attempt to infiltrate the "enemy" ranks. He and Mowgli are both mesmerized by the beat and fluidity of Louie's kingdom. Taking the boy by the hand, King Louie, sporting a familiar black-coded voice, sings to him his famous song, "I Wanna Be Like You." Once we make the obvious connection between King Louie and African Americanism—at least the African Americanism dear to white bourgeois liberal culture—the lyrics of his song become a humiliating revelation, for King Louie sings of his desire to be a man "and stroll right into town . . . ooo—I want to be like you." According to Disney, "an ape can learn to be human too."

In addition to racial references accomplished in such lyrics, *Jungle Book* frequently relies on verbal class and gender stereotyping for its "innocent" fun, displacing the visual black and white of *Song of the South* onto aural stereotypes. The film invariably endows regal mannerisms and posh British accents to characters with power, whether they are beneficent or malevolent: Shere Khan the tiger, the most feared of the jungle's denizens; Colonel Hathi, the leader of the pachyderm parade and the representative of the military in the film; and Bagheera, the dignified panther who takes the responsibility for both educating Mowgli and seeing to it that he reaches his final destination. The vultures, on the other hand, scavengers and outcasts from jungle society, speak in various lower-class British accents. The Black-coded characters speak a jazz lingo that reflects the most stereotypic African American dialect. (More precisely, this is the argot of Mailer's white negro, since the voices for these obviously black-coded characters were performed by the white entertainers Louis Prima and Phil Harris.) But the film further distinguishes among its entitlements, assuring the ultimate primacy of the "man" whom Mowgli is to become. According to Bagheera, King Louie is beneath contempt, while Baloo is a "shiftless, stupid, jungle bum," an epithet whose language invokes both classist and racist commonplaces. Moreover, Bagheera suggests to Baloo, in another demonstration of jungle classism/racism, that "birds of a feather flock together; *you wouldn't marry a panther would you?*" (emphasis added).

This vague reference to marriage stands out largely because female characters are so conspicuously absent from this Boy's Life adventure. Bagheera's opening narration recalls that he had no worries about Mowgli first being accepted into the wolf family by its mother, "because of the mothering instinct." Between this easily constructed Natural allusion to female "instinct" and the movie's romantic conclusion, the only appearance by a female character is that made by the junior league edition wife of Colonel Hathi of the elephant brigade, who becomes a loud nag only when she identifies with motherhood and the quest to recover Mowgli: "What if that were *our* boy lost in the jungle?" Consequently, when Mowgli sights the man-village, we are not consciously surprised that he hesitates to enter it. In fact, we may root for him to resist the coquettish young girl who settles his choice of "jungle" vs. "man" worlds by beguiling him. But he yields. Enticed by her flirtatiousness and charmed by her song, with a shrug of his shoulders Mowgli hoists the water jug she "accidentally" drops and ambles after the girl, just as Hall's "tiny family man" must [above]. Apparently, given the brevity of their appearances and the seeming inevitability of their bothersome qualities, women are an Other that Mowgli will never figure out. The misogyny of the movie's choral ending in the girl's song predicts the postponed world we must live in, in its most basic bourgeois outlines: father hunts, mother cooks, and the girl carries water. When she is grown with a husband and a daughter, the bourgeois outline repeats itself: "I'll send her to fetch the water, I'll be cooking in the home." Women not only receive short shrift in *Jungle Book* but are significant only as props in conventional patriarchal the-atre. As Baloo warns, and as we imagine Mowgli's lot given his gender edu-cation in the jungle out there, "they're nothin' but trouble."

Of course we're entirely aware that we may appear to have misrepresented *Song of the South* and *Jungle Book*, that we raise "nothin' but trouble" in these summaries. Despite the NAACP's and others' for-now definitive ob-jections to *Song of the South*, and despite the obvious use of stereotyped race- and class-coded experience to fund the humor of *Jungle Book*, an important case might as easily be made that especially in the eyes of inexperienced chil-dren, both films are exactly what either a conservative or liberal parent would wish its child to see and absorb.

A different summary of *Song of the South* could note that it portrays a white child bonding with young and old African Americans of much stronger character than their white counterparts, and that this youngster is loyal to a lower-class girl who herself shows that no one needs to be "kept down" by origins when the proper meritocratic energy is applied to their limits. Ginny's mother, exemplifying correct motherly ability to "make do," sacrifices her wedding dress to make a frock worthy of Johnny's mother's exclusive party. It is after all the tenant family whose briefly viewed reunion after its father's absence is warm, open and loving. That father, unlike Johnny's, seems easily capable of restoring discipline and order to his child-ren and genuine peace of mind to his wife. And Johnny's family, dysfunc-tional as it may be, does at least assert the priorities of love over work, home over public conflict, that keep us centered in "our" special independence.

In addition, African Americans represent the only obvious competence displayed in *Song of the South*. The primary focus on Uncle Remus's shaman-ism is mirrored as Johnny's young companion, Toby, teaches him how to play with frogs and models appropriate rural skills. Tempy's lightning-quick making of a pie is worthy of Julia Child on her best day; Uncle Remus and Grandmother together, rather like an old couple, understand the problems of both generations of children whom they take in, comfort, and eventually teach how to behave. What may appear to be Uncle Remus's unaccountable retreat from the plantation after Mother Sally separates him and his mythic wisdom from Johnny is, in fact, his character's additional realization that in a defunct slavery replaced by money culture, he is a weak old man. He is both economically "useless" in industrial production and socially estranged from the formerly integrated plantation "family" that historically mingled slave and master generations. Grown children, in the person of Sally, reject not just his stories for their children, but in this new world he understands too well, they will go so far as to order him to stay away from a child, in a clearly reprehensible destruction of traditional Southern society.

Similarly, Mowgli's repeated encounters with difference and the Other in *Jungle Book* are models of diversity. As an archetypal developing boy, he learns the important skills that require making distinctions, and his traveling mentors also openly show him how to distinguish false from authentic persuasion in the deceptive oratory he encounters. Mowgli's repeated giggles at the antics of elephants, monkeys, and especially Baloo the bear reassure us that he is learning precisely the important lesson that all children need, to balance play against safety. The overt message of the film, in song and image, is clearly pro-natural growth under the protection of wise parental figures who responsibly protect the child from nature's excesses. Both of these movies tell us, and show children, that people left to "nature" will acquire multiple perspectives, equipment for making choices and distinctions that they need not only for survival, but for fully conscious and socially skilled lives.

These alternative summaries do not entirely stick in our throats, for they are indeed the "text itself" of each film, and supply warrants for Disney's usually accepted didactic claims to teach "pure" values to children in any of its productions. In fact, if we are to argue successfully that these films contribute not only to the production of racist, sexist, and classist cultural scripts, but to abilities in all of us to write and rewrite them, it is imperative that we avoid monolithic interpretations of their actions and language. Overt and implied prejudices in each film are contextualized in home truths accepted along the breadth of what is commonly taken to be Western political and social spectra. It is precisely the mutuality of these alternate summaries of the "text itself" that enables their success as a cultural pedagogy, a way of teaching "middles and muddles" as ways of thinking and talking that reproduce a discriminatory, hierarchical culture while they can appear to resist it.

The Movie You Don't See

It may seem that so far we have taken permission from our actual collaboration to move unhindered from one to another casual use of second-person pronouns—the "we" that is actually "us" as writers; another "we" of adult childhood whom we implicate in dual summaries of the films; and again a "you" who see and do not see, each quite precisely, the films before "our" eyes. We have, however, exact rhetorical purposes for these terms of self-exposure and address. They emphasize the creation of a particular culturally positioned identity and the ongoing conflict within it that is suggested by

Susan Miller and Greg Rode

our bifurcated summaries of these films. These terms of self-exposure and address also emphasize how important it is to specify the situated audiences that receive such productions, at least if we are to understand how rhetoric, understood as discovering "all the available means of persuasion" (Aristotle, *Rhetoric*, I), reveals their less visible but more decisively successful pedagogic strategies. As consuming adults, as nostalgic and still politically immature "adult children," and as children in the actual public situation in which these films were first seen, we have recursively learned ways to compose culture so that we sustain, even when we would critique, its problematic norms.

Obviously, it is too simple to say that *Song of the South* and *Jungle Book* are "for children," no matter if it is "the kid in us" who can hum "Zip-a-Dee Doo-Dah" and "The Bare Necessities" and recall those images of brooms, deserts and animals making Cinderella's dress for the ball. Disney must "sell" to designated teacher/parent/caretakers, adults with money to spend, who may never see the products they buy. Frances Clarke Sayers claims that Disney "never addressed himself to children once in his life; [his] material is made to reach an adult audience" (qtd. in Russo 1992, 24). But this judgment on Disney, the man *and* the conglomerate, oversimplifies the cultural work that these films accomplish. This view suggests, that is, that a unified consciousness literally directs only the movies, the "content" of representations whose ambivalence we have outlined, to make but one mercantile appeal. Either focus, on adults or on children as audience, hides the complexity of this particular way of teaching and of learning.

It is useful, consequently, to keep in mind a distinction between multiple uses *for* Disney films and multiple purposes *in* them. The purposes *for* Disney films, like the purposes for textbooks that must be sold to teachers rather than students, focus on adults who will both predict and replay them in memory. Their published and informal reviews and interpretation praise and blame them, as does the constant Wall Street notice of the rising and falling economy around their production and its variations in the profits from renting the video, buying the tickets and the popcorn, or stuffing videos and their spin-off artifacts in stockings at Christmas. (Disney products do not feel like Chanukah presents or celebrations of any vividly "different" cultural holiday.) We imagine this adult audience, some of whom may not even see the films they provide to children, as mature versions of the youngsters who are first persuaded by "Disney." This grown-up audience is usually brought into play at the films' releases and re-releases, especially by long and now commonplace journalistic accounts of the dual difficulty, but downright horseplay-at-a-boys-club *fun*, that everyone experienced while planning and animating a film. As a recent *New York Times* celebration of the retirements

The Movie You See, The Movie You Don't

of Disney artists describes, "When a movie was finished, some of the animators would have a contest. They would throw [r]eels on the floor, jump on them and see how far they could slide down the hall of the animation building" (Harmetz 1993, 18). A mature audience, those who pay, is invoked by such stories, which regularly highlight both this hysterical spirit and the technical difficulty of the work, and of working with Disney himself. This audience may imagine the "grown-up," painstaking, minutely repetitive skill involved in drawing and otherwise producing these presents for its children. But it more significantly can also find safety in the purification of cultural purposes *in* the films that is accomplished by the ways that such accounts dismiss analyses of them with images of horseplay and statements like "reaching 'inside the human heart' is hindsight nonsense" (Harmetz 1993, 29). The adults whose purposes *for* these films are financial and cultural provisions, can in this context accept the studio's response to charges of racism in *Song of the South*, "that the film 'was not trying to put across any message but was making a sincere effort to depict American folklore, to put the Uncle Remus stories into pictures' " (qtd. in Thompson 1986, 18).

These cultural productions and their success are worth paying for, or so such narratives of their making and intentions persuade us. They appear to be for the "kids," the children it is our duty to entertain. Yet Disney himself is represented as always enormously concerned with this mature audience, displacing onto its aesthetic response the monolithic profit motive that we might, with facile Marxist oversimplification, readily attribute to him. His concern about grown-ups was most powerfully visible at premiers, where it seems Disney was fervently anxious about whether the audience of actors, reviewers, and VIPs would respond appropriately. He could not sit through openings, or so it is told, for fear that someone might cough:

> I want to know what Atlantans think of [*Song of the South*] but please don't ask me to see it with you. I can't stand it. I suffer too much. It's a failing of mine. Once somebody coughed at a preview of *Fantasia* and I was sick. I knew they didn't like it. And once there was a laugh at the wrong place in another one of my pictures and I thought I'd go crazy. . . . When [*Song of the South*] is previewed in Atlanta I know I'll spend all my time in the men's room suffering. (Thompson 1986, 18)

Stories like these about the work, play and fears of "Disney people" explain a great deal about the production of the audience that does not see itself as seeing Disney films. This cultural phenomenon is a constructed social space that collects sanctioned, universalized values, operations that have nurtured both Young Republican and New Leftist sensibilities in adults who send children to them and, at least in the case of the currently available *Jungle Book*, bring them home for re-viewing. In the adult space of economically grounded cultural work that such narrative details portray, respect for expertise and belief in adult duty to children fit many versions of bourgeois family values, a category seemingly larger than political affiliations, whose language relies on "respect" and "belief" in specific ways. This constructed *audience* we do not see is comprised of dutiful adults who relay Disney movies to children. Whether ideologically situated on the left or the right, these responsible adults share a high modernist appreciation of technical acumen and the films' inventions, of work that is not really "hard" work, of personal sensitivity to an audience's reactions, and especially of nostalgia for an (always absent) space of recently "classic" childhood. Like Uncle Remus and Mowgli's mentors, it wants to provide simultaneously an expertly produced and a fantastically protected world for all children, which is also its own memorial space where remembered images remain purified by simultaneously exuberant and neat technology. This adult audience is consequently implicated in the cultural work of Disney if only because the publicity around each re-release offers it a matured realm of identification with Disney's avowed and regularly re-instituted projects: mastery of "our" cultural heritage represented by stated didactic goals *for* the films, and esteem for the well-executed technical achievements *in* them. These two elements of cultural capital invoked by the managed publicity that sells and resells these movies both construct adults as extracurricular teachers. They provide movies as cultural texts, the handmaids to their own teachers/surrogates, the Disney stable of artists, producers, voices and actors. Consequently, we all over time recursively participate in the "authorship" of these films. They are productions delivered and redelivered by expert "grown-ups," metonymically represented by Disney himself. As culturally consuming "parents," we provide and reprovide them. Yet adults and "Disney" may also be imagined and re-imagined as mythic "authors," respected canonical transmitters of cultural beliefs.

How then do these films first prepare us as actual children with elementary lessons in cultural authorship? This rhetorical analysis requires that we recall a specific historical setting in which this persuasion occurs, which in the cases of *Song of the South* and *Jungle Book* was literally at the movies. In the precisely pre-video but post-war era in which both were first released, they were part of the Saturday afternoon sending to the movies that some of us remember so well—a safer time when many children were regularly allowed to be unsupervised. First "marketed" to children in this particular viewing situation, *Song of the South* and *Jungle Book* were films that parents might take their children to see, but might as likely drop them off to see. We learned as a culture to use TV to baby-sit by being left at such Saturday matinees. They previewed technology creating social spaces that over the last forty years have elaborated the ways in which both adults and children have and have not assimilated each other's traditions.

These films thereby exposed wartime, post-war and cold-war children to a newly acceptable intervention in formerly more discrete, if never entirely isolated, home languages. The newly technologized and acceptable "voice over" discourses of cinematic value enlarged the range of sources that had "always" comprised cultural transmissions like the books by Joel Chandler Harris and Rudyard Kipling used as their bases. Saturday movies were places where children learned in ways that cooperate with the "content" of these films, both of which portray children outside the supervision of biological parents. They learned at these movies to be alone, apart from their families but with surrogates for them (the ticket seller, the "ushers," and the dread "manager"), and to be with peers in organized public spaces outside school.[2] These sites offered, consequently, a place to learn about what appeared to be another world, populated with the "others" of *Song of the South* and *Jungle Book* whom we would never meet. We went to the movies to learn, we imagined, more than our parents taught us, to see more than our parents saw and could show us, to hear language our parents didn't speak and to imagine alternative futures they might not imagine. For some, parents didn't care at all what the movie was "about" so long as their children would be entertained (and away for a few hours), and neither did many of us. We went to eat a box of Good & Plenty, candy we never desired or noticed elsewhere, slowly, one piece at a time, while in the dark we saw other illuminations.

This setting in extracurricular classrooms holds the final version of answers to our original and continuing questions about how Disney gives us bifurcated do's, how this cultural site produces and reproduces us as authors of the clashing agendas that Ruth Warrick so precisely voiced. This context for their telling creates movies we do not notice, memories that are inculcated not as a script but as the ability to reiterate culture for ourselves. It prepares us for the many instances in which we take the part, not of a Mother Sally or a Mowgli, but of the actress at her premiere and versions of Disney himself.

Of course this context of telling is not material circumstances alone. The grammatical deep structure of cultural maintenance does not depend on the reinforcing lessons learned by venturing into public as a child, either to go to the neighborhood theatre or to the plantation and jungle of the films. Both films, wherever they are seen by children, contextualize their plots in

Susan Miller and Greg Rode

a framework so obvious it may be overlooked, the context of learning and teaching. These tales assure that their youngest viewers learn that experience is strategically bifurcated, in ways that will specifically exempt them from responsibility for it, especially when it involves encounters with visually "different" races, classes, genders—even species. Both films, that is, enact constitutive binary splits in the form of separations between events and persistent commentaries on these events, which act as their organizing aesthetic principles. As Ian Hunter says of divisions between what happens in an aesthetic production and what it must be made to "mean" morally and ethically, they put into question "the individual's 'ordinary' relation to *all* spheres of existence" (1992, 351). Framed events and their interpretations, "doings" and immediate explanations of them, work together to reconstitute both events and interpretations as always insufficient, always incomplete.

In *Song of the South,* this constitutive rupture is obvious in the difference between frame and tale, human actors and animated cartoons, which appears to a young child as magic that Uncle Remus and the act of storytelling itself can perform. This split between social "reality" and the animated social Darwinism of the Brers is precisely where "the movie you don't see," the one that teaches, occurs. These divisions themselves—between "child" and "man," aestheticized "folktale" and a mundane, "troublesome" world of adult conflict and parental restrictions—offer the necessary model for "inner" and "outer," "then" and "now" realms of identity, the regions that persistently take us away from "ourselves" and our ordinary relation to existence, into one or another *conflicted* mode of experience. This oscillation in the film, that is, is precisely the "story" that children learn from it, a story about being that writes identity in a binary separation of its external circumstance from the internal "self," which is thereby trained to be an observer, not an instigator, of that circumstance. This binary both requires and is reinforced by constructed ("Natural") oppositions between child and adult, black and white, women and men. This is precisely where the impact of Disney's "special magic" takes hold, producing the subjectivity capable of racism, classism, and sexism despite its love for Uncle Remus, attachments to Ginny, and reliance on the competence of both Grandmother and Hattie McDaniel. It is here that we learn to say "some of my best friends are Black," to accept competitive meritocracy as the Natural lot of the lower classes who would "improve" themselves as Ginny does, and equally to desire and fear powerful women. This constitutive narrative bifurcation, the way we tell a story as a teaching and thus organize our own experience, finally and powerfully de-politicizes the "individual." It offers a public world of competition, estrangement and exploitation, about which nothing can be done (in a precise passive construction), and a private world in which we can chase frogs with Toby, find romance "beneath ourselves," and realize our supposedly true selves "where we belong," back on the idealized farm, not in the demands for public articulation in legitimate contests of the city. In its professionalization, this simple division between "child" and "adult" spheres has generated discussion of who, *exactly*, Disney films address, in respect for the artificial divisions between supposed audiences for these films.

Jungle Book, on the other hand, disperses such unintended, obliquely stated lessons throughout its cartoon acceptance of division between bosses and workers, expertise and class-coded ignorance. But its primary pedagogy divides the worlds of Nature and Nurture so that they may be conflicted, marginalizing the "man-village" but replacing it in a persistent tension in the jungle, not between its story's animals but between the story-telling play of song and the verbal work of interpretation that Mowgli's "serious" father-surrogate, Bagheera, promotes. Its grammar of self-division consequently depends on oppositions between the child's mentors, here Bagheera and Baloo, "sensible" and "irresponsible" poles that war to restrain or liberate the child in a typical parental opposition. This constitutive split in telling Mowgli the "story of life" and telling his young viewers the story of that learning is not portrayed visually, as in *Song of the South*, but in the music that signals narrative demarcations throughout the film. Whenever Mowgli's most important "lessons" emerge, the teacher/character imparting the knowledge bursts into song, a phenomenon only peripherally exploited in *Song of the South*, where the Oscar-winning "Zippity-Doo-Dah" coincides with the first animated sequence. In the "Zippity-Doo-Dah" segments of both films, the depoliticized realm of the private, relaxed self, "everything is satisfactual." Baloo's recurring theme song, "The Bare Necessities," is *Jungle Book*'s "Zippity-Doo-Dah." In it, Baloo advises Mowgli to "try and relax . . . cool it . . . fall apart in my backyard." "Forget about your worries and your strife," he instructs him. Mowgli should learn to be satisfied with his modeled bare [bear] necessities, which will surely come his way if he learns to "rest at ease." Baloo's song recommends taking it easy in an infantilizing space of adventure, where, as Stephen M. Fjellman points out about all the "determinedly middlebrow" Disney songs, "fractious adults do not exist" (1992, 267). This tune tells us to equate relaxation with dissociating ourselves from the work of "looking around" that might require us to change the circumstances in a public, conflicted world that excludes mindless fulfillment. Like the civil society that Johnny's father apparently returns to by mistake in *Song of the South*, the man-world imagined in "The Bare Necessities" is full of worries and strife. Cultural conundrums such as the disposition of

Susan Miller and Greg Rode

power and the potential to problematize racial, gender, and class relations appear to be the "something that can't be found," that which "you can live without" and "go along not thinkin' about."

The telling lesson of *and* in both films, we are arguing, is that "reality" is always a *mediated* reality, a "story" that shows one or another binary pole of experience, either work or play, patriarchal family society or cartoon violence, but not the actual vexed complexity of ordinary encounters. We learn from these films, that is, how to imagine societies that can be kept blind to unjust social relations and incapable of problematizing them precisely because they are constituted by individual selves who exist outside their social relations and authentic plans for changing them. "Personal" places and friendships thereby become the only sites of "true" identity. We may not remember that the women in *Song of the South* wear tight bodices and display cleavage if they are objects of desire, "ladies," and that they wear high buttoned collars if they are not. But we certainly remember that Brer Rabbit wants to be in the briar patch even though he pleads to avoid it. We remember, that is, the lesson that we all have a space of exemption where "individuals" can assert falsely private permission to sit out the hierarchies, prejudices, and seemingly temporary conflicts on which these films rely.

Consequently, we take these films quite seriously, but not primarily because of their obviously stereotypical "messages" about race, class, and gender. Instead, we remain fixed on their entirely permeating extracurricular identity-schooling, lessons in how to "be." As in schools, neither child-hero is learning "listen to this" subject matter. Both tiny family men learn, as do counterparts of either sex in their multiple audiences, that experience, *especially* insofar as it involves encountering marginal worlds and people, always requires and in fact *is equal to* an interpretation. The constitutive split that this cinematic cultural pedagogy enacts visually and aurally on its youngest viewers, one certainly reinforced in the structure of formal schooling and certain organized religious teachings, is a difference *within* the supposedly unified and universalized subjectivity that dominant culture already acknowledges as legitimately separating its inner from outer experiences and identities. It is imperative, if the culture that produced and still buys these films is to be maintained, that this nationalized yet isolated identity that encompasses North and South, Liberal and Conservative will hold two simultaneous certainties: that it is a unified observer who encounters *plotted* experience, and that direct encounters with "ordinary life" must immediately be placed in some always available "frame of reference."

Another way to say this is that these Disney movies prepare children to be, precisely, *schooled*. Children learn from them and their counterparts that whatever anxieties, dangers, or fun they encounter, a grown-up "voice," in the person of a film's teacher-surrogate, provides a running commentary on these encounters, which might otherwise constitute examples of actually fragmentary and contradictory life. It is this pedagogical voice, the comfort of Uncle Remus or the bifurcated wisdom and distancing play of Bagheera/Baloo, that they internalize, wrapping it in a gauze of memory that assures its repeated coherent interventions in their reactions to prejudice. Certainly Ruth Warrick felt outraged that James Baskett did not attend the Atlanta premiere of *Song of the South,* just as she was unselfconsciously committed to her inability to *do* anything about his absence, even refuse to attend. But reasons for Baskett's absence were located in an outer, public world of "opinion," not "hers." These reasons were, as Baloo taught us, part of what you hope to "go along not thinkin' about." When you must encounter them, you have learned that acting against them is "the something you want that can't be found."

Notes

1. Disney paid Harris's heirs only $10,000, a paltry sum even in the 1940s.
2. We do not mean to suggest that no such socialization was available before motion pictures, but rather to emphasize their prominence at this time.

References

Althusser, Louis. 1971. "Ideology and Ideological State Apparatuses: Notes toward an Investigation." In *Lenin and Philosophy and Other Essays,* trans. Ben Brewster. London: New Left Books.

Eliot, Marc. 1993. *Walt Disney: Hollywood's Dark Prince.* New York: Birch Lane Press.

Fjellman, Stephen M. 1992. *Vinyl Leaves: Walt Disney World and America.* Boulder: Westview Press.

Hall, Stuart. 1988. *The Hard Road to Renewal: Thatcherism and the Crisis of the Left.* London: Verso.

Harmetz, Aljean. 1993. "Disney's 'Old Men' Savor the Vintage Years." *New York Times,* 4 July.

Hunter, Ian. 1992. "Aesthetics and Cultural Studies." In *Cultural Studies,* ed. Lawrence Grossberg, Cary Nelson, and Paula Treichler. New York: Routledge.

Kantrowitz, Barbara. 1986. "A Film Unfit for the Kids?" *Newsweek,* 22 December.

Russo, Peggy. 1992. "Uncle Walt's Uncle Remus: Disney's Distortion of Harris's Hero." *Southern Literary Journal* 24 (Fall): 19–32.

Sayers, Frances Clarke. 1965. "Walt Disney Accused." *Horn Book Magazine* 41: 602–11.

Thompson, Frank. 1986. "Animating the South." *Southline,* 12 November.

II.

Contestations/Disney Film as Gender Construction

Somatexts at the Disney Shop
Constructing the Pentimentos of Women's Animated Bodies

Elizabeth Bell

Old paint on canvas, as it ages, sometimes becomes transparent. When that happens it is possible, in some pictures, to see the original lines: a tree will show through a woman's dress, a child makes way for a dog, a large boat is no longer on an open sea. That is called pentimento because the painter "repented," changed his mind. Perhaps it would be as well to say that the old conception, replaced by a later choice, is a way of seeing and then seeing again. (Hellman, 1973)

The early Disney shop, not unlike other organizations in the 1930s, strictly divided labor into that performed by men and that relegated to women. From "storymen," "gagmen," art directors, lyricists, animators, and "in-be-tweeners," to background artists, layout artists, and camera operators, the production staff was overwhelmingly male except for 200 women in the Painting and Inking Department. These women applied paint to the artists' tracings on each individual "cel" of film, yielding, on the average, 250,000 paintings for each animated feature film.[1] When the company became so large that direct communication among all the production facets was difficult, a second gendered labor practice began. In "sweatbox" sessions (re-views of works in progress in a small, windowless screening room), a woman stenographer recorded the conversations and produced typed transcripts for distribution to all departments. The hands of women, painting and tran-scribing the creative efforts of men, performed the tedious, repetitive, la-bor-intensive housework of the Disney enterprise.

Those collective, creative efforts resulted in the nest eggs of Disney's em-pire—*Snow White and the Seven Dwarfs* (1937), *Cinderella* (1950), and *Sleep-ing Beauty* (1959)—the transformations of western folktales into animated films. Thirty years later, under the creative auspices of Howard Ashman and Alan Menken, Disney returned to these folk roots with *The Little Mermaid* (1989), *Beauty and the Beast* (1991), and *Aladdin* (1992). These six tales, out of thirty-five full-length animated features, are the signatures and legacy of Walt Disney. With the logo "Walt Disney Pictures," Disney wrote his name and ownership on the folk stories of women, creating indelible images of the feminine:

> Cinema has a way of leaving the images of certain faces and bodies permanently inscribed in our memories. . . . Perhaps no aspect of the cinema is more powerful—or more potentially troubling—than its capacity to confront viewers with such moving bodies and faces, larger than life, images projected in motion and in time. (Pyle 1993, 227)

Although Pyle is describing the cyborg futurism of *Blade Runner* and *The Terminator*, his observation is equally applicable to the images of women created by the Disney shop. Kay Stone's 1975 survey of British and American women for their recollections of fairy-tale girls found that Disney's versions of Snow White, Cinderella, and the Sleeping Beauty were the indelibly inscribed memories. But long before cyborgs dreamed of electric sheep, Disney artists created "cyborg" women composed of the language and bodies of others, rendered "larger than life" only when their images were "projected in motion and in time."

Animation, perhaps more than any other graphic art form, relies on motion and time to give life and efficacy to its images. Despite its popular association with children's cartoons, Disney animation is not an innocent art form: nothing accidental or serendipitous occurs in animation as each *second* of action on screen is rendered in twenty-four different still paintings. The exacting, communally created images of women by men are consistently rendered in a somatic triumvirate of bodily forms and snapshots of the aging process. The teenaged heroine at the idealized height of puberty's graceful promenade is individuated in Snow White, Cinderella, Princess Aurora, Ariel, and Belle. Female wickedness—embodied in Snow White's stepmother, Lady Trumaine, Maleficent, and Ursula—is rendered as middle-aged beauty at its peak of sexuality and authority. Feminine sacrifice and nurturing is drawn in pear-shaped, old women past menopause, spry and comical, as the good fairies, godmothers, and servants in the tales.

More than a somatic time-line of physical changes, Disney's animated women are pentimentos, paintings layered upon paintings, images drawn on images, in a cultural accumulation of representations of good girls, bad women, and doting servants. The first layer of the pentimento, the folktale templates of Perrault, the Grimms, and Andersen, can be punned and dismissed as painted ciphers—characters with no weight or influence. But as the painting accrues, with layers of contemporaneous film and popular images of women, live-action models for the characters, and cinematic conventions of representing women, the levels become increasingly coded and complex. Disney's drawn women are transformed from weightless ciphers, drawn in black and white by men, into a second definition of cipher, texts encoded to conceal their meaning, when the women of the Painting and Inking Department add the palette of hues.

This essay explores the "semiotic layering" in the construction of women's bodies in Disney animation.[2] As cultural artifacts, their meanings are not fixed, but invite a diagnosis of the encoded possibilities of multitextual iconographies in animation. Within the language of Disney animation, the constructed bodies of women are somatic, cinematic and cultural codes that attempt to align audience sympathies and allegiance with the beginning and end of the feminine life cycle, marking the middle as a dangerous, consumptive, and transgressive realm.

Disney's Dancing Girls

The bodies of Disney's teenaged heroines begin as thumbnail sketches for kind and beautiful young girls in the literary tales. Snow White in the Grimms' tale is "white as snow, and as red as blood, and her hair was as black as ebony. . . . When she was seven years old she was as beautiful as the day" (1972, 249, 250). Charles Perrault first describes Cinderella with an "exceptionally sweet and gentle nature" who was "a hundred times more beautiful than her sisters" (1961, 58, 60). Under the bad fairy's spell, the princess in *Sleeping Beauty* seems to be dead, but "the trance had not taken away the lovely colour of her complexion. Her cheeks were flushed, her lips like coral" (p. 4). Andersen describes the little mermaid, the youngest of six sisters, as "the prettiest of all, her skin was soft and delicate as a rose-leaf, her eyes as blue as the deepest sea" (1945, 87).

Disney artists sketched the flesh and blood on these folktale templates with contemporaneous popular images of feminine beauty and youth, their sources ranging from the silent screen to glossy pin-ups. The 1937 Snow White, with large expressive eyes, pouty mouth, and broadly drawn features, is reminiscent of the *ingenue* of silent movies.[3] In the animators' earliest renderings in 1934, Disney "had to decree that their Snow White figure was really too young for the tempests of love (she must have looked about 8!), and that they should add a few years to her age. . . . Disney opted for girl-next-door prettiness" (Grant 1993, 151). Later production notes describe her as "Janet Gaynor type—14 years old" (Finch 1975, 66).[4] The 1950 Cinderella, cultured and stately even in her work clothes, is reminiscent of the sophisticated elegance of Grace Kelly, another girl next door destined for royalty. Roger Ebert claims Cinderella, like "the bland post-war 1950s . . . looks like the 'Draw Me Girl' " (1989, 115). Princess Aurora, the sixteen-year-old of *Sleeping Beauty* (1959), has been described as Disney's most beautiful heroine (Solomon 1989, 198). Comparisons of this statuesque blonde to the contemporaneous Barbie doll are difficult to avoid. Production work for *The Little Mermaid* began in 1985. Ariel, too, is sixteen years old. Her huge blue eyes, upturned nose, and excessive bangs recall the '70s wholesomely lithe pin-up girl, Farrah Fawcett.

The constructed bodies of the young women in Disney's three earliest tales, however, are not drawn in prosaic strokes of cartoon corporeality, but in the formal and poetic lines of classical ballet. Although the actresses and singers who voiced the characters are given screen credits in the latter films, the live-action models for the teenaged heroines are lesser known and remain largely unacknowledged outside Disney histories. Marjorie (Belcher) Champion at 18 years old modeled for Snow White, and Helene Stanley for Cinderella; the entire film of *Sleeping Beauty* was filmed in live action before drawn (Maltin 1980, 74). Disney's early teenaged heroines were constructed on the bodies of professional dancers.

The transformation of dancers into whimsical characters and animated choreography was an early motif in the Disney repertoire. Films of classical ballet dancers, actual choreography, and Jules Engles's familiarity with the world of dance were translated in the lyric *Nutcracker Suite* and comic *Dance of the Hours* in Disney's third full-length feature *Fantasia* (1940) (Maltin 1980, 62). Feild innocently relates that Hyacinth, the prima ballerina hippopotamus in *Dance of the Hours*, was troublesome to animate until

> a Negress weighing more than two hundred pounds was found who tripped with lumbering grace over the live-action stage while the cameramen recorded the least quiver of her flesh, noticing those parts of her anatomy that were subjected to the greatest stress and strain. (1942, 214)

While Disney historiographer John Grant describes the *Dance of the Hours* as "an affectionate parody of the pretensions of classical ballet" (1993, 177), the ciphers of folktales are transformed into conflicting codes of race, class, and gendered performance in Disney's dancing girls.

The animation of race and ethnicity was unproblematic in the early Disney shop. Animated heroines were individuated in fair-skinned, fair-eyed, anglo-saxon features of eurocentric loveliness, both conforming to and perfecting Hollywood's beauty boundaries.[5] The markers of class, however, are covertly embodied in the metaphors of classical dance. Royal lineage and bearing are personified in the erect, ceremonial carriage of ballet and manifested not only in the dance sequences, but in the heroines' graceful solitude and poised interactions with others. Classical dance carriage and royal bearing are interchangeable in Disney animation; once a body is drawn in those lines, the form is inescapable. Prima ballerina Gelsey Kirkland, for example, relates that in one rehearsal of Jerome Robbins's *Scherzo Fantastique*, Robbins stopped the rehearsal,

> blaring over the theatre microphone: "Miss Kirkland, will you take that goddamn tiara off your head!" I had nothing on my head. What he was complaining about was the overly proper way I was carrying myself. I was too stiff, too much of a "princess." (1986, 78)

Disney's early heroines cannot escape from the pentimento of their constructions, their rendering as "too much of a princess." Even Briar Rose, unaware of her royal status as princess Aurora, and Cinderella, before marriage/ascension, move through their worlds seemingly *en pointe* and turned out. Dance physician L. M. Vincent notes that even if one "takes away the dance bag and the chignon, the walk is still a dead giveaway. The walking apparatus of the ballet dancer is not mutated; rather the peculiar stride results from external rotation of the hips" (1979, 3). This "peculiar stride" captured on film is then translated into pencil drawings by Disney animators. The language of ballet, and its coded conventions for spectatorship of "high" art, are embedded in the bodies of young Disney women.

To mark class and privilege with the studied, tensive grace of classical dance is further problematized when the teenage years of sexual maturation are marked by the same metaphors. The formal carriage of the animated heroines is constructed on the bodies of actual women, shaped by the strenuous rigors and artful artificiality of classical ballet. Classical dance has always maneuvered natural body positions into unnatural ones; only the culturally coded ways of looking at ballet transform and render these stances and movements as "natural" grace, form, and line. Borrowing the forms of classical dance and grafting them onto teenaged fairy-tale heroines, Disney artists ask viewers to elide from established and elitist conventions for spectatorship to the animated, politically "innocent," and popular conventions of song and dance. Indeed, the Disney apparatus buys into and then sells the twofold fantasy of little girls who want to grow up to be princesses *and* ballerinas.

While musicals have always broken the narrative conventions of film, the bodies of Disney's classical dancers are troublesome in that they argue with the formulaic characterization of girls in folktales. Marcia Lieberman (1987)

Elizabeth Bell

sketches a composite drawing of young femininity in western tales: beauty, helplessness, and passivity are the catalysts and rewards for destined marriage and money. Goodness is linked to victimage and martyrdom. For Ruth Bottigheimer, the bodies of Grimms' heroines are voiceless ones: "the pattern of discourse in *Grimms' Tales* discriminates against 'good' girls and produces functionally silent heroines" (1977, 53). Carol Gilligan's work with adolescent girls (1991) finds behavioral parallels to these folktale motifs, as the onset of puberty finds active, verbal, and confident girls suddenly quiet and reticent, internalizing and enacting newly realized cultural cues for womanhood.

The young Disney women, at the rate of twenty-four still drawings a second, undergo these same plot and personality requisites. Their bodies, however, built on the disciplined, expressive "naturalness" of dancers, have backbone. In animating Snow White, Cinderella, and Aurora, Disney artists have created a somatic mixed message. While the characterizations of Disney heroines adhere to the fairy-tale templates of passivity and victimage, their bodies are portraits of strength, discipline, and control, performing the dancing roles of princesses.

On the other hand, the ugly stepsisters, attitudinal counterpoints to Cinderella, are animated as antitheses to correct dance carriage and movement. Their strides are always heel first, bent knee exaggerations of incorrect ballet postures and movements. Indeed, in most ballet productions of *Cinderella*, the dancing roles of the wicked stepsisters are performed by men in drag, parodying and disrupting gendered constructions of classical dance roles. Disney's Anastasia and Drizella, with their flat chests, huge bustles, and awkward curtsies, could as well be read as comic drag acts in this balletic fantasy. The stepsisters serve as animated commoners to Cinderella's royal body, gender benders to Cinderella's enactment of ballerina.

In the Disney landscape, the dancing heroines are partnered by the silent ciphers of nineteenth-century classical ballet. The art of *pas de deux* is drawn in its technical and aesthetic contours: the dancers are "suitably matched for height and weight . . . to convey the truth of the partnership between boy and girl" (Serrebrenikov and Lawson 1989, 5). Indeed, Disney is reported to have chosen dancer Louis Hightower to model for Prince Charming because "Disney liked his sturdy legs" (Grant 1993, 150). Dressed in tights and tunics, Disney princes fulfill the gendered expectations taught in partnering class:

> Girls learn to trust that their partners will be there when they need
> them, and boys learn to live up to that trust. They learn how to support
> an arabesque, how to lift and catch a girl, how to stop a pirouetting prin-
> cess so that she faces the audience, and how to present her to their public

as though she is the most important jewel in his collection. Adagio class is where the boys get experience in handling girls, and where girls get used to being handled. (Hurford 1987, 69)

If Disney animators draw teenaged heroines that are "too much of a princess," then Disney princes enact their ballet roles with equally accurate excess, an excess that renders them silent, dramatic "cardboard" (Grant 1993, 253).

In the *pas de deux*, the romantic centerpiece in the Disney repertoire of fairy tale turned ballet, the physical requirements of classical dance are accurately rendered, but the encoded asexuality of performance creeps through the layered construction. The "classic embrace" of the waltz, featured in *Cinderella*, *Sleeping Beauty*, and *Beauty and the Beast*, conveys "elegance and regal bearing, giving a balletic quality to glamour and beauty. . . . Here the upper body is stressed, accomplished through elongated necks and accentuated backs, his militarily straight, [hers] arched" (Peters 1991, 149). The elegant tensiveness of the *pas de deux* is carefully constructed, but always couched as the "natural" expression of love—the seamless quality of the dance at once representing and replacing the sexual act. The carefully encoded and constructed aesthetic of eroticism is transformed ultimately into (an)aesthetic asexuality:

> Dancing represents sex in its least costly form, free from imprisonment and free to a great extent from the emotional responsibility and, above all, as a sure thing, independent of someone else's pleasure. In other words, it means freedom from sex. . . . In a strange transmutation dancing is a form of asceticism—almost a form of celibacy. (Agnes de Mille qtd. in Vincent 1979, 150)

The *drawing* of dance would seem to cost even less. The pains and politics of partnering, lifted from their real world enactment and captured on film, are replaced by two-dimensional paintings. The aesthetic conventions for viewing classical dance and the (an)aesthetic conventions of dance asexuality are both encoded in the Disney dance sequences.

Sherri Stoner, the live-action model for both Ariel and Belle of *Beauty and the Beast*, is a departure from the classical ballerina template for teen body.[6] Instead, Stoner was a member of the Los Angeles improvisational group, the Groundlings (Jackson 1991, 50). Chosen from the group for her expressive face and small frame (she stands 5'2" and weighs ninety-two pounds), Stoner worked with Disney animators twice a week for two years in the ongoing construction of Ariel. For both Ariel and Belle, Disney storymen departed from the gendered stereotypes of the tales. Both are active, intelligent young women in pursuit of their dreams against the wishes of the parent figures in the films. The Disney Studio, too, changed tactics, employing Linda Woolverton for *Beauty and the Beast*, the first Disney tale/film screenplay written by a woman.

While critics applauded both films for their accurate portrayals of teenage petulance, the teenaged bodies moved from the realms of classic dance aesthetics to popular conventions of cheesecake. For Pauline Kael, Ariel is "a teen-age tootsie in a flirty seashell bra" (1981, 140). Like its live-action Touchstone predecessor, *Splash* (1984), the costuming of a mermaid is problematic. "Disney as Corporation" was not quite ready for a bare-breasted Darryl Hannah; costumers taped her hair strategically to her breasts (Grover 1991, 16). Disney artists, too, played with the costuming conventions of mermaidhood. The first frame of Ariel finds her peering over the broken mast of a shipwreck, her breasts covered by the horizontal mast. This coquettish striptease pose, both postponing the discovery and heightening the audience's curiosity, is quickly resolved, but later recalled. When Ariel finds herself with legs and no clothes, she dresses and poses in a sailcloth rag to the omniscient soundtrack's accompanying wolf whistle.

While the earliest folk heroines move in the stilted lines of classical dance, the latest folk heroines tease with the conventions of burlesque. While the first approach distances the audience in the guise of artificiality and elitism, the second approach entices with the implicit warning, "look, but don't touch." Instead of the lush soundtracks of classical music and their accompanying balletic *pas de deux*, both *The Little Mermaid* and *Beauty and the Beast* recall and reenact the elaborate filmed fantasies of Busby Berkeley. Sea creatures and household objects take the place of women in Ashman/Menken Berkeley-esque numbers, but the spirit of display remains:

> American eroticism has always been a different provenance and complexion than the European variety, an enjoyment both furtive and bland that is closer to a blushing cartoon than sensual celebration. There is a titillation in the *faux-innocence* of Busby Berkeley's banana'd bathing beauties. . . . His was a vision of women as sex objects raised to a kind of comic sublimity, a state of formal grace. (Haskell 1987, 21, 146)

Both Belle and Ariel are positioned as the viewers of these fantastic spectacles, distancing themselves as commodities in the Disney burlesque economy. The tales, however, still narrate and fulfill their destiny as marriage/reward for the prince/beast; their commodification in the marriage plot overwhelms the animated *jouissance* of the musical numbers.

As Disney artists draw dancers' bodies onto folktale templates, the results are fissured gaps in the paintings, images leaking through the surface, confusing the ways of seeing folk heroines, dancers, and sexuality. The "backbone" of dance argues with the weakness of the narratized girls; romantic interludes are ultimately asexual and (an)aesthetized; the titillation of burlesque underscores the commodification of the heroines in the marriage plot, while distancing them from complicit participation in those plots. These semiotic layers result in a formal unreadability in these teenaged bodies: dancers assuming roles of princesses and strippers working with props and costumes. Disney artists have rendered a paradoxical level of performance affectation. Like *Who Framed Roger Rabbit?*'s Jessica who claims "I'm not bad, I'm just drawn that way," the bodies of Disney teenagers make a similar, if unspoken, self-reflexive claim: "I'm not weak, I just talk that way."

Disney's *Femmes Fatales*

Disney's evil women, the beautiful witches, queens, and stepmothers, evidence a similar performance affection, but the metaphors are not borrowed from the bodies of classical dancers. Instead, Disney transforms the vain, active, and wicked woman of folktales into the *femme fatale*, the "deadly woman" of silent film and of Hollywood classic film. Colette, writing in 1918 "A Short Manual for the Aspiring Scenario Writer," describes the *femme fatale* as a "shattering revelation" characterized by decolleté, a "clinging black velvet dress," and weaponry. She catches the spectator in her gaze, "sinuously turns her serpent's neck . . . and—having first revealed enormously wide eyes, she slowly veils them with soft lids" (Virmaux and Virmaux 1980, 47). In silent film, the *diva* is characterized by "exaggerated movements of the hips and arms, with the head thrown back, her hair suddenly spilling down her back, contortions, rolling eyes" (Sadoul qtd. in Doane 1991, 124–25). Describing the "vamp" of American films in the 1930s, Molly Haskell claims these representations of the treacherous feminine are "meant to represent demonic natural forces that, like a cyclone, threaten to uproot man from himself" (1987, 103). Mary Ann Doane summarizes the *femme fatale*'s most striking characteristic as "the fact that she never really is what she seems to be. She harbors a threat which is not entirely legible, predictable, or manageable" (1991, 1).

The *readability* of the *femme fatale*, painted in beautiful and shapely strokes on the bodies of Disney's Wicked Queen, Lady Trumain, Maleficent, and Ursula, is evident in the careful cosmetics of paint, cowls, jewelry, and "clinging black dresses." The deliberateness of these choices is apparent in Disney historiographies. Grant relates that one essay in *Photoplay* maintains that "experiments on [*Snow White*'s wicked Queen's] lovely cruel mouth and eyes alone represent drawings enough to paper a house" (1993, 152). Production notes describe her "beauty [as] sinister, mature, plenty of curves" (Finch 1975, 66). The Disney official account of Ursula's creation for *The Little Mermaid* is that she was modeled on *Sunset Boulevard*'s *femme fatale*, Norma Desmond.[7] Live-action models for the wicked women are not noted in Disney historiographies, but their voices become interchangeable auralities in the Disney lexicon. Lucille LaVerne voiced both Snow White's Stepmother Queen and her alter ego the Witch.[8] Eleanor Audley voiced both *Sleeping Beauty*'s Maleficent and *Cinderella*'s wicked Stepmother. Pat Carroll's Ursula is a contemporary shift to well-known performers as voice talent in Disney animation.[9]

More than aural and visual similarities among the animated characters, the pleasurable and duplicitous ways of looking at Garbo and Dietrich are inscribed on the drawn bodies of Disney's evil women. The pleasure derives from their power and authority as *femmes fatales*, living and thinking only for themselves as sexual subjects, not sexual objects; the duplicity derives from the animated perfection that subverts their authority even while fetishizing it—these deadly women are also doomed women. But unlike the conflicting somatexts of Disney's heroines, the caricature and melodramatics of the *femme fatale* are iconic and congruous cinematic codes that inscribe middle age as a time of treachery, consumption, and danger in the feminine life cycle.

Disney artists appropriate and enlarge a common convention in cinema, the extreme close-up of the *femme fatale*. Doane summarizes the significance of the close-up, especially of the female face, as

> that bodily part not accessible to the subject's own gaze (or accessible only as a virtual image in a mirror)—hence its over-representation as *the* instance of subjectivity. But the face is not taken in at a glance—it already problematizes the motion of a pure surface since it points to an interior, a depth. The face is the most *readable* space of the body. (1991, 47)

The evil women of Disney films are the only female characters rendered in close-ups. Moreover, they are the only characters who address the camera directly, both advancing the narrative diegesis and confronting the spectator's gaze with their own. But Disney enlarges the cinematic code for the face of the *femme fatale* with a special effect: the face and background fade to black and the eyes are painted as gold, glowing orbs, narrowing tightly on the intended victim/heroine. This special effect is an intensification of not only the women's evil natures—their unknowable interiors—but it recalls primal fears and animal phobias, transforming their faces to the exterior icons of wolves and cats whose eyes glow in the dark.

While the signatures of a witch are clearly written on Disney evil women—their familiars, caldrons, and spells—the construction of their bodies on predatory animals heightens the dangerous consumptive powers of the *femme fatale*. Marc Davis, chief animator of Maleficent in *Sleeping Beauty*, explains that "she was designed like a giant vampire bat to create a feeling of menace" (qtd. in Solomon 1989, 182). For the climactic battle scene with Prince Phillip, animator Eric Cleworth modeled their encounter on a striking rattlesnake: "The dragon's motions have a ponderous, reptilian grace that suggests powerful muscles moving a bulky body over the rocky terrain. The long neck and narrow head dart with serpentine fluidity" (Solomon 1989, 200). Disney's famous decree for *Snow White*'s wicked queen, that she be "a mixture of Lady Macbeth and the Big Bad Wolf" (Finch 1975, 66), not only crosses literary and folk genres, but enlarges her *femme fatale* iconography with predatory powers. Ursula, originally envisioned as a "scorpion fish" (Sanez 1989, 124), not only captures the melodramatic, languorous, and rapacious movement of the *diva*, but her octopus tentacles physically manifest the enveloping, consumptive sexuality of the deadly woman.

While the *femme fatale* of *film noir* directs her catastrophic powers at a man who is powerless under her fatal force, Disney's deadly women cast their spells, not only on their young women victims, but on the entire society from which they are excluded. Whether societies of merpeople or kingdoms, their excess of sexuality and agency is drawn as evil: "It is this evil which scandalizes whenever woman plays out her sex in order to evade the word and the law" (Montrelay 1978, 93). This performative scandal is heightened by the contrasted construction of the bodies of kings in the Disney iconography. The typical Disney king is a short, stout, balding, blustering "hollow crown," encapsulized in the admonition used in both *Sleeping Beauty* and *Jungle Book* (1967): "You pompous old wind-bag!" The narrative diegesis constantly points to the fact that they exert no control over their children, their lackeys, their castles, or their kingdoms. In middle age, they are drawn as physically and symbolically impotent in contrast to the evil women's sexual potency and powers.

Through animation, Disney artists have constructed a powerful critique of patriarchial discourses: the inefficacy of divine right of kings is both drawn and storied in contrast to the potency of women's evil and their dangerous and carnivorous threats to order. The *femme fatale* construction of feminine excess begins the wicked pentimento of Disney evil; the layers of rapacious animal imagery align women's powers with predatory nature, marking the *femme fatale*'s gaze as not just interiority, but as a well of power beyond comprehension. If Disney heroines are somatic contradictions, then Disney's evil women are somatic congruities. Each layer of their construction—from the cosmetics of their vanity, the affectations of their movement, and the confrontation of their gaze to the animals that define their "natural" predatory natures—the accumulative paintings mark feminine sexuality "as terrifying; it is an earthquake, a volcanic eruption, a tidal wave" (Gauthier 1981, 202). The fated doom of the predatory, animated *femme fatale* is always marked by two events: the collective and unified efforts of all other characters in the films, and the upheaval of natural forces—rock slides, ocean storms, and cliff precipices. Together they reestablish the control and stability of the cultural and natural order in the destruction of the transgressive feminine.

Disney's Grandmothers

While the dancing *ingenue* of the stage and the *femme fatale* of the cinema are familiar representations of women, Disney artists fill a relatively empty cultural category with their depictions of feminine nurturing and sacrifice in their depictions of good fairies, godmothers, and servants in the fairy-tale films. In the depiction of supernatural feminine goodness, Disney artists adhere to the fairy-tale templates of physical and temporal separation. That is, the "helpful crone and fairy godmother" appear and disappear at whim, evidencing a "protective power [that] is always and ever present within the sanctuary of the heart" (Campbell 1968, 71–72). Flora, Fauna, and Merriweather of *Sleeping Beauty*, Cinderella's fairy godmother, Carlotta of *The Little Mermaid,* and Mrs. Potts of *Beauty and the Beast* all are narrated with dutiful servant's capacity to be on call without being underfoot, never needful in their own rights, but consistently helpful and protective of their charges.

On the blank sketch pads of Disney artists, feminine nurturing and sacrifice are consistently drawn in contrast to the *femme fatale*. Unlike the shapely and mature curves of wickedness, Disney grandmothers are pear-shaped or apple-shaped. As endomorphs, they fulfill the physical somatype/ stereotype as calm, relaxed, cooperative, affable, warm, forgiving, sympathetic, soft-hearted, generous, affectionate, and kind (Cortex and Gotti 1965). With none of the painted vanities of evil, they wear no cosmetics, jewelry, or adornment; indeed, they have no lips. Their hair, gray, silver or white, is covered. Their bountiful arms and torsos cradle, bathe, and dress the heroines of the tales. Feminine sacrifice is drawn not in the middle-aged peak of sexuality and authority, but in the postmenopausal script of asexuality. In the cultural biologic timeline, they are grandmothers whose bodies are nonthreatening, unavailable, and harmless. They reestablish and maintain the order that the *femme fatale* destroys.

Many comic moments in the films center on the initial ineptness of their maintenance: the fairy godmother forgets where she put her magic wand; the good fairies fumble through Princess Aurora's birthday cake and dress; Carlotta serves the horrified Ariel crab for lunch. The comedic value of the bodies of old women is evident in Frank Thomas's description of the attention he gave to animating the good fairies of *Sleeping Beauty*:

> I found that when old ladies move, they bounce like mechanical toys. They paddle, paddle, paddle on their way. They stand straight, and their arm movements are jerky. Their hands fly out from the body. The reason for this is that they're afraid to get off-balance, afraid they will fall. (Qtd. in Thomas 1991, 105)

Solomon describes the good fairies of *Sleeping Beauty* as "dear, if slightly befuddled, spinster aunts" (1989, 198). Solomon's observation is well placed; animator Thomas found models for Flora, Fauna, and Merriweather while spending time "at the supermarket observing rotund old ladies, usually at the dog-food counter" (Thomas 1991, 105).

Disney artists distance the good women from the evil women of the tales, not just in their physical construction, but in their divergent productivity. Doane maintains, "It is appropriate that the *femme fatale* is represented as the antithesis of the maternal—sterile or barren, she produces nothing in a society which fetishizes production" (1991, 2). The good Disney women produce, not children, but the perfected enactment of motherhood as fostering grandmotherhood. Removed from a "natural" blood relationship to the child/heroine, their sacrifices are deemed even purer in their selflessness. Sacrifice and nurturing, lifted from the realm of necessity, become a matter of choice.

These grandmothers have potent powers and manifest their magic in "Disney dust," those colorful sparkles that mark good magic in the Disney lexicon. As protectors and guides, Disney grandmothers appear and produce magic and service at crucial moments of transition in the world of women: childbirth, sexual maturation, and marriage. As caretakers and healers, witches employ a white magic drawn not in the material certainty of herbs and plants, but in the immateriality and charm of special effects. This fetishized perfection and mystification of powerful goodness is localized in the somatic timeline of feminine old age. As Gilligan describes one adolescent girl's relationship to her grandmother, she "has taken in, in the name of love, an image of perfection, exemplified by her grandmother . . . the stillness at the center of this frozen image" (1991, 32). The borders surrounding "this frozen image" conscribe codes of sacrificial mothering, of women's magic as mystical and charming (apart from the cold tools of science and medicine), and of goods that transcend materiality.

The power of feminine goodness, rooted in matriarchal healing, comfort, and sacrifice, contrasts well with constructions of Disney bureaucrats: the prim, proper, angular lackeys of kings. The Grand Duke of *Cinderella* and adviser Grimsby of *The Little Mermaid* are painfully thin, rule-bound middle managers, invested with "beyond the throne" power. This institutional empowerment is no match for the magic of Disney women. "Disney dust" and service substantively change matter and lives; the symbolic power of bureaucrats changes nothing. Daniel Lawrence O'Keefe claims that magic has the capacity "to counter the terrors of the symbolic world that man has created and to get some control over it" (1983, 39). Disney artists have drawn the unknowable and unnameable, outside the orders of science and technology, divinity and religion, bureaucracy and hierarchy, not simply in the gaze of the *femme fatale*, but in the bodies of magical grandmothers.

The Disney Magic Recast

The pentimentos of Disney women, like Lillian Hellman's description, ask viewers "to see and to see again" through the layered constructions of the animation process. The tales that prescribe the characters of women are not fixed texts, but are starting points for cultural constructions of the feminine. The ownership and repeatability of the tales—whether as oral art, written texts, or films—not only speak to the parameters of cultural production, but echo the concordance of voices that perpetuate them. Karen Rowe explains that

> in the history of folktale and fairy tale, women as storytellers have woven or spun their yarns, speaking at one level to a total culture, at another to a sisterhood of readers who will understand the language, the secret revelations of the tale. (1986, 57)

While Disney artists have captured the characterology of beautiful victims, active wickedness, and feminine goodness sketched in the tales of the Grimms, Perrault, and Andersen, they have also captured performative enactments of gender and cultural codes for feminine sexuality and agency.

The young heroines are typical of "the perfect girl," whose body, voice, and destiny are a "mesmerizing presence" through which "girls [enter] the world of the hero legend, and experience the imposition of a framework which seemingly comes out of nowhere—a worldview superimposed on girls but grounded in the psychology of men" (Gilligan 1991, 33). But Disney artists constructed their "perfect" girls on the bodies of real women; bodies that produce cracks in the animated perfection and offer sites of physicality and performance that resist the psychology of men and idealizations of women. The wicked women harbor depths of power that are ultimately unknowable but bespeak a cultural trepidation for unchecked femininity. That Disney artists resorted to the coded cinematic representations of the *femme fatale* for feminine agency speaks to the lack of conventions for encompassing such incomprehensible power. In animation, these filmic conventions are denaturalized; their artificiality and encoding are made visible. Of the good women in fairy tales as consistently aligned with the supernatural, Marcia Lieberman asks an important question: "A girl may hope to become a princess, but can she ever become a fairy?" (1987, 196). In the Disney lexicon of power, the magic of grandmotherhood is possible.

The "secret revelations of the tale" are graphically depicted in the Disney films. It is the worlds of women—worlds of song and power and care—that offer alternatives to institutional hierarchy, science and technology, and divine rights of kings. The women in these films are not bifurcated into good and bad, but represent a continuum of cultural representations of women's powers and performances; the films celebrate the ambiguity, the diversity, and potency of women's bodies, and the multiple sites and sources of their cultural construction. Moreover, these constructed performances are rooted in a physical timeline that decrees that these bodies will change: from the tentative strength of youth, to the confident carriage of middle age, to the aplomb of old age.

During the 1993 summer re-release of *Snow White*, movie theatre lobbies blossomed with point-of-sale advertising for the film. The six-foot-tall, free-standing "billboard" was dominated by the beautiful wicked Queen. Her cold, stately beauty and her direct gaze confronted the audience members waiting in line; her black cloak spread to encompass and to backdrop the figures beneath her. Below her, Snow White beamed lovingly at the dwarfs at her feet. The composition and arrangement of these figures was new. The film contains no such physically direct juxtaposition between Snow White and her stepmother, but their physical similarities were remarkable. The coloring of their hair, lips, and skin, and the construction of their bodies, were identical—with the exception of twenty-five or so years. On the Disney cultural and somatic timeline, the young heroines will become their stepmoth-

Elizabeth Bell

ers; the stepmothers, too, will become the good fairies and godmothers. They in turn will care for the next generation of young heroines, lovingly and carefully, telling their tales to the "sisterhood of readers who will understand the language. . . because only for women does the thread, which spins out the lore itself, create a tapestry to be fully read and understood" (Rowe 1986, 68–71). The Disney film fabric is not made of threads, but of celluloid. The women of the Painting and Inking Department, lovingly and carefully, paint the pentimentos.

Notes

1. The Disney Studio was not alone in this gendered labor practice. In one fanciful chart of the animation process, Hanna-Barbera cartoon characters mark the production stages: Huckleberry Hound writes the script; Barney Rubble creates the storyboards; Yogi Bear reads the track; Fred Flintstone directs. Betty Rubble, brush in hand, paints the cels (Madsen 1990, 356).

2. Maureen Turim defines "semiotic layering" as "the accrual and transformations of meanings associated with an artifact as it passes through history, or as it is presented in different versions" (in Erens 1990, 109).

3. In 1932, Disney hired Don Graham to conduct art classes at the Hyperion studio. Part of this training included watching live-action films, especially the silent-screen films of Charlie Chaplin and other silent comedians (Maltin 1980, 43).

4. Molly Haskell describes Janet Gaynor as "one of the most ethereal of the angel-heroines" of the silent films of the 1920s (1987, 50).

5. 1992's *Aladdin*, however, was problematic. The length of noses, color of skin, and shape of eyes for the two young protagonists, Jasmine and Aladdin, were all hotly debated in the Disney shop (Avins 1992, 11).

6. Bob Thomas in *Disney's Art of Animation* spells her name as Shari.

7. "The Making of the Little Mermaid," aired on the Disney Channel in 1991.

8. Ollie Johnston and Frank Thomas relate that Ms. LaVerne achieved the "rough" quality of the crone's voice by removing her false teeth (1993, 56).

9. Roger Ebert, in a review of *Cinderella*, claims he much prefers "Disney's policy of using unfamiliar voices for the dubbing, instead of the studio's guess-that-voice derbies of recent years" (1989, 115). Pat Carroll, however, is an interesting example of intertextuality. In 1965, she performed the role of wicked stepsister Prunella in Rodgers and Hammerstein's televised production of *Cinderella*.

References

Andersen, Hans Christian. 1945. "The Mermaid." *Fairy Tales*. London: Oxford University Press.

Avins, Mimi. 1992. "*Aladdin*." *Premiere*, December: 65–70, 111.

Bottigheimer, Ruth. 1977. *Grimms' Bad Girls and Bold Boys: The Moral and Social Vision of the Tales.* New Haven: Yale University Press.

Campbell, Joseph. 1968. *The Hero with a Thousand Faces.* Princeton: Princeton University Press.

Collins, Jim, Hilary Radner, and Ava Preacher Collins, eds. 1993. *Film Theory Goes to the Movies.* New York: Routledge.

Cortex, J. B., and F. M. Gotti. 1965. "Physique and Self Description of Temperament." *Journal of Consulting Psychology* 29: 404–14.

Doane, Mary Ann. 1991. *Femmes Fatales: Feminism, Film Theory, Psychoanalysis.* New York: Routledge.

Ebert, Roger. 1989. *Roger Ebert's Movie Home Companion.* Kansas City: Andrews and McMeel.

Erens, Patricia, ed. 1990. *Issues in Feminist Film Criticism.* Bloomington: Indiana University Press.

Feild, R. D. 1942. *The Art of Walt Disney.* New York: Macmillan.

Finch, Christopher. 1975. *The Art of Walt Disney: From Mickey Mouse to the Magic Kingdom.* New York: Abrams.

Gauthier, Xavier. 1981. "Why Witches?" In *New French Feminisms*, ed. Elaine Marks and Isabella de Courtivron. New York: Schocken.

Gilligan, Carol. 1991. "Joining the Resistance: Psychology, Politics, Girls and Women." In *The Female Body: Figures, Styles, Speculations*, ed. Laurence Goldstein. Ann Arbor: University of Michigan Press.

Grant, John. 1993. *Encyclopedia of Walt Disney's Animated Characters.* 2nd ed. New York: Hyperion.

Grimm, Jacob, and Wilheim Grimm. 1972. *The Complete Grimm's Fairy Tales.* New York: Pantheon.

Grover, Ron. 1991. *The Disney Touch.* Homewood, IL: Business One Irwin.

Haskell, Molly. 1987. *From Reverence to Rape: The Treatment of Women in the Movies.* 2nd ed. Chicago: University of Chicago Press.

Hellman, Lillian. 1973. *Pentimento.* New York: Signet.

Hurford, Daphne. 1987. *The Right Moves: A Dancer's Training.* New York: Atlantic Monthly Press.

Jackson, D. 1991. "Sherri Stoner, Animation Model." *Premiere*, November: 50.

Johnston, Ollie, and Frank Thomas. 1993. *The Disney Villain.* New York: Hyperion.

Kael, Pauline. 1981. "The Current Cinema: Busty, Twisty, Fishy." *New Yorker*, 11 December: 136, 140.

Kirkland, Gelsey. 1986. *Dancing on My Grave.* Garden City, NY: Doubleday.

Lieberman, Marcia. 1987. "Some Day My Prince Will Come: Female Acculturation through the Fairy Tale." In *Don't Bet on the Prince*, ed. Jack Zipes. New York: Routledge.

Madsen, Roy Paul. 1990. *Working Cinema: Learning from the Masters.* Belmont, CA: Wadsworth.

Maltin, Leonard. 1980. *Of Mice and Magic: A History of American Animated Cartoons.* New York: McGraw-Hill.

Montrelay, Michele. 1978. "Inquiry into Femininity." *m/f* 1: 91–92.

O'Keefe, Daniel Lawrence. 1983. *Stolen Lightning: The Social Theory of Magic.* New York: Vintage.

Perrault, Charles. 1961. *Complete Fairy Tales.* New York: Dodd, Mead.

Peters, Sally. 1991. "From Eroticism to Transcendance: Ballroom Dance and the Female

Body." In *The Female Body: Figures, Styles, Speculations*, ed. Laurence Goldstein. Ann Arbor: University of Michigan Press.

Pyle, Forest. 1993. "Making Cyborgs, Making Humans: Of Terminators and Blade Runners." In *Film Theory Goes to the Movies*, ed. Jim Collins, Hilary Radner, and Ava Preacher Collins. New York: Routledge.

Rowe, Karen. 1986. "To Spin a Yarn: The Female Voice in Folklore and Fairy Tale." In *Fairy Tales and Society: Illusion, Allusion, and Paradigm*, ed. Ruth Bottigheimer. Philadelphia: University of Pennsylvania Press.

Sanez, C. 1989. "Those Faces! Those Voices! Behind *The Little Mermaid*." *People*, 11 December: 120–24.

Serrebrenikov, Nicolai, and Joan Lawson. 1989. *The Art of Pas de Deux*. Princeton: Prince Book.

Solomon, Charles. 1989. *The History of Animation: Enchanted Drawings*. New York: Knopf.

Stone, Kay. 1975. "Things Walt Disney Never Told Us." In *Women and Folklore*, ed. C. R. Farrer. Austin: University of Texas Press.

Thomas, Bob. 1991. *Disney's Art of Animation: From Mickey Mouse to Beauty and the Beast*. New York: Hyperion.

Vincent, L. M. 1979. *Competing with the Sylph: The Quest for the Perfect Dance Body*. 2nd ed. Princeton: Princeton Book Company.

Virmaux, Alain, and Odette Virmaux, eds. 1980. *Colette at the Movies: Criticism and Screenplays*. New York: Frederick Ungar.

Seven

"The Whole Wide World Was Scrubbed Clean"

The Androcentric Animation of Denatured Disney

Patrick D. Murphy

A May 25th, 1993, *Chicago Tribune* column by Anna Quindlen on the recent royal marriage in Japan was titled " '90s Princesshood: What Happened to Happily Ever After?" The notion that marrying a prince ought to be a woman's highest ambition has recently been dashed on the gems of British and other royalty. Yet, the Walt Disney Company has attempted to persuade us otherwise in its most recent animated films. Despite Disney's recent corporate changes, the motto for the animation division should be: "The more things change the more we stay the same." The trailer for the videocassette edition of *The Jungle Book* (1967) evidences such an implicit motto. Jeffrey Katzenberg, chairman of movie and television operations, introduces clips from the production of *Beauty and the Beast* (1991) and promises that it is "pure Disney imagination." Architect of the Touchstone R-rated repertoire, Katzenberg seems to be assuring parents that even if the live-action films are a departure, the animated ones remain true to the Disney ethos (see Taylor 1987, 217–18, 239–43).

But is that ethos worth maintaining? From the 1930s *Snow White and the Seven Dwarfs* through the 1960s *101 Dalmatians* and *The Jungle Book*, the 1980s *Rescuers* films, and the very recent *The Little Mermaid* and *Beauty and the Beast*, Disney's full-length animated films reveal a consistent, although incoherent, worldview on nature and women that is escapist and androcentric. The escapism is based on denying wild nature as an integral part of the biosphere at the world level and as part of individual character at the personal level. The denial of *wild* nature serves the fabrication of a timeless, universal, and unchanging order articulated in part by means of cultural values and generalizations. The cyclical re-release strategy for key Disney animations is

Patrick D. Murphy

based on the claim that these timeless "classics" will appeal to, and should be seen by, each new generation.

The establishment of such order depends on a belief in, and maintenance of, social stasis. And wild and static are mutually exclusive structures. As Gary Snyder expresses it, "wilderness is a *place* where the wild potential is fully expressed, a diversity of living and nonliving beings flourishing according to their own sorts of order. In ecology we speak of 'wild systems' " (1990, 12). While we may speak of wilderness as place, we must speak of wild as process, with its active manifestations contingent, indeterminate, and contextually particularistic, and thus continuous demonstrations of the principle of difference.[1] The Disney ethos promotes escapism from the indeterminacy of "wild systems" through denial of process and difference.

It is not coincidental that Disney animation consistently displays static, absolute depictions of both nature and women, rather than just one or the other. Ecological feminism, more commonly known as ecofeminism, argues as its starting point that the oppression of women and the exploitation of nature are inextricably linked in the history of western and other patriarchal civilizations.[2] Both are based on androcentric hierarchies and dichotomies, with women and nature objectified for the benefit of the male subject. While the mutual objectification and subordination occur consistently, they are not always identified with one another. Women and nature are in many historical periods simultaneously portrayed as identical and oppositional, just as the "virgin/whore" dichotomy is a mainstay of dominant American culture. Hence, the claim that the androcentrism of Disney animation is consistent *and* incoherent. The consistency resides in the objectification and subordination; the incoherence in the philosophical justifications and ideological formations that naturalize them. For example, Disney consistently attempts to reflect a sense of "virginal" innocence, promoting the "magic" of childhood often through characters' friendships or ability to communicate with animals, while at the same time reflecting the cultural drive toward the conquest of nature through promoting a capitalist work ethic among dwarfs, princes, mice, servants, and heavily anthropomorphized animals.

Significantly, Walt Disney's first major creation demonstrates such incoherence. Richard Schickel notes:

> In The Mouse, as he was conceived by Disney, all conflict that the animal's real nature might have caused was resolved by an act of creative will: reality was simply ignored. . . . All inner conflicts about the nature of the land were similarly resolved in Disney's other films: he always, and only, showed us a clean land. Indeed, the whole wide world was scrubbed clean when we saw it through his eyes. (1968, 53)

"The Whole Wide World Was Scrubbed Clean"

Similarly, women receive the same subjection to the "act of creative will" in their caricaturization and stereotypic limitation, whether it be body imagery or personal ambitions.

The Disney ethos both reflects and promotes particular elements of the dominant ideology of United States culture. And one finds a demonstration of this overlap of reflection and promotion in the preface to *Storming the Magic Kingdom* (Taylor 1987). Writing of the 1984 hostile takeover attempt of Disney, Taylor claims:

> To accept it was unthinkable. Walt Disney Productions was not just another corporate entity, not just some holding company in a cyclical industry like natural gas or forestry that suffered from overcapacity and therefore needed to be rationalized by liquidation of its assets to achieve maximum value for the shareholders. . . . The company's executives saw Disney as a force shaping the imaginative life of children around the world. It was woven into the very fabric of American culture. Indeed, its mission—and it did, they believed, have a mission as important as making money for its stockholders—was to celebrate and nurture American values. (1987, viii)

Taylor first delineates the hierarchical dichotomy between nature and culture, "natural gas" and "forestry" being *only* natural resource industries and Disney productions being *significantly* a culture industry and therefore superior. He then equates national values with human values by approvingly depicting Disney's efforts to inculcate "American" values worldwide.

By the time of *Snow White* (1937), Walt Disney was seeking exceptionally realistic detail in animation. But only the details should be real, not behavior, not nonhuman difference from the male image of the world. In reviewing the first release of the film, Otis Ferguson makes a telling comparison. He approvingly comments on how the movements of the young deer are "shrewdly carried over from the common cat" (qtd. in Schickel 1968, 219). How can one approve of making a deer behave like a cat and call that realistic? Only through the lens of androcentrism can one imagine that *all* animals are meant to be domesticated and will prove willing objects of domination. When Snow White awakens after fleeing into the woods, all sorts of kindly and there-to-assist animals take her to the dwarfs' house. The animals also volunteer to help clean up the place.

Anthropocentrism is certainly not a problem unique to Disney, nor is sexism. But in *Snow White*, as elsewhere in Disney, androcentrism combines these two ideological formations and extends them to nonhuman nature. It is not simply that humans are conceptualized as the center of the universe, but rather that men are the universal center. The exclusive reliance on the male-normative viewpoint throughout the film not only restricts heroism to males and limits "good" females to domesticity, but also subordinates non-human nature to human agency, whether evil or good. In viewing *Snow White*, young boys may be assured that when all is right with the world, women and nature remain ready to serve them, no matter how messy they may be, since women are a domesticating and civilizing presence and non-human nature is a resource pool to provide beasts of burden.

101 Dalmatians (1961) presents two significant variations from what has become standard Disney animation: characters who resolve their own crises rather than being saved by another character; and the presence of functional, rather than dysfunctional, heterosexual families (a problem no longer explainable through resort to Walt Disney's biography). In regard to the former, we could say that *Dalmatians* deviates from the norm because the *Snow White* plot becomes the fundamental structure of story development, rather than the *Dumbo* (1941) structure. In almost all of the other animated films, a human rather than nonhuman character in crisis, who undergoes no significant change or development, is rescued by another human or heavily anthropomorphized animal, who also undergoes no real individual development. Evil disrupts static lives, but only long enough to move the characters from one situational plateau to another; e.g., Snow White and Ariel marry, while Penny of *The Rescuers* (1977) gets adopted, but none of them really changes.

In regard to the latter, the *Dalmatians* variation actually reinforces the dysfunctional norm because the main function of marriage seems to be to produce offspring to make the father proud—the male dalmatian, Pongo, is credited by the human husband as the driving force behind the female dalmatian's ability to give birth to fifteen puppies. And because Perdita tires in the process, one pup is dying; but, as if to underscore that males are the true generative force, the human husband brings the pup back to life.

Unlike these variations, the incarnation of evil is typical. Cruella Deville, a powerful, autonomous and "wild" woman, is vain, selfish, and greedy. In his song, Roger identifies her as an "inhuman beast," so that the human female antagonist, with no interest in animals except for their fur, is identified more strongly with nonhuman nature—apparently predatory and rapacious—than the couple who care for the dogs. In contrast, the dalmatians are depicted anthropomorphically, more in line with the civilized cultural norms that Cruella flouts. The animals are most noble when most nearly "human," while the human is most ignoble when most nearly "inhuman" (see Plumwood 1991, 10).

This human/inhuman dichotomy is reinforced in various gender-stereotypic ways. As good females, Perdita and the housekeeper are permitted only to take initiative when doing so in defense of the pups. The other prominent females are the dairy cows who provide milk to the hungry pups. Only as mothers, real or surrogate, are females depicted as doing anything positive in this film, and, of course, they do it instinctively; the canine males, however, analyze and calculate.

The film isolates evil as the personification of the independent woman, who resorts not only to cruelty but also theft. While reinforcing patriarchy and androcentrism, the use of the isolated female also enables an escapist, rather than allegorical, viewing of the film. The issue of the daily commercial destruction of millions of animals, whether for food, clothing, or cosmetics testing, need never come up. Cruella's wearing furs and blowing smoke are, like her loud, brash voice, symptomatic of her individual excess and aggressiveness rather than a class or cultural problem; unlike the dalmatians who are integrated with a class of other valuable "purchased" dogs throughout the rescue effort, Cruella remains a unique and isolated figure. Indeed, there is only a conflict because Cruella resorts to theft of the fifteen after failing to purchase them as disposable properties, which she has done with the other eighty-six puppies. While Roger and Anita will not break up their human-canine extended family for money, the conflict is limited to that between individual goodness and individual wickedness, not between opposing systems of objectification, valorization, or ownership. After all, Roger capitalizes on Anita's friendship with Cruella to render her an object of ridicule by means of his song, which becomes a highly marketable commodity.

Released within a year of Walt Disney's death, *The Jungle Book* (1967) was touted as a fitting tribute to the man and proof of the continuation of the basic values and techniques that established Disney's greatness. After thirty years of full-length animation, audiences seemed to "know" the Disney ethos and could judge the degree to which a particular film realized it. And "knowledge" becomes a crucial commodity in this film. Will Wright observes accurately that "knowledge is always a *legitimating* idea, in the sense that assertions of knowledge always assert what is correct, what is proper, what is legitimate" (1992, 6). What, exactly, is the knowledge asserted in the jungle, and who makes these assertions?

As with *101 Dalmatians*, the film has voice-over narration by a participant animal character; yet, while in the former film the viewpoint was explicitly presented as canine, nothing in Bagheera the panther's remarks suggests anything other than an androcentric perspective. Like Roger, Bagheera acts as the generative force by saving the infant's life. Viewers quickly learn that the ten-year-old boy must leave the jungle because Shere Khan has returned and will surely kill him—not because the wild tiger is a predator but because he has developed the anthropomorphic emotion of hatred for humans. One must studiously avoid the incoherence of inconsistent attribution of qualities among characters here to suspend disbelief. (The wolves can protect the boy from every other predator except the tiger? Tigers that do not feel hatred are no threat to humans? Panthers like people and are not threatened by hunters? Wolves, not to mention a North American bear, are major players in the jungles of India?) The leader of the Dawn Patrol makes clear that the human/nature dichotomy dominates the conceptualization of the film. He states unequivocally that the "man-cub" does not belong in the jungle. Well, just where are all the villages supposed to be in this part of the world? The idea that the villages are in opposition to the jungle rather than in relationship with it demonstrates a culture/nature split that universalizes all human habitation on the basis of the western alienated model.

The racism of the monkey kidnapping of Mowgli should not go unnoticed by any viewer of the film. But it also highlights the movie's androcentrism in that up to this point only males speak. Later there are only two exceptions: the wife of the lead elephant speaks from a mother's perspective to urge the other elephants to search for Mowgli (the kind of female initiative already treated as acceptable in *Dalmatians*), and the girl sings Mowgli into the village. The jungle is a "man's world" but also a nonhuman habitat. Mowgli should fit right in as a male among the other males in this jungle. And yet, as a human, he does not belong because he is not wild enough to survive.

Near the end Baloo assures Mowgli that no one will come between them, since they have engaged in male bonding through shared violence. Yet everyone knows what comes between males and the wild: women. With a typical misogynist remark, "They're nothing but trouble," Baloo warns Mowgli. Yet, heterosexual attraction is stronger, even allegedly at the age of ten, than male bonding, as proven by the female's ability to lure Mowgli into domestic life. The few female characters in *The Jungle Book* stand as civilizing figures— never wild ones. The maternal, then, is not so much natural here as cultural, and its utility limited to early childhood.

The Rescuers and *The Rescuers Down Under* (1990) introduce some tactical variations from previous films, such as the cross-species rescue in both. And while the changing roles of women in American society are acknowledged in *Rescuers*, the unconverted character of the acknowledgment is emphasized through the woman's *needing* a male chaperon for the mission. Medusa in the first film and McLeach in the second are basically Cruella types motivated by personal greed, while the lackeys of the evil individual have been transformed from humans to reptiles to depict more conveniently the evil-human/rapacious-nature identity already established. While the antagonist in *Rescuers Down Under* is male, this seems a by-product of the setting more than anything else, with the difference reduced by switching the animal cohort from male, as in *Rescuers*, to female.

In both "Rescuers" films, the mouse characters never become animalistic, but always remain anthropomorphic with the characters modeled on the two actors, Eva Gabor and Bob Newhart, who voice their lines. Other animals remain only animals, and the evil reptiles do not "speak" the language of the "good" animals. But in *Rescuers Down Under* a significant "good" character is also denied access to the community of animal speakers: the mother bird, whose capture initiates the conflict between McLeach and Cody. Here the incoherence of the dominant ideology leads to contradictions in the construction of the imaginary world in the film. Except for this bird, all of the voiceless animals are depicted as subordinate creatures in the animal-character hierarchy. Why?

First, despite this giant bird's being female and having a nest of eggs to which she must return, the character looks like an eagle, associating it with an extremely powerful masculine symbol in American culture. To let an eagle speak in a female voice, particularly a blatantly motherly one, might generate confusion about the linkage of masculinity and power in the minds of the audience. Female viewers might find it easier to identify with this bold, free-flying character than with Bianca, who by film's end is committed to marrying Bernard. Cody, the young male protagonist, establishes a clear bond with this bird, and too heavy an inter-gender relationship might be a turnoff for male viewers busy trying to generate a sense of autonomy from their mothers, and hoping to remain bachelors without becoming dwarfs.

Second, the significance of motherhood and nurturance as natural is undercut here as in other Disney animated films. The boy's faceless, anonymous mother serves only as a failed inhibitor of Cody's adventurous spirit at the start of the film. The bird, whose mothering cannot be defined as specifically cultural rather than natural, is depicted at the end as bonding with Cody as mutual free-flyer and autonomous subject rather than assuming responsibility for her own offspring. The male albatross who has flown the rescuers to Australia ends up brooding the eggs. Reminiscent of Roger's rejuvenation of the puppy and Bagheera's saving of Mowgli, this male hatching of the young, coupled with the boy's initial rescue of the mother, equates generative power with male rather than female capabilities. By having a female bird never depicted in any way as feminine, the animators maintain the character type necessary for plot development, while at the same time reinforcing dominant male images of power and autonomy. While female viewers may applaud the bird's resistance to capture, any further identification leads toward a negative affirmation of subordination of the female to a male-dominated world. Unlike Mowgli, the male protagonist of *Rescuers Down Under* appears at film's end flying off unchanged, riding on the back of the bird, into the stars free of mother and culture, free of the threat of domestication and denaturalization.

But if the sexual tension and its attendant threat of domestication are missing from the future for Cody, they return with a vengeance for the heroines of *The Little Mermaid* (1989) and *Beauty and the Beast* (1991). Ariel lives in a strangely inconsistent world. The merpeople are "people," in the sense of having a clear, hierarchical, established social order, but some of the sea creatures participate in it while others do not. The good characters, Flounder the young fish and Sebastian the crab, speak the same language as the merpeople. Yet the evil shark that chases Ariel is excluded from language and community, while the underlings Flotsam and Jetsam speak, although with a strongly "snakelike" accent reminiscent of Kaa in *The Jungle Book*. Perhaps such voicing is possible because both snake and eels are communicating with people immersed in more primitive/natural conditions than human civilization, emphasizing Mowgli's and Ariel's need to enter a more "productive" world.

Ariel is attracted to the surface world by the consumer goods of early capitalist production. She remarks that "I don't see how a world that makes such wonderful things can be bad." But doesn't her world make things? According to the song "Under the Sea," apparently not, since Sebastian makes it quite explicit that this Caribbean-equivalent, underdeveloped aquatic state does not engage in significant labor. Merpeople just sing and dance, while humans work. This racist and colonialist perspective reinforces the human/nonhuman and culture/nature dichotomies by associating the merpeople, and by implication Caribbean and other equatorial peoples, with a closer-to-nature, live-off-the-land indigenous lifestyle inferior to the industrial lifestyle—because advanced humans make things, i.e., they transform nature to serve them rather than adapt themselves to cohabitate with the rest of their environment.

Actually, this transform-nature worldview fits quite well with the "love-at-first-sight" cliché that dominates the storyline. It too is based on a concept of transformation that supposedly results in stasis. Both also involve commodity fetishism. Love-at-first-sight depends upon marketable products: physical beauty, acculturation, singular traits. In this case, the commodity consists of Ariel's voice, which the evil Ursula turns into an object of exchange to make Ariel less marketable. Without her voice, Ariel cannot immediately re-enchant Prince Eric. So Sebastian attempts to commodify her remaining physical attributes by encouraging her to be coquettish. But since Eric's "love" is based on a single attribute, the enchanting singing voice, Ursula is able to steal him away.

Near the end Eric impales Ursula on the mast of a death ship—how conveniently phallic. But even so, we do not yet have a "happy" ending. Incoherence and contradiction across Disney films is revealed when Triton uses his magic to turn Ariel into a human so that she can marry her prince. When women have wielded magic, such as the Queen in *Snow White* and Ursula, it has been portrayed as a perversion of the natural; but in *The Little Mermaid*, the unnatural transformation of Ariel is approved, since it elevates her to a higher nature through participation in a more progressive—because industrial—world. Women do not need to speak to men to engage in building human-to-human relationships, but only need to seduce and serenade them into a male-female cultural order. Since her prince is already acculturated and ready for marriage, Ariel does not pose the threat of domestication. Rather, Eric will "treat" her to the joys of colonial assimilation, with her deculturation following necessarily from her loss of power due to denaturalization. The escapist character of the film omits any possibility of a problem arising if Ariel's former friend Flounder shows up on the dinner table one evening.

In *Beauty and the Beast* the roles at first appear to be reversed. Belle will acculturate the Beast, saving him from his tragic fate through domestication. But who really gets domesticated and whose nature is really transformed in the course of this film?

Much of the landscape and even the forest is animated relatively realistically, but the castle is highly stylized. Along with this, the voice-over nonparticipant narration and story book stills at the beginning encourage an allegorical reading. We do not, however, end up with a significant degree of transference to contemporary life. Belle is supposedly a "smart" woman who reads books, but her sense of possible destinies for women is based on romances. When, after eluding Gaston, Belle sings of wanting more from life than to be a wife, the camera "pans" the landscape as if to suggest she wants to see the wider world, but—as the clock and candlestick know—she is just a "girl," not a woman. By film's end she has chosen a life of living in the castle as a princess, where she will have endless hours to read the romance novels collected in the library that the Beast-Prince has already given her. The abandonment of that wider world in exchange for princesshood reinscribes the validity of androcentric promotion of escapism as the answer to the contemporary cultural debate about the nature of gender relationships—[the smart woman gets the prince not by dint of her intellect but by means of her self-sacrificing devotion and selfless love.]While the Beast-Prince undergoes significant change, it remains the means-to-an-end within the context of the curse. The curse requires that someone love him, not that he love someone else.

The Beast-Prince represents the culture/nature dichotomy in that he is turned into a beast because he has failed to be fully human, and he becomes fully human only through love. Yet the representation of love here contradicts that of *The Little Mermaid*. There it was instinctual and physiological and accordingly immediate; here it is cultural and emotional and accordingly developmental. The contradictory treatment from film to film of "love" demonstrates the conceptual incoherence of a consistent ideological position on gender relationships and culturally appropriate behavior. The end result of repeating the cliché for women that "someday my prince will come" justifies the contradictory depictions of love and relationships. The appearance of such contradiction between two films released only three years apart seems more indicative of the degree to which feminism has problematized the successful representation of the marriage plot of patriarchy than it says about any possible Disney cultural awareness. *The Little Mermaid* replicates the *Snow White* structure with *Beauty and the Beast* not far behind. Janet Ames notes that "*Snow White* reflects a set of assumptions about femininity, about motherhood, that no longer hold for the world we live in" (1993, 94). The same must be said for these recent films, with no excuses given because of their dates of production.

The heroes of Disney animated features are almost always produced by circumstance rather than by design: Snow White does not antagonize the Queen to get out of the castle; Penny and Cody do not seek to become embroiled with kidnapping jewel thieves and poachers; Belle does not go looking for a prince to marry. Thrown into situations in which they participate in, but do not engineer, their own rescues, they conclude their adventures with only their circumstances altered; their characters remain fundamentally unchanged. Since the films do not empower their characters, they cannot possibly empower their audiences. But is this the destiny of popular full-length animated films? No. *The Land Before Time* (Universal/MCA, 1988) and *Fern Gully* (20th Century Fox, 1992), two recent non-Disney animations, show the possibilities for a different destiny and an empowering happy ending. *The Land Before Time* comes from Don Bluth, who left Disney in 1979. The nonparticipant narration encourages an allegorical rather than escapist approach to the film. "Evil" is explained in terms of a necessary conflict between herbivores and carnivores rather than some individual excess. In any wild system, some members will always be food for others. Although Littlefoot is the central character for the story, the plot depends on a team of baby dinosaurs working together and changing their attitudes and behaviors in the process. Also, nature is a character, or at least agent of change, in the film, and far more attention to landscape as a factor in events appears here than in the recent Disney films. While Littlefoot loses his mother early in the film, she remains a significant influence through her nurturing and teaching—unlike the absent nonentities of Disney. Although the theme focuses on reuniting families, this can only occur as a result of adapting to changing natural conditions and recognizing their significance.

Fern Gully: The Last Rainforest is an overtly ecological film, with a female lead. The ecological necessity of defending the rainforests is developed clearly, and the responsibility of industrialized societies for changing their behaviors is stated explicitly in the end without being overly didactic. These are the film's strengths, but they are partially offset by significant weaknesses. The first is the Snow White syndrome, i.e., the idea that women have to clean up after men. Zak is part of the problem until Crysta patiently straightens him out and works to correct the damage he has participated in creating. The second is the Vanished Indian syndrome, i.e., the idea that indigenous peoples belong to history, not contemporaneity. The film shows no humans in the rainforest except the industrialized destroyers. The third is the "Women and Gaia are one" syndrome, i.e., women are essentially and automatically closer to nature and more in tune with it. This version of biological essentialism represented by Crysta becoming the new Magie dovetails with the first syndrome and promotes the idea that women are not as ideologically and culturally conditioned as men within a patriarchal society. Nevertheless, *Fern Gully* and *The Land Before Time* demonstrate, even if they do not fully realize, agent-initiated revisioning of the animation ethos dominated by Disney.

Both of these films have "happy endings," but they are constructive rather than escapist. Marrying a prince will not save the rainforest or reunite a family sundered by environmental changes. Only those fully invested in the maintenance of the androcentric status quo can risk the luxury of escapist entertainment; yet such people are likely to be a far higher percentage of its producers than its consumers. As Schickel rightly observes, what we see in Disney animation is "a popular nostalgia for the life of an imagined past" (1968, 210). But what Schickel fails to observe is the degree to which efforts to depict that nostalgia on screen contribute to the realization of that imagi-

Patrick D. Murphy

nary past in the present, the degree to which they reflect and promote the dominant ideology of United States culture, consistently and incoherently. And if the image does not play with this generation, Disney can try again with the next. But will there still be a receptive audience?

Notes

1. In "A Social Theory of Differences," Will Wright discusses the idea of a "principle of difference," distinguishing it from a commitment to a specific difference: "The social commitment could not be to a 'true' set of specific *kinds* of people. . . . Rather, the social commitment must be to legitimating the *principle* of difference, to encouraging and multiplying different kinds of people and positions and values for their own sake, within the bounds of social order, because it would be through the legitimacy of difference that new and necessary forms of rationality would emerge" (1992, 212).

2. For introductions to the principal characteristics of ecofeminism, including the significant theoretical differences within it, see Diamond and Orenstein (1990); Plant (1989); and Warren (1991).

References

Ames, Janet. 1993. "*Snow White* Revisited." *Ladies' Home Journal*, August: 92, 94.

Diamond, Irene, and Gloria Feman Orenstein, eds. 1990. *Reweaving the World: The Emergence of Ecofeminism*. San Francisco: Sierra Club.

Plant, Judith, ed. 1989. *Healing the Wounds: The Promise of Ecofeminism*. Philadelphia: New Society.

Plumwood, Val. 1991. "Nature, Self, and Gender: Feminism, Environmental Philosophy, and the Critique of Rationalism." *Hypatia* (6)1: 3–27.

Quindlen, Anna. 1993. " '90s Princesshood: What Happened to Happily Ever After?" *Chicago Tribune*, 25 May, Sec. 1: 19.

Schickel, Richard. 1968. *The Disney Version: The Life, Times, Art and Commerce of Walt Disney*. New York: Simon and Schuster.

Snyder, Gary. 1990. *The Practice of the Wild*. San Francisco: North Point.

Taylor, John. 1987. *Storming the Magic Kingdom: Wall Street, the Raiders, and the Battle for Disney*. New York: Knopf.

Warren, Karen J., guest ed. 1991. "Ecological Feminism," Special Issue. *Hypatia* 6(1).

Wright, Will. 1992. *Wild Knowledge: Science, Language, and Social Life in a Fragile Environment*. Minneapolis: University of Minnesota Press.

Eight

Bambi

David Payne

Technoscience and science fiction collapse into the sun of their radiant (ir)reality—war. (Haraway 1991, 185)

My father is a wise and gentle man. He was never drunk, loud, violent, abusive, competitive, aggressive, unfaithful, or impatient. He never, in my presence or to my knowledge, made a fool of himself trying to prove that he was a man.

Until he was drafted into the army just after World War II, my father had never left the panhandle of western Oklahoma where he was born to a displaced Missouri farmer and Nora Jones, child of a half-Cherokee father. My father had avoided going to war through a farm deferment, graciously awarded even during war years to the last remaining son on a farm. In the army, he typed paychecks for his committed time, and then returned to the clay-red bluffs and coarse panhandle grasslands to become what every man raised there became: a farmer. After the birth of his second son, me, he decided what countless others in 1952 decided, and moved his young family to the city where he was to do factory work for most of the next thirty years. In Wichita, Kansas, he built and repaired the large bombers for Boeing Aircraft. He sired two more sons, but no daughters.

While my father is a man of uncommon intelligence, he tells that he spent little time in the one-room schoolhouse afforded the children of Camargo, Oklahoma. He also apparently enjoyed great freedom from the supervision of his parents, as he spent much of his youth hunting in the woods and fields along the South Canadian river that winds through that country. That land taught him things that were not being recited in the schoolhouse. As a hunter, a farmer, and a contemplative soul, he learned about nature, about relations among seasons, weather, growth, animals, wildlife, and domestication. He never wanted to leave that country and still today imagines that he wants to return.

As a boy beside him, I could feel that he was most himself, most at peace, and most a man, when he and Grandad drove and walked across the fields to look over the cattle herd, or to examine the heads of ripening milo, or to appreciate the fresh radiant green of sprouting sweet clover. Unlike my brothers, I never once passed up a chance to go with him, to walk beside and behind him, to work with him when at Grandad's farm, or those of my uncles, or the small farm we ourselves worked for a short year when Dad was laid-off from the factory. These were times when he taught me with patience, when he loved being my father and I his son. Often, he would squat down on his haunches, pull a stem of grass to chew, and watch and listen in silence. I would imitate every action, sitting, pulling my own stem and squinting my eyes just so, looking where he looked, wishing I could see what he saw as he stared across the fields and cattle. I don't think I ever complained of boredom, or asked him to take me home, or ever thought there was anything else we should be doing but being father and son, being men, in this way.

While the scientists and technicians in the industrialized countries of the world were preparing for World War II, the artists at Disney were working on the production of *Bambi*. Largely finished by 1941, but not released until August 1942, *Bambi* was easily the most monumental project that the animated sciences had yet conceived. As early as 1935, Disney had secured the rights to Felix Salten's charming little characterology of forest animals (1929), and over the next six years the project, like the dialogue of war itself, proceeded at an on-again, off-again pace, although "it rarely came to a complete halt" (Grant 1993, 189).

In the Disney guild, technical and metaphysical ambitions combined to create a vision of the film that allowed the scenic properties of nature to nearly overtake all other elements of the story. Deer fawns were brought to the studio for artists to study; copious footage of animals and their forest habitat was filmed. Intense scenic realism became the technical psychosis of the animators, while natural realism became the metaphysical breakthrough this technical accomplishment would permit:

> It was decided that the animals must be allowed to tell their own story as far as it was possible! The continuity must be based not upon what man has read into nature but upon what man can learn from nature of those things they share in common. The whole *Bambi* unit surrendered to the spirit of the wild; countless thousands of drawings were made in all mediums, of all sizes, under all conditions, on the off chance of some secret's being captured that would make it possible to see the story more truthfully. Life and death took on new meaning; the influence of the seasons manifested itself in unrecognized ways. Imperceptible transitions between night and day, the mysterious persistency with which storms can

build up or disappear at a moment's notice, perhaps leaving the earth re-invigorated or temporarily prostrate, all became a part of the story con-trol. (Feild 1942, 197)

In the marvelous dramaturgy of technical realism, nature would [herself] be turned into motivated action; absolute scenic fidelity would transform "nature" into agent, allowing "her to tell her own story" (Feild 1942, 176).

One wonders whether there isn't a rather direct correlation between re-alism and war; not that war causes realism or that realism causes war, of course, but literally that a co-relationship exists between them. Both war and realism are in some sense possibilities that play among the mutable dialogues of human purpose and at times they appear to play together in a cooperative spirit. Justifications and preparations for war take on a dramatic proportion-ality similar to that in *Bambi*: taking action depends upon a "realistic" as-sessment of the circumstances, the scene, as the proper context for such ac-tions. Ultimate actions, as those that align the members of a nation for war, depend upon ultimately "realistic" assessments of scene to transform the members into a single character, ready to execute the ultimate actions of killing the enemy, so as to transform the scene and restore it to its "natural" harmonic relations. War itself is a dramatic vocabulary of "the real," insofar as watching death and destruction up close involves a religious self-enforce-ment that this is real, this is necessity, this is the natural condition of men, and these realities must be kept at the forefront of one's mind. To let go of any of these insistences when killing makes it impossible to act. When one lets go of the realistic frame in watching the imagery of battle, war doesn't provide any escape; it becomes *surreal*—more than real—but never a fiction. This is also true when one is hunting and killing game—the animal in your hands is dead, and if even for a moment you let go of the reasons and right-ness of killing, the animal does not come back to life. Like the "realities" of war, the death of the animal is undeniably real. One cannot escape that reality, one can only find ways to subvert or to reinforce it.

So, too, in *Bambi*. To let go of the realism that the text obviously speaks as its context does not allow one to return it to fiction, certainly not to escapism (to which other film texts during the Depression-War era, especially Disney's fantasies, can easily be released). When one lets go of the realist presumption in *Bambi*, it becomes surreal more than real. The "truth" *Bambi*'s creators obviously sought to depict does not dissipate into a fiction, it becomes surrealistic; it becomes the "Truth," a decontextualized realism that reveals the pious warpages of how we construct the "real."

One should not assume from this argument that the coincidence of

David Payne

Bambi's release and World War II made the film a success. Rather, it is reported that the 1942 release was a "financial disaster" and that perhaps this was due to the war itself (Grant 1993, 189). But *Bambi* did go on to become an important film in the Disney *oeuvre*, and a very important film in the experiences of children in the 1950s and early 1960s. *Bambi* is often recalled as the most memorable film of people's youth, not only for its charm and natural wonders, but because there children learned about death. The emotional impact of Bambi's mother being shot, and of hearing the little fawn's long, mournful calling for her, could have few parallels in children's literature or filmic experience. The politics of "Nature vs. Man" in the film are such that the anti-hunting sentiment in America came to be called, perhaps fairly, "The Bambi Syndrome."

Bambi is a story about the birth and maturation of a young male deer. The film opens with the birth of the fawn, and the stir the event causes among the forest citizens. "Come quickly!", "It has happened!", "The new Prince is born!" the small creatures urge the old Owl, who seems to be the great uncle of the woodland family. Bambi's privileged birth is certified by the excitement, and by the absent patriarch, the old Prince, the great Stag, who we soon see is standing on a hillside overlooking the nativity scene. There he strikes the regal pose of dominion that becomes the icon of maleness in the film. There he surveys his domain and takes property ownership of the birth of his heir.

The story that emerges from this opening gesture is a story of animals who live in a human society—almost. The children are reared in a neighborhood (the thicket) of endearing creatures, where mothers chat and the broods converse in cross-specific harmony, and absent fathers retain the voice of family authority: ("[Thumper,] what did your father tell you about eating greens?" "What did your father tell you [about being nice]?") At a given time Bambi and mother encounter the larger society of deer in the meadow, where Bambi is pursued by the more aggressive female child, Faline, until he sees two young Bucks fighting and turns on Faline in a hostile imitation of his male gender model. In the meadow, the young male deer spar and chase and run until they stop, all deer freeze in motionless silence. The Great Stag, the Prince of the Forest, enters the scene to display his status. He struts slowly, regally, inspecting the young deer until he comes to Bambi. Without a word, the Stag examines Bambi with mortifying gaze and walks away. "Why was he looking at me, mother?" "Because, Bambi, he's your father, the Great Prince of the Forest."

Is this nature's story? The election of the deer as the royal species of nature seems curious, running counter to the more traditional metaphor of large cats, the predators, as "King." Deer are not predatory, of course, but are relatively passive prey for larger predators. The cross-specific dominion of the deer in *Bambi* include only nonpredatory species: rabbits, squirrels, birds, and skunks. Deer, as it turns out, are principally prey for "Man," the hunters, civilization, who invade the harmonious hierarchy of deerhood with their weapons. The meadow scene ends with shots being fired from hunters. Led by the Great Stag, the deer escape into the forest. When winter comes, Bambi and mother visit the meadow once again in search of food. The Great Stag comes to them to warn that "Man is in the forest." The threesome run, shots again are heard, the mother is killed. As Bambi arrives unharmed in the thicket he calls repeatedly, "mother, mother." Soon, through the falling snow, the outline of the Great Stag appears to tell Bambi his mother is dead. "Come," the Stag orders in a solemn voice. The film, an animation, draws a picture of a blank screen for several seconds.

Bambi is certified as "nature's story," it would appear, primarily because of the politics it displays wherein nature is a unity because it is ravaged and violated by "Man." It is not so much nature's story, then, as nature's drama, the realism of which is supplied by the agonism of humankind's anti-nature, an antithesis which is likely to resonate with the pieties and guilts of twentieth-century audiences. But in this agonism, a deft substitution is supplied, wherein nature is purified by contrast to "Man," yet nature as feminine is reoccupied by a patriarchal social system that is the fullest perfection of Man's wish: a single male patriarch with absolute dominion and property ownership of all that transpires in the society, a privilege earned by longevity and wisdom, by the survival and fitness that is the epideictic consummation of scientific realism; which, curiously, is the language of nature invented *by Man* for nature's own preservation (see Haraway 1991).

With rare exceptions, the only times my father hunted, and I with him, were when we would visit Oklahoma. We were strictly bird hunters, and Thanksgiving and Christmas visits coincided with quail hunting season. As a small boy, of course, I was not permitted to go along with the men as they rose early, drank their coffee, donned their warm clothes, and secured their weapons. As I grew older, I was sometimes allowed to accompany them under very strict rules of both the explicit and tacit kind. Explicitly, I could not carry a weapon and must follow directly behind my father, obeying his every command to stop, to be silent, or to pay attention. Tacitly, I could never complain of cold feet, tired legs, hunger, or of my intense desire to participate as an equal, all of which I experienced regularly during these outings. In short, I must not be a child nor bother the men in this most serious of manly enterprises, rules which coincided with my own heart's desires perfectly.

Learning to hunt is a rite of passage to manhood in the culture we revisited when we returned to Oklahoma. It was also part of the culture of many of my Kansas cohorts, but that was not a culture in which we participated in our "usual" life. Hunting, and the desire to hunt, became affixed to my father's "return" to the "natural" narrative of his life, the one where he felt belonging, and the one he lamented sacrificing for the middle-class emergence of his family. It was a narrative lived by my uncles and cousins undisturbed by the progressive and, when in their presences, conspicuous forces that were turning my father's sons into "city kids." My completion of the rites of passage in this secondary culture was partial, sporadic, and insufficient. But like all boys, I desperately wanted my father's acceptance, to be a man on his terms, and those terms always found me as a hunter wanting. I was never punished for this want, mind you, verbally or otherwise, but it was something I felt nonetheless.

I recall one incident that typifies for me the desire, the passage, and, notably, the *ethic* that is hunting. By the time I was fourteen or so, my father would take me and my older brother hunting by ourselves, for we were not yet sufficiently indoctrinated to go with the "men," although boys our age from that culture surely would be. My brother was the first, naturally, to have his own shotgun. I carried my grandfather's small .410 gauge until the arrival of my own fifteenth birthday when I received a Stevens 20 gauge shotgun just like my brother's.

I had never, at this time, actually hit a bird. To make matters worse, my brother had killed several, a few even that day if I recall. Next to the abandoned farmhouse on my Grandfather's land, we could nearly always scare up a large covey of birds. This day we found them in the grain stubble not far from the old house, and even without a dog, startled them into flight. When twenty quail take flight, the moment is so startling and chaotic, the flutter of those speedy wings so surprising and loud, that it requires quick reactions and steely nerves to execute a shot that has a chance of hitting a bird.

When the quail flushed, I shot without aim or object. The small spray of pellets from my .410 probably came near no birds. This time, however, one bird flew up a few feet above ground, and went down. He then flew again, ascending only a few feet and then returned to ground zero. "I got one!" I hollered, as though my long night of exclusion had come to an end. My father managed to trap the still flailing bird on the ground, and I ran up to see my trophy.

When a bird has been wounded rather than killed outright by a shotgun blast, which is rare enough, one immediately puts the animal out of its suffering. This my father would do by deftly twisting the head off in a smooth motion, exhibiting no evidence of the stomach cramps I always had when watching him do that.

This time Dad held the bird until I arrived. The piteous creature stared back at me with eyes full of life. Upon inspection, it seems that there was a pellet of buckshot in the bird's wing, explaining its crippled flight. The wound was old, surrounded by the greenish discoloration of lead poisoning, and there was no blood. Obviously, the bird had been wounded by an earlier encounter with a hunter and had managed to stay with the covey. Also obvious was that I hadn't hit the bird at all, but my father did not point this out. Rather, he allowed me to examine the bird without comment. He told me that if I thought I had shot this bird, then he would kill it. If not, then we would let it go. I hesitated for a moment and looked again at the bird's frightened eyes. As much as I wanted and needed that kill, I could not perpetuate a hoax with such questionable consequences. I shook my head and my dad released the bird. Walking away I asked him what would happen to the bird, whether it would live. "Oh, a coyote will probably get it" he said, and we walked on. I think we both agreed that what I did was more manly than having hit the bird in the first place, although we didn't say so, and as we walked I began to feel pretty good about the whole thing.

There are rules to hunting that have to do with sportsmanship, I guess, but that itself is no shallow thing. Those rules, sportsmanship itself, have something to do with the rights of nature and the rights of the animals, if that doesn't sound too ironic. Oddly, and hunters defending themselves often say this, hunting is a way of expressing piety and respect for nature. It is a way for men (usually, but less so all the time) to participate in nature, to participate in a relationship with nature that goes back to the beginning (our family, at least, only killed what it wanted to eat). The rules, rituals, acumen, and observances of hunting are a worked-out relationship between men (+) and nature, however perverse they may seem, or in this day and age are, and despite the fact that they are perversely disregarded by too many people carrying weapons in a wild they do not know or respect.

While I went on to kill a few birds in my brief and mostly adolescent career as a hunter, I was never much good at it nor in my heart completely comfortable with killing (fishing doesn't bother me). My father today says that he will never hunt again, which I think is only a recognition that the nature he loves and our relationship to it have changed oh so drastically since he, and I, were boys.

Bambi reinscribes nature with a patriarchal language certified by scientific, natural realism: it is a human society the animals live—almost; "almost" because it is only a mythopoeic perfection of human society and its patriarchal myth. There are no "Great Stags" in human societies, there is only the mythic place for one at the head of the patriarchal entelechy; there are only would-be pretenders to Great Staghood, none of whom have achieved the singularity and authority of the Great Stag, and none who ever will. Human societies will not allow there to be a single, authoritative "Great Stag," but the possibility of "nature's story" opened up by *Bambi*'s technical realism allows that metaphysical ambition to be realized; Man is perfected in that which is not-Man, in that which Man kills. The feminine of nature, always dualistically opposed to "man," "culture," "civilization," is reoccupied by killing her: Bambi's mother is our mother, this violation of nature is only overcome by recommitment to the "natural" patriarchy, the perfection of the patriarchal urge that is natural science. Human society is flawed, there is no "natural" order to it, there is no Great Stag, which is perhaps why those men were hunting in the forest that day: to reaffirm their manhood and authority by respecting nature through killing her.

That said, however, human societies are not wanting for pretenders to the Great Stag role. Great Stags *are* possible in the societies of *men*—notably, the military. The society of deer in the meadow that first day of Bambi's emergence from the thicket is a society of men, with women and children clearly at the margins. The young bucks are engaged in Spartan military exercise, the expression of fraternal culture, when the Great Stag enters from his lofty mountain perch and freezes them at "attention." The slow, strutting inspection he delivers is not merely regal, but military. The gaze he fixes upon Bambi is not paternal-familial, but patriarchal-familial; the son who must pass muster as a new recruit and so not shame his father, the general. The Great Stag speaks neither to Bambi *nor* to his bride. The role of women in such a society is reproduction of men; the role of the patriarch is to own the means of reproduction.

One of the original advertising posters for *Bambi* bills the film as a "love story." Indeed, from the point in the film when Bambi's mother is killed, the story is largely the maturation of Bambi through his romance with "Faline," the female fawn he met on his first day in the meadow. The sexual politics of this romance are suitable material for an essay that is beyond the spatial and thematic limitations imposed here. They may be summarized as Bambi's emergent masculinity discovered in combat, heroism, and survival, all of which are inspired by, even manipulated by, his desire to win Faline for his mate (from other deer) and to protect her from the ravages of survival (the evils of hunters, the forest fire caused by invading "Man").

The structure of the film narrative was intended to mimic the seasonal cycles of nature—told through the reproductive cycle of females. The film begins in the lush procreative abundance of Spring with the birth of Bambi, moves to the Summer encounter with deer society in the meadow, and then to Winter with the death of Bambi's mother. After the death scene, when Bambi goes with his father to some mysterious masculine quarters for his remaining childhood rearing, the film returns to Spring. Bambi and his childhood cohorts are now adolescents, who learn about the perils of romance from the initiating old Owl. The Owl instructs them at length about "twitterpation," the hypnotic willess surrender to which female seduction will reduce them. The film then illustrates the sequential seduction of each teen boy by the wily females of their respective species, whose sole purpose in life seems to be the initiation of the reproductive process. Faline, luring Bambi into his first tender kiss, helplessly follows a more mature young stag off to mate, entrapping Bambi in fierce combat. Having vanquished his challenger, Bambi strikes the iconic, erect pose of his Princely father, and Faline sidles beside him in pure devoted admiration and submission.

The Spring's enactment of reproductive heroism turns almost imperceptibly to Fall, and the hunters return. Bambi must protect Faline in even more dangerous combat against a pack of hunting dogs. The hunter's campfire spreads to a disastrous forest fire, traumatizing the entire forest population, and Bambi must again rise to heroism, with some help from father, to save Faline and to secure their survival. The forest is destroyed, the greatest evil of "Man" against "nature" is displayed, and Bambi and Faline are bonded in love. The Winter that follows is not pictured as the narrative returns us to Spring and to the rebirth of the forest. The cycle of nature, and its tremendous healing power, is completed as the opening scene of the movie is replicated in detail. The small animals again flurry to announce that "It's happened!" Again the old Owl is stirred to take his place as overseer of the birth scene of the royal family. Again a mother deer is found nestled with her offspring, this time twins, a boy and a girl. Again, the old Owl hoots his approval and blessing while the matrons and broods of other species look on admiringly. This time it is Faline who has given birth to Bambi's children, and this time it is Bambi who is missing from the hallowed event. The frame of the film, just as in the original enactment of Bambi's birth, moves slowly upward to the hillside where the patriarch oversees his property and his naturally guaranteed replication. This time, it is Bambi *and* the old stag who survey the domain below in their erect pose. The old stag begins to fade, turns and steps slowly into invisibility. Bambi takes one step forward and strikes the royal pose of the old patriarch, his form swelling to perfectly fill the outline left by the disappearing Prince. The cycle of nature is completed perfectly, *by the perfect replication of the social order that governs it*. There the film ends.

I have discussed the matter with my family, and we can't remember whether Mother took us to see *Bambi* when we were children or not. My older brother and I both remember the forest fire scene most vividly, but that may be a result of its reproduction on Smokey the Bear commercials admonishing us against starting forest fires. Of course we are familiar with Thumper and Flower and the other creatures, but these may seem familiar because these characters appeared on Disney's television show, watched religiously on Sundays throughout our youth.

The first viewing of *Bambi* that I can recall occurred a few years ago. My son was not yet born, and my daughter was not yet three years old. Our family had not yet begun to rent videos for the child(ren), nor to build our personal collection of Disney tapes which is now complete and frequently reviewed. *Bambi* was the first tape I rented to watch with Meredith, who I recall thinking might be old enough to sustain interest in a longer narrative and who might be charmed by the cute, furry little characters that I viewed as the substance of the film's entertainment. I had forgotten completely about the traumatic scene where Bambi's mother is shot, and would not have rented it had I remembered.

As it turns out, Meredith was not yet old enough, or trained enough, to sustain interest in such a long show. She was distracted during the scene where Bambi calls mournfully for his mother, and I was spared explaining about hunters or death or any of those topics that seem to be coming up frequently now that she is older. But Meredith's reaction to the opening scene of the film is what inspired this essay. When the film first focused on the birth scene where newborn Bambi lay nestled against his mother, Meredith cooed, "Oh, *she's* little," enacting the very common pleasure small children have in seeing babies of any species in books or on television.

In that moment, I was struck that Meredith had no cultural training that would prevent her from expecting that the newborn fawn would be, like her, a female child. I wondered whether to correct her, and explain that Bambi was a boy, and I became interested in when she would learn and whether she would react to the realization of Bambi's gender. As a father, I became interested in the film as a story of a male, not in the least expecting that the film we were watching was nothing more than the story of a male and a spectacle of gender politics where the male achieves dominion over women and all of nature. As a father, I began to experience a heightened concern for the truth of feminist claims about the exclusion of female heroism and agency in the literature young women experience.

Like Bambi, I am a father now. I have both a female and a male child. I probably will never take either of them hunting. Grandfather's farm was sold at an estate auction long ago. We live in lush country surrounds, and I can take them fishing in the small pond behind our house. There is something I want to teach them about nature, something that won't be included in the ecology lessons they get at their school, something different from what they will learn from the saturation of Disney-inspired nature narratives that fill the curricula of our Public Broadcasting Stations. There is a story about nature that my father not so much told me as he taught me to hear: it was not a story of contest, sexuality, and war. It is not a story told with language.

References

Feild, R. D. 1942. *The Art of Walt Disney*. New York: Macmillan.

Grant, John. 1993. *Encyclopedia of Walt Disney's Animated Characters*. 2nd ed. New York: Hyperion.

Haraway, Donna. 1991. *Simians, Cyborgs, and Women*. New York: Routledge.

Nine

Beyond Captain Nemo
Disney's Science Fiction

Brian Attebery

A science fiction story by Howard Waldrop describes the accidental activation of three robots in a post-holocaust landscape. The three were intended as attractions in a late twentieth-century amusement park. After a stroke of lightning wakes them in the abandoned factory, they take their bearings:

> "Gawrsh," said one of them. "It shore is dark in here!"
> "Well, huh-huh, we can always use the infrared they gave us."
> "Wak Wak Wak!" said the third. "What's the big idea?" (Waldrop 1986, 168)

Thus Goofy, Mickey, and Donald enter the world of science fiction as mechanical simulacra of their cartoon selves. In the radically transformed environment of the story, the animated figures turn into absurdist heroes, playing out their preprogrammed roles, like characters in a Beckett play, in a wasteland.

Waldrop's story reveals how bizarre those familiar images really are. They are—have always been—unnatural, isolated, sexually ambiguous, alien beings. What is surprising is that we could have forgotten the fact, could ever have accepted them as ordinary suburban males. A giant mouse living in a ranch house? With a dog for a pet? Only the extreme ordinariness of the surroundings, the safe, bland environment that was a Disney specialty both on film and in his theme parks, allows us to suppress our awareness of the anarchic energy hidden in the notion of the guy down the street who happens to be a talking mouse or duck. Waldrop's science fiction frame simply unleashes the covert disruptions.

Walt Disney is not usually thought of in connection with science fiction, with either the scientific and sociological extrapolation characteristic of written science fiction or the special-effects monstrosities of the cinematic form. Yet Waldrop's story calls attention to the fact that the cartoon characters have always had an affiliation with science fiction: they are creatures of technology, assembled from machine-made recordings of drawings and voices and later disseminated by other machines. To turn them into robots is merely to further the process, using more machines to mimic weight and depth and volition just as film mimics surface and motion and sound.

Science fiction is, among other things, fiction about technology, about human attempts to remake the universe and ourselves through our machines.[1] One form of technology that has powerfully affected our sense of selfhood is the technology of film, which, as psychoanalytic critics such as Christian Metz have pointed out, intervenes in some of the most fundamental aspects of human subjectivity, such as the transformation of biological drives into culturally channeled desires (1982, 61–64). The technology that constructs the image of Mickey Mouse also constructs larger-than-life images of masculinity and femininity which then become part of our apparatus for interpreting the world and ourselves. According to Teresa de Lauretis, "the construction of gender goes on today through the various technologies of gender (e.g., cinema) . . . with power to control the field of social meaning and thus produce, promote, and 'implant' representations of gender" (1987, 18). Our notions of who we are, whom and how we desire, how we watch others and are watched, whether we speak or remain silent: all of this is largely determined by the gender roles we have been taught to inhabit, and one of the primary teachers is the cinema.

In most Hollywood movies, both animated and live-action, the technological nature of the medium is concealed by such conventions as limiting the visible space to one side of a 180 degree line, opening each scene with an establishing shot, and using shots of a leading character alternately with shots of what he or she is presumed to be looking at (shot/reverse shot): collectively these techniques are called continuity editing (Bordwell and Thompson 1986, 210–13). The same editing conventions are, not coincidentally, part of the mechanism by which movies seduce the audience into identifying with their characters, thereby internalizing the norms, the ways of thinking and desiring, and the gendered identities presented on screen (Silverman 1983, 201–205). But when the conventions of realism are replaced—or rather overwritten—by those of science fiction, the technological nature of the film medium, in the form of "special effects," is highlighted. The fantastic machines we see on the screen can stand, in part, for the machines that made the images. Because science fiction brings technology into the foreground and at the same time defamiliarizes it, the effect of technology on the individual psyche becomes a possible topic for consideration.

In addition, as the example of the Waldrop story demonstrates, science fiction or SF,[2] with its radical transformations of society and the individual, can denaturalize the link between role and subject. Even though the only apparent difference between Mickey and Minnie Mouse is the absence or presence of oversized high heels and false eyelashes, we usually allow them to stand in for human male and female and expect them to behave accordingly. When Waldrop presents Mickey as an explicitly artificial construct, however, our expectations about gender-marked behavior drop away. With the technological basis of selfhood rendered explicit, the constructedness of gender likewise becomes visible and revisable, at least in Waldrop's rendering of Disney images. Do similar things happen when the Disney studio itself ventures into science fiction?

As pointed out above, Disney is not usually thought of as a SF-oriented studio. Yet beginning with *20,000 Leagues Under the Sea* in 1954, Disney and its subsidiary Touchstone have produced upwards of twenty-four films that can be classed as science fiction, even using a fairly conservative definition of that term: stories presenting a world that departs from our present consensus reality in ways that reflect science's techniques for observing, categorizing, and manipulating the physical universe.

Disney films are, for the most part, not great SF, neither original in their use of scientific ideas nor rigorously worked out with regard to social implications. Of the twenty-four, only one, *Tron* (1982), merits mention in *Screening Space*, Vivian Sobchack's (1987) history of recent science fiction film. Peter Nichols's comprehensive survey of *The World of Fantastic Films* discusses several Disney fantasies in detail (notably *Popeye* [1980], *Dragonslayer* [1981], and *Something Wicked This Way Comes* [1982]), but mentions only three SF films from the studio, and one of those, *The Black Hole* (1979), is cited primarily as a major disappointment (1984, 130). What is most interesting about Disney SF is not that it advances the genre in any significant way (although a case can be made for visual elements in *Tron*), but that there is so much of it and that it is so much alike.

The interest of the Disney corporation in science fiction could almost have been predicted from the gadget-filled early cartoons and from such brushes with SF iconography as the dinosaur segment of *Fantasia* (1940), the airborne warfare of *Victory Through Air Power* (1943), and the shrinking machine of *Babes in Toyland* (1961). The early nature films, with their fictionalized science and their emphasis on strange environments, also bore a family resemblance to SF, and in fact the studio's first overt venture into SF, *20,000 Leagues*, was originally planned as an underwater nature documentary (Finch 1973, 363). Disney theme parks have always included science fictional elements, not only in the Tomorrowland sectors but also in their transportation systems and other examples of environmental engineering. Indeed, the popular imagination so strongly associates Disney with futuristic tech-

Beyond Captain Nemo

nology that it has produced an urban legend about the cryogenic preservation of Walt's dying body (Waldrep 1993, 142).

Disney's SF is able to draw on the formidable technical resources developed for these other Disney products. It is no wonder then that the primary emphasis in most of the SF films is on plots that allow the filmmakers to show off their special-effects skills. The typical Disney SF film is a modest comedy or comic adventure involving improbable gadgets (*The Absent-Minded Professor* [1961], *The Rocketeer* [1991]), visiting aliens (*Escape to Witch Mountain* [1975], *Spaced Invaders* [1990]), or both. *Tron*'s major character is a computer program created by the hero, demonstrating that the gadget can also be the alien.

Aliens and miraculous machines are common SF elements; it is not immediately noticeable how many equally common themes are completely missing from the Disney *oeuvre*. There are no alien worlds, no mutations, no trips to the future, no dramatically estranged societies, either utopian or dystopian. None of the Disney films display the kind of vision that can translate such themes into indelible images, like those in Fritz Lang's *Metropolis* (1926), Stanley Kubrick's *A Clockwork Orange* (1971), Andrei Tarkovsky's *Solaris* (1972), Ridley Scott's *Blade Runner* (1982), and Terry Gilliam's *Brazil* (1985). Even if the studio were prepared to invoke the radical social visions of these SF classics, it has been unwilling to invest the money needed to bring them to the screen.

Disney live-action pictures have generally been low-budget efforts, especially after the remarkable success of *The Shaggy Dog* (1959), shot in black and white for just over a million dollars and earning nine million in its first release (Schickel 1968, 299). Low-budget films do not have stars, big-name directors, or, most significantly for SF, elaborate and inventive sets. Within SF film, a low budget has always meant shooting on the back lot or on a nearby location: hence the giant ants marching across the California desert. The Disney option has generally been the back lot or a small town location, which means that alienness is brought onto the domestic scene. The suburb or farmhouse becomes the site for some sort of disruption, either by technology or by alien invasion. Thus the modest production values of most Disney SF dictate the use of the elements mentioned above, though not necessarily the plot formulas built upon them. These formulas might be labeled the Exploding Gadget and the Stranded Extraterrestrial.

In Exploding Gadget movies, the gadget does not literally explode; rather it sends out emotional and social shock waves until the hero can disarm it at the end. The hero is a boyish inventor (whether as young as Tommy Kirk in *The Misadventures of Merlin Jones* [1964], or as old as Fred MacMurray in

Son of Flubber [1963], he is still boyish) who creates or acquires the Gadget, which flies, reads minds, transforms things, or causes people to behave in inappropriate ways. When the Gadget is made public, it leads to the temporary estrangement of the hero's girlfriend or wife and subjects him to pursuit by various agents of the government, the military, or the business world. In the end, the Gadget's powers are tamed, the roused military-industrial establishment is appeased or evaded, and the hero's personal life settles down. The comic plot is resolved without requiring any examination of underlying tensions, such as those between the hero's scientific interests and the community's mistrust of intellectuals. As is common in Hollywood plots, a romantic resolution substitutes for the social change that the initial situation seemed to demand.

It is the second formula, the Stranded Extraterrestrial, that leads to a more unsettling depiction of American middle-class life. Just as the SF framework of Howard Waldrop's story defamiliarizes cartoon characters we are accustomed to seeing as stylized versions of the small town or suburban man, the presence of a literal alien in the midst of the cozy community forces an acknowledgment of alienation already at work there. In the Stranded ET formula, the same boyish inventor who operates the gadget in the Gadget formula is brought face-to-face with an alien Other, whom he must assist in repairing a space ship or finding a way home. The execution of the plot closely resembles that of the Gadget plot: the extraterrestrial's actions lead to various misunderstandings with the neighbors, family members, girlfriends, and the military, and attract the attention of unscrupulous businessmen and/or master criminals who wish to exploit the alien's powers. But because the disruptive agent is an individual rather than a mere gadget, the hero's social and psychological tensions can be acknowledged by being displaced onto the Extraterrestrial, rather than being buried in a comic resolution. In addition, the most significant interaction within the plot is between the hero and the alien, so it is not so easy for erotic satisfaction to substitute for social change. In these movies, the hero ends up romantically linked either with the alien or with no one at all.

Versions of the Stranded Extraterrestrial plot can be found not only in Disney SF films but in a number of non-Disney films that are deliberate or unconscious homages to Disney, most notably Steven Spielberg's *E.T. The Extra-terrestrial* (1982). Spielberg has repeatedly acknowledged his debt to Disney, and underscores the fact in *E.T.* by quoting cinematically from *Peter Pan* (Nichols 1984, 111). Among Disney's own ET's are *Escape to Witch Mountain* (1975); *Return from Witch Mountain* (1978); *The Watcher in the Woods* (1981); *Splash* (1984), a blend of SF and fantasy in which the alien comes from the ocean rather than outer space; *Spaced Invaders* (1990); and the three films that I am going to examine in detail: *Moon Pilot* (1962), *The Cat from Outer Space* (1978), and *Flight of the Navigator* (1986).

The last three are virtually the same movie three times over, and both the repetitions and the variations offer insight into some of the ways social identity is formed within American culture, particularly masculine identity, and the changes that occurred within gender coding between the 1960s and the 1980s. Masculinity is foregrounded in these films as a result of making the heroes male. The heroes are male because that has been the unconsidered choice, the norm, for American selfhood. Woman is the exception; man is the default setting.

That is the statement made by the Disney filmmakers in trying to make no statement. The dynamics of the Stranded ET film require that the alienness of the extraterrestrial be counterbalanced by the most ordinary of earthlings, and so such categories as women, gays, ethnically identifiable Americans, non-Americans, the rich, and the poor are not so much eliminated as never considered in the first place. The surprising fact is that even within the remaining category—middle-class white males—the films discover a powerful response of identification with the alien. This response grows out of a sense that the masculine hero, too, is out of place, eccentric, in disguise. His identity begins to break apart when he is confronted by the alien, who embodies all the aspects of the self that the masculine role excludes.

The first of these films, *Moon Pilot*, is the most surprising as a product both of the Disney studio and of its period. Though the astronaut theme was a natural enough choice, given the popularity of the Mercury space program and the need for a movie tie-in for Disneyland's rocket ship, the movie's writers chose not to emphasize the hyper-male image of the test-pilot/astronaut (Tom Wolfe's "right stuff") but rather the reverse.

Tom Tryon stars in the movie as reluctant astronaut Richmond Talbot. Talbot's part in the space program seems to be taking care of the chimpanzee Charlie. He is not particularly well suited to the role of moon pilot, since he dislikes flying, nearly falls out of the hatch of a rescue plane, and gets airsick even on a commercial flight. There is no indication that he knows how to pilot a plane; we never even see him driving a car. Though his scientific knowledge gives him a place on the team, his status is low until he unintentionally volunteers (when jabbed with a fork by Charlie) to be the first human to be launched into lunar orbit.

The atmosphere at NASA/Air Force is heavily macho. Uniformed men surround themselves with phallic rocket models and bark orders to one another. The only woman on the scene is relegated to the role of nutritionist, or technologized mother. Even she is asked to leave the room when the men discuss sexuality—a discussion which is so discreet that Talbot misses the point, that he is not to have sexual relations during the brief leave he has been granted before his mission. When he does catch on, he reaffirms his secondary status by admitting that, "I don't have a real steady girlfriend anyway." This opens the way for the General to play Dad, which he does throughout the rest of the movie.

Talbot uses his leave to go home to visit Mom. On the way there his dissatisfaction with his social role is externalized in the form of the alien woman Lyrae (Dany Saval). She approaches him on the airplane and offers him pills to cure his airsickness (one of the signs of his socially imposed impotency). Her alienness is expressed through a strong accent, unconventional clothing and hairstyle, and an open and even sexually aggressive demeanor.

When Talbot's brother Walt arrives to pick him up at the airport, Talbot instructs him to drive away quickly from the pursuing Lyrae. In the exchange that follows, Walt (Tommy Kirk) establishes himself as the perfectly conventional male role model: he boasts about his job as "new assistant second foreman of Daisy Fresh Frozen Foods," where he expects to be in charge in thirty years or so. He offers to induct his brother into the masculine mysteries, suggesting that he can find him both a job and a date. Talbot cannot accept either offer: we don't know whether he is tempted.

When Talbot arrives at his mother's suburban house, she scolds him since this is her bridge night and he hasn't called ahead to warn her. Like the General, she has effectively reduced Talbot to age twelve or so, and he responds by changing out of his uniform into a tight gray suit and red bow tie—an outfit whose symbolic significance was later exploited by Paul Rubens in creating the perpetually prepubescent Pee-Wee Herman.

After Lyrae reappears and Talbot flees to the city, he becomes the object of surveillance from a number of sides. The Air Force is watching him, the FBI is called in, and Lyrae herself admits that her people "have been watching you for centuries." These various gazes serve both to control Talbot and turn him into a sexual object as, for instance, when Lyrae shows up in his hotel room while he is preparing to take a shower. The long and appreciative look she gives his bare chest makes him pull his robe together uncomfortably.

Voyeurism is a staple of the cinema, but it is nearly always posed in terms of male watcher and female spectacle, with the audience invited to position itself with the watcher (Mulvey 1975, 33). Reversing the relationship feminizes Talbot, unleashing his and the audience's anxiety but ultimately establishing the grounds for his self-redefinition. For Lyrae offers to let Talbot be the looker as well as the object of the gaze. She "materializes" for him a vision of the future: a child that will be born to the two of them. The sexual associations of vision are made explicit when Talbot wonders how she can convince the General and others: she can't go around materializing for them because "it wouldn't be decent."

When Talbot reenters the masculine world of the General, he is no longer in a subservient and juvenilized position. (He has even exchanged his bow tie for a long one.) At a police line-up that is intended to identify Lyrae from among "every female beatnik in the town," the General is reduced to watching Talbot watching the women. It is no surprise thereafter that Talbot is able to dictate the terms of his return to the space program.

The movie's ending shows him and a stowaway Lyrae in his space capsule. As they prepare to divert the craft to Lyrae's home world, they ignore the General's repeated demands for an explanation, and Talbot parodies his own earlier juvenile role by saying, "I just wanted you to know that I'll be a little late getting back." As the final credits roll, Lyrae teaches Talbot a song about the seven moons of Beta Lyrae, "all made for love."

By singing the song, Talbot identifies himself as no longer part of the male world of uniforms and hierarchies. Whereas the typical movie astronaut, as Vivian Sobchack has pointed out, is both colorless and asexual (1985, 46), Talbot has been inducted by Lyrae into adult sexuality, autonomy, and even paternity. He has achieved a form of masculinity without having to apprentice himself to the General or follow his brother up the corporate ladder. Unlike the other men in the story, he does not define himself through external symbols, institutionalized behaviors, and denial of the feminine— indeed, for him masculinity is achieved through accommodating himself to the apparently secure feminine identity represented by Lyrae.

Moon Pilot sets up not only the basic plot scenario for the Stranded ET movie but also lays out some of the key symbols through which the masculine image is questioned in those films. These include the hero's body, sexuality, economic status, position within corporate or military hierarchies, interactions with literal and symbolic parents, and active or passive role in surveillance. Talbot's relation to all of these elements is initially unsatisfactory and restrictive; when he accepts the unconventional lifestyle and outsider role represented by Lyrae, all of the dissatisfactions are resolved.

By 1978, when *The Cat from Outer Space* appeared, the counter-culture no longer seemed a safe way out of the masculine dilemma. The plot of this film differs from *Moon Pilot* in three main respects: the stranded ET is not an attractive woman but an animal, the hero is not part of the military establishment but is instead a scientist tenuously connected with a private space research facility, and the resolution leaves both hero and alien earthbound.

Ken Berry, playing the hero Frank Wilson, begins in approximately the same cultural position that *Moon Pilot*'s Richmond Talbot ended in. He is outside both the military and the business establishments: though he is working for a research corporation, he is neither dependent on nor loyal to its hierarchy, since he is merely "on loan" from Cal Tech. He speaks and behaves with whimsical eccentricity. His lab and his apartment show him to be neither pragmatic nor conventionally masculine. In the lab is a Rube Goldberg-style apparatus that harnesses mouse-power to make coffee. He also keeps a cello and a flute, which he presumably plays during work time.

The sexual partnership Talbot could find only with an alien is already offered to Wilson in the person of Dr. Elizabeth Bartlett (Sandy Duncan), who works in his division, lives in his apartment house, car pools with him, reads his scientific papers, and is obviously interested in him. He has interesting work, a comfortable income, and the benign neglect, if not the respect, of the masculine establishment of the Energy Research Laboratory. He is apparently at ease.

Only when the extraterrestrial comes on the scene do Frank's discontents manifest themselves. Zunar J5, or Jake, is the cat-shaped alien of the title. Jake has plenty of reason for discontent. His broken ship has left him stranded on earth. His "mother ship" (speaking in a stern maternal voice) threatens to abandon him. The military "fathers" try to gain control over his ship—a shot of four nearly identical military men staring at his ship through four sets of binoculars could stand as a textbook example of the coercive phallic gaze hypothesized by Lacanian psychoanalysis. Jake cannot function in earth society because of his feline appearance, and he cannot make the needed repairs himself because, despite his superior intelligence and nearly magical powers, he has no hands to manipulate machinery. His best prospect is to be left alone as something decorative and useless, a pet.

(Useless) intellectuals and (powerless) outsiders, Frank and Jake are thus natural allies. When Jake uses his mental powers to play the musical instruments in Frank's lab, he proves not only his alienness but also his aesthetic sympathies. In contrast, Frank's only human friend Link (McLean Stevenson) is completely out of touch with aesthetic interests. When he loses a sports bet, he says disgustedly, "I should have bet on the Metropolitan Opera."

The movie's plot indicates two different possible solutions to Jake's/ Frank's problems. One route is for Frank to imitate Link and assimilate himself to the world of manly interests and activities: watching football, gambling, playing pool, driving various vehicles, dressing up in uniform, rescuing a woman in distress (Liz Bartlett having in the meantime given up all pretense at scientific competence and gender equality). The other, less obvious route is the growing intimacy between Frank and Jake. Whereas the romantic scenes between Frank and Liz are both awkward and perfunctory, the scenes between Frank and Jake are relaxed and pleasurable. They share interests in such matters as the nature of the "primal mainstream," and when Jake teaches Frank to tune into that mainstream with his mind, the result is that Frank learns to fly, an experience that so exhilarates him that he nearly forgets to complete the repair of the space ship.

The relationship between man and cat is platonic, but it does have sexual overtones. Even male cats are usually coded feminine in American society, and Jake's appearance is further feminized by the diamond necklace he wears. Frank spends a lot of time holding and petting Jake (probably a necessity in filming scenes with a cat). When Liz tries to take over Jake's care, Frank jealously shouts, "Liz, butt out!" In the end, Jake gives up his opportunity to return to the Mother and stays with Frank: their union is formalized with a civil ceremony, not a wedding but a citizenship hearing for the alien cat. No such union with Liz is indicated.

Whereas in *Moon Pilot*, the reconfigured masculine identity is achieved by the hero's sexual involvement with an alien woman, in *The Cat from Outer Space* sexuality is fetishized, translated into activities like flying and mental telepathy and redirected to such objects as a cat and a necklace that confer mental powers. In the third film of the sequence, *Flight of the Navigator*, the fetishizing goes further, from animal to machine.

The hero of *Flight of the Navigator* is literally what the heroes of the other two films are figuratively: a preadolescent boy. He is David Freeman (Joey Cramer), who, soon after the movie opens, mysteriously vanishes for eight years and reappears unchanged. From this point on, he represents both the twelve-year-old boy he looks like and the twenty-year-old man he would have been: the two different identities show up in his reactions as well as his role in the plot.

When David returns in 1986 he finds it difficult to be with his parents. They look old and haggard and their responses seem awkward and exaggerated. When they reach for him, he draws back. When scientists from NASA come looking for David, who has revealed unconscious knowledge of an alien spaceship, the Freemans let him be taken away for "treatment."

It is no wonder that David hears a voice in his sleep: "He's hurt. He's calling me." The voice belongs to the spaceship, but the hurt might well be David's. To the NASA investigator Faraday (Howard Hesseman), David and the ship are equally alien, equally suspect. David is imprisoned in a room with a one-way mirror; the ship is imprisoned in a hangar (it looks exactly like the one in *The Cat from Outer Space*) and watched over monitors.

Even the sympathetic young intern played by Sarah Jessica Parker makes David into the object of surveillance. Like Lyrae in *Moon Pilot*, she looks him over admiringly: "You know, you're cute. Did a girl ever tell you that before?" But unlike Talbot, David is not ready to accept a sexually challenging gaze, any more than he wants to accept the controlling eye of Faraday's scientific monitors.

When David escapes and makes contact with the ship, he finds a more manageable outlet for his desires. As in *The Cat from Outer Space*, the alien is both a double for the hero and a displaced sexual object. It doubles for him in being lost, naive, and spied upon. It expresses his unformed desires by being a welcoming space (the interior is a jeweled womb), and providing him the two forms of erotic experience he is ready to accept: dreamlike flight and voyeuristic vision. Once David is inside the ship, the wall in front of him becomes transparent, from the inside only. Instead of being watched, he is now the unseen watcher. Together David and the ship, which he names Max, escape from the NASA compound, and a considerable part of the movie concerns the wild ride Max takes David on. In case the audience has missed the sexual subtext, the ship prepares for its flight by undergoing a highly suggestive transformation from its original seashell shape to a longer, sleeker, more potent design.

David does not merely escape in the ship, but ultimately becomes a working component of it—the Navigator—after allowing its mind to fuse with his own. SF often depicts telepathic communication in sexualized terms, with echoes of seduction or rape. In this case the ship is the seducer, David the reluctant receiver of its attentions. But though it is David whose mental boundaries are breached, both partners are "fertilized" by the procedure. From Max, David gains access to the information planted in his unconscious mind and can now pilot the ship. Max acquires from David a new individuality and volition. One sign of the latter change is that Max's voice, which had been that of an adult male, becomes high and squeaky—at this point it becomes obvious that an uncredited Paul Rubens is providing the voice. As in Rubens's series, *Pee-wee's Playhouse*, that voice signals a transgression of adult sexual difference and its accompanying anxieties (Penley 1989, 160).

The ship now combines childlike fluidity with greater-than-adult powers, leaving it free to complete its mission. David, too, finds that the answer to his dilemma is to become a hybrid of child and machine, a sort of junior cyborg. The powerful technology imprinted on his brain gives him control over the phallic power of the ship, without the emotional strains that accompany adult sexuality. He uses his power to go back in time to 1978, retreating to a safer era. He elects not to grow up, at least not yet, but instead to become a preternaturally knowing innocent like Max—or Pee-wee or Mickey Mouse.

Together, these films represent three attempts at finding a satisfactory masculine identity: first, through entering into sexual partnership with the alien; second, through deflection of sexuality into symbolic forms while still paying lip-service to the heterosexual ideal; and third, through essentially becoming the alien artifact, which involves rejecting adult sexuality. As the Disney studio moved from *Moon Pilot* to *Flight of the Navigator*, its science fiction was assimilated to the model of displaced sexuality that has always marked its other products. The hero has finally become yet another Disney cartoon.

When Disney filmed Jules Verne's *20,000 Leagues Under the Sea*, a second hero, Ned Land, was provided as a foil to Captain Nemo, who seemed too intellectual and too strange for audience identification (Finch 1973, 370–71). Since that time, though, it is the virile and self-assured Ned Land who has become difficult to identify with, while Nemo's counterparts have taken over as audience favorites even while growing more and more alien. Similar changes have occurred in non-Disney SF films: according to Vivian Sobchack, during the last decade,

> Alien Others have become less other—be they extraterrestrial teddy
> bears, starmen, brothers from another planet, robots, androids, or repli-
> cants. They have become our familiars, our simulacra, embodied as liter-
> ally alienated images of our alienated selves. (1987, 293)

Thus the middle-class ordinariness of the Disney hero converges curiously with the marginalized figures of such art films as *Brother from Another Planet* (1984) and *Liquid Sky* (1983). What Disney seems to be saying is that the norm—the masculine self—has disappeared, and the only way to reconstruct it is to become the technological Other, to imitate the alien and merge with the machine.

Notes

1. Even before Hugo Gernsback coined the term *science fiction* in 1929, people were trying to define the genre. Gary K. Wolfe, in his *Critical Terms for Science Fiction and Fantasy*, lists thirty-three such definitions ranging from Gernsback's "a charming romance intermingled with scientific fact and prophetic vision" to Brian Aldiss's "the search for a

definition of man and his status in the universe which will stand in our advanced but confused state of knowledge (science)" (1986, 108–11). The definitions in this essay are my own.

2. SF has become the standard abbreviation for science fiction within academic discussions of the genre, partly because it can also be made to stand for such related terms as *speculative fiction* and *science fantasy. Sci-fi*, common in the popular media, is often considered to have a pejorative connotation.

References

Bordwell, David, and Kristin Thompson. 1986. *Film Art: An Introduction.* 2nd ed. New York: Knopf.

de Lauretis, Teresa. 1987. *Technologies of Gender: Essays on Theory, Film, and Fiction.* Bloomington: Indiana University Press.

Finch, Christopher. 1973. *The Art of Walt Disney: From Mickey Mouse to the Magic Kingdom.* New York: Abrams.

Metz, Christian. 1982. *The Imaginary Signifier: Psychoanalysis and the Cinema.* Trans. Celia Britton, Annwyl Williams, Ben Brewster, and Alfred Guzzetti. Bloomington: Indiana University Press.

Mulvey, Laura. [1975] 1990. "Visual Pleasure and Narrative Cinema." In *Issues in Feminist Film Criticism,* ed. Patricia Erens. Bloomington: Indiana University Press.

Nichols, Peter. 1984. *The World of Fantastic Films: An Illustrated Survey.* New York: Dodd.

Penley, Constance. 1989. *The Future of an Illusion: Film, Feminism, and Psychoanalysis.* Minneapolis: University of Minnesota Press.

Schickel, Richard. 1968. *The Disney Version: The Life, Times, Art, and Commerce of Walt Disney.* New York: Simon.

Silverman, Kaja. 1983. *The Subject of Semiotics.* New York: Oxford University Press.

Sobchack, Vivian. 1985. "The Virginity of Astronauts: Sex and the Science Fiction Film." In *Shadows of the Magic Lamp: Fantasy and Science Fiction in Film,* ed. George Slusser and Eric R. Rabkin. Carbondale: Southern Illinois University Press.

———. 1987. *Screening Space: The American Science Fiction Film.* New York: Ungar.

Waldrep, Shelton. 1993. "The Contemporary Future of Tomorrow." *South Atlantic Quarterly* 92(1): 139–55.

Waldrop, Howard. 1986. "Heirs of the Perisphere." *Howard Who?* Garden City, NY: Doubleday.

Wolfe, Gary K. 1986. *Critical Terms for Science Fiction and Fantasy: A Glossary and Guide to Scholarship.* Westport, CT: Greenwood.

Ten

The Curse of Masculinity
Disney's *Beauty and the Beast*

Susan Jeffords

The only real addition Ronald Reagan made to Richard Nixon's agenda for the 1980s was a focus on the family and the moral values that, for those on the far right, defined it. But while Reagan was able to keep the disparate and potentially contradictory interests in a hard-boiled militarism and a warm-hearted familialism in check, largely through the force of his personal image, George Bush could not manage the same feat. The Republican ticket for 1988 revealed the divisions between these elements of the right, as Bush campaigned on his experience as vice president, as former CIA chief, as former U.S. ambassador, and as personal friend of foreign leaders, while Dan Quayle campaigned on his defense of family values and moral principles. This evidence of a splintering of the conservative movement was supported by other divisions, particularly the "gender gap," as Republican women began to become more vocal about their oppositional stances on abortion and women's rights in the workforce. But with the economy declining, the national debt skyrocketing, and the militaristic reason for many such expenses disappearing, the Reagan emphasis on family seemed to provide the only secure legacy of the Reagan ideology. At the same time, it provided a popular and facile site for retaining a sense of American superiority in the face of Japanese and European economic competition.

In such a context, it would seem quite logical that the hard-edged masculinity that had been so closely affiliated with the foreign policy angles of the Reagan era would now shift toward domestic policies, emphasizing the family and personal values over market achievements. With a good deal of bravado, these new male heroes would thumb their noses at an economic superiority that they did not have and return to the families they had neglected before. Leonard Reitman's 1990 film, *Kindergarten Cop*, for example, starring one of the 1980s' most muscular and hardened heroes, Arnold Schwarzenegger, shows how the transition to this new masculine heroism was to be sketched out.

At the beginning of the film, John Kimball *is* the '80s man, the lethal weapon *par excellence*. He is a tough, unshaved, brutal, determined police officer who holds the single-minded goal of imprisoning Cullen Crisp, an expert drug dealer and murderer who is backed up by his evil, overprotective single mother. When legal police procedures prevent his partner from detaining the only witness to Crisp's crime, Kimball chases after her on his own, breaking down doors, blowing away furniture with a special-make shotgun, and brutalizing anyone who comes between him and his witness. For Kimball, as for all '80s action-adventure heroes, the legal system is only an impediment to getting things done and putting criminals away. In the mold of Martin Riggs or Dirty Harry, Kimball is a loner, a single-minded law officer who writes the rules as he goes along, a tough guy who needs no family or partners, and a brutal, violent, and unfeeling man. He is, in other words, the typical '80s action hero.

But by the end of the film, Kimball has given up being a police officer in favor of teaching kindergarten. He has broken through his emotional barriers to tell Joyce, another teacher, that he doesn't want to lose her or her son, Dominic. He feels guilty when he punches an abusive father and promises from now on to let the law punish such men. His life is most threatened, not by another super-macho, special combat male enemy (like Mr. Joshua in *Lethal Weapon*), but by a determined mother who is out to revenge the death of her son. And his life is saved, not by a fancy weapon or an effective body blow, but by his partner, a short woman with a baseball bat. What happened to turn that relentless, law-making, brutalizing cop into a nurturing, playful, and loving kindergarten teacher?

It takes only one word: Family. John Kimball, the cop, had a wife and child, but his wife left him many years ago and has since remarried a "nice man" who now raises Kimball's son. One of the reasons Kimball devotes his life to police work is simply that he has no other life to go to. He has, audiences are invited to psychologize, used the violence and confrontation of his job to block out the pain he feels about the loss of his family. It is only when he is reintroduced to children (who are coincidentally about the age of his son when they were separated), that he begins to remember this pain and realize how the loss has affected his life. When his police assignment invites him not only to have contact with another mother and son but to guard and protect them from the sadistic drug-dealing Crisp, Kimball's lost-family emotions are given full play, and he learns that he does not want to lose yet another opportunity to have a family. Consequently, when all the bad guys are caught and Kimball's battle wounds have begun to heal, he returns, not to the police station to tag yet another criminal, but to his newly found family and the life of a full-time father, both as parent and as kindergarten

The Curse of Masculinity

teacher. The message? The emotionally whole and physically healed man of the '80s wants nothing more than to be a father, not a warrior/cop, after all.

Kindergarten Cop anticipates the endings of many 1991 films that are resolved through a man's return to his family. When the character played by Billy Crystal in *City Slickers* finds himself on a cattle ranch and discovers the meaning of life, the "one thing" he learns is that he must return to his family, accompanied by his own "child," a calf that he birthed on the trail and subsequently saved from the slaughterhouse. Michael Keaton's character in *One Good Cop* is excused for the crime of theft that he committed and welcomed back onto the police force because he took the money in order to provide a house for his family. Steve Brooks (Steve Perry/Ellen Barkin) gains a pardon for his treatment of women and entrance into heaven when s/he gives birth to a daughter in *Switch*. And even though the Terminator "dies" in *Terminator 2*, it does so to insure the survival of its new family, Sarah and John Connor. In these films, families provide both the motivation for and the resolution of changing masculine heroisms.

In addition to laying the outline for the male transformation of the '90s, *Kindergarten Cop* identifies how the issues of manhood are to be addressed and defined in the next decade. One of the clearest messages to come out of *Kindergarten Cop* is that the tough, hard-driving, violent, and individualistic man of the '80s is not like that by choice. Kimball was, like the police officer of *One Good Cop*, the radio announcer of *The Fisher King*, the lawyer of *Regarding Henry*, or even the machine-programmed Terminator, trying to do his job, and doing it the way the job had been defined by a social-climbing, crime-conscious, techno-consumer society. The problem all these men confront in their narratives is that they did their jobs too well, at the expense of their relationships with their families. Spending so much time tracking criminals and making money left little time for having, let alone raising, children or meeting, let alone relating to, women. And, as *Kindergarten Cop* makes so clear, while these men were doing their jobs, they were unhappy, lonely, and often in pain.

Retroactively, the men of the '80s were being given feelings, feelings that were, presumably, hidden behind their confrontational violence. While '80s action-adventure films gloried in spectacular scenes of destruction, '90s films are telling audiences that these men were actually being self-destructive. At the cost of their personal and family lives, '80s heroes were rescuing armies, corporations, and ancient artifacts. Now, they're out to save themselves.

But didn't they bring all this loneliness and suffering on themselves? Were *they* not the ones who picked up the guns and went for the high-powered

Susan Jeffords

jobs? Were *they* not the ones who spent time at the office (or firing range) instead of at home? According to these films, not exactly. Nineties films had already carved out a space for their heroes that allowed them always to be reacting to some outside force rather than acting from their own internal needs for violence or action (Reagan was always "defending" the U.S. against Soviet aggression). In each case, it was their jobs, their nations, or their friends who made it necessary to enter into these violent confrontations. It was not, these films conclude, the wishes of the men themselves.

But many '90s films go even farther than this, suggesting that it wasn't just the jobs or social obligations that brought these men to betray their own feelings and families. It was, in an odd way, their very bodies themselves, those heroic exteriors that made it possible for them to do what other people could not. One of the plot features of a number of '90s films is a discovery by the male lead that his body has failed him in some way, whether through wounds, disease, or programming. The body that he thought was "his," the body he had been taught to value as fulfilling some version of a masculine heroic ideal—suddenly that body became transformed into a separate entity that was betraying the true internal feelings of the man it contained. *Robocop 2* led the way here in 1990 by showing the distress brought about in its hero's life by the conflicts between Robocop's bullet-proof exterior and his memories of his family. The indestructible body that was to make Robocop invincible led not to a machine-like insensitivity but to deep pain and isolation at the loss of love. *Robocop* makes clear that behind the tough bodies of these male heroes lies, not cheap insensitivity and lusty brutality, but a caring, troubled, and suffering individual. But what 1991 films provide that *Robocop* did not is a happy ending, where the betrayed body is transformed, either back to its "original" loving owner, or into a body that is now in tune with the internal goodness that the film's narrative has revealed.

And while many 1991 films by black male directors about black men's lives emphasize families and masculinities as well—John Singleton's *Boyz n the Hood*, Matty Rich's *Straight Out of Brooklyn*, Spike Lee's *Jungle Fever*—the thematics of internalization and bodily betrayal are not present as they are in Hollywood films about white male leads, largely because the action-adventure heroism of the '80s was never meant to figure black men's bodies in the first place.[1] While, for example, Martin Riggs (Mel Gibson) *is* the "lethal weapon" in the films named for his body, Roger Murtaugh's body (Danny Glover) is never depicted as "lethal" at all. The audience's first shot of him is in a bathtub, surrounded by his loving family, all of whom tell him he looks old. And Riggs has to insist that Murtaugh shoot, not to maim, but to kill, since the enemies you maim always come back to haunt you. Under

The Curse of Masculinity

Riggs's tutelage, Murtaugh is able, at the end of *Lethal Weapon 2*, to fire point blank and kill the chief enemy of the film, Argen Rudd, a South African diplomat whose immunity, Murtaugh declares, has just been "revoked." The safe, nonlethal, aging image of an African-American police officer who kills only when provoked by true evil is an appealing screen character for white mainstream audiences who can be assured that assimilated black men will enforce rather than challenge U.S. systems. Murtaugh does not have to "discover" his feelings for or through a family, since he has one intact at the beginning of the film. His job, or more pointedly, his masculinity, has not taken him away from his family, largely because, such films imply, he has not been out saving countries, artifacts, or corporations. He has not, in other words, been carrying the white man's burden, or, by implication, his masculinity.

There is, consequently, a dangerous racial subtext to all this Hollywood body shifting and internal reform. As has historically been the case in dominant U.S. cultures, masculinity is defined in and through the white male body and against the racially marked body. Action films of the '80s reinforce these assumptions in their characterizations of heroism, individualism, and bodily integrity as centered in the white body. And though '90s films repudiate many of the characteristics of that body—its violence, its isolation, its lack of emotion, and its presence—they do not challenge the whiteness of that body, nor the "special" figuration that body demands. If, these films suggest, there is a body that has been betrayed, victimized, burdened by the society that surrounds it, it is not the body of color, the body that has been historically marked by the continuous betrayals of a social, political, and cultural system that has marginalized and abused it. It is, instead, the body of the white man who is suffering because he has been unloved.

No one, certainly, seems to have been less loved than the hero of the Walt Disney Studio's 1991 film, *Beauty and the Beast*, bringing to the screen an updated version of Marie de Beaumont's eighteenth-century tale. While animated film versions of classic fairy tales have been a Disney staple for decades (*Snow White* [1937] and *Cinderella* [1950], for example), the Disney corporation has also had success in recent years with animated features that develop new characters, such as *The Rescuers Down Under* (1990). But in a time when children's animated features are one of the sure markets of the film and, more pointedly, the home video industry, why would Disney return to a 250-year-old fairy tale? At least part of the answer lies in the fact that this tale helps to forward the image of unloved and unhappy white men who need kindness and affection, rather than criticism and reform, in order to become their "true" selves again.

Susan Jeffords

In this context, it's worth looking at the changes Disney made to the original "Beauty and the Beast" story. Briefly, in its earlier versions, the beautiful daughter of the merchant is asked to take her father's place as the prisoner of a horrible Beast as punishment for the father plucking a rose from the Beast's garden. Her every whim satisfied at the Beast's enchanted castle, Beauty is soon more impressed by the Beast's generosity, kindness, and intelligence than by his animalistic appearance, though she continues to refuse his nightly request to marry him. When Beauty discovers that her father is ill, the Beast allows her to return home under the provision that she will return voluntarily in a specified time. When Beauty fails to return, she learns of the Beast's suffering through a dream (or enchanted mirror) and returns to the castle, only to find him (and there's never any question that the Beast is male) dying. Beauty declares her love and agrees to marry the Beast, only to find that the Beast has disappeared and a handsome prince has taken his place. The prince then explains that a wicked fairy cast a spell over him that could be released only when a beautiful woman would love him for himself and agree to marry him (equally, there is never any question in any of the stories that the spell could have been broken by the open-hearted affection and love of a man, Beauty's father, for example). The prince is restored to his wealth and power, and Beauty lives happily ever after.

The Disney version follows much the same plot, with several key differences. First, and most importantly for the subject of masculinity, the enchanted curse is altered. In none of the other versions of the story that I read was the curse explained anywhere except at the end, when Beauty has already vowed her love for the Beast. In some stories, the Beast is even forbidden to tell of the curse before it is broken. And while the Disney version adheres to this plot pattern in keeping the Beast's enchanted state from Beauty, it doesn't hesitate to tell the audience what's at stake in this picture. As the opening scenes of the film explain, a selfish young prince refuses shelter to an old beggar woman. An enchantress in disguise, the woman condemns him for his selfishness: "I have seen that there is no love in your heart. . . . That makes you no better than a beast—and so you shall *become* a beast!" And, she goes on to explain, "The only way to break [the spell] is to love another person and earn that person's love in return" (Singer 1992, 2–3). To heighten the tension of the narrative, she adds that he must do so before his twenty-first birthday, after which time he will remain a beast forever.

There are several important consequences of this change. Most important, it is to make this movie really the story of the Beast, and not of

Beauty—or Belle, as she is called in the Disney movie—at all. The older tales only introduce the Beast well into the story, when the father has trespassed upon the Beast's property, and he is only seen then *as* a Beast, as a horrible and frightening creature who endangers those around him. The story throughout is Beauty's, telling of her goodness and kindness, her love for and devotion to her father, and her ability to transform through her love even the most miserable of circumstances. In contrast, Belle's equal kindness and love for her father are made secondary to the young prince's dilemma. Will he learn to love someone before his twenty-first birthday? How can someone love him when all are frightened by the sight of him? Who will break the spell?

Belle is less the focus of the narrative here—will she ever see her father again? will she escape the Beast's castle? will she remain good in the face of such horror?—than she is the mechanism for solving the Beast's "dilemma." And in case the audience doesn't understand this narrative setup from the plot arrangement, some of the most appealing characters in the film offer this information straightforwardly. For here's another change. While the older versions isolate the Beast in his castle, having all of Beauty's needs filled by enchanted magic, the Disney tale adds its own trademark to the tale— inanimate objects come to life, the objects that have intrigued audiences since *Snow White*'s talking mirror (1937), *Cinderella*'s dazzling pumpkin (1950), and *Fantasia*'s dancing brooms (1940). In the updated *Beauty and the Beast*, all of the prince's servants are sharing in his plight, having been turned themselves into household objects: clocks, candalabras, teacups, pots, feather dusters, and wardrobes. Not only then are audiences to be concerned about the Beast's impending twenty-first birthday, but about the fate of all of those innocent servants as well. Even if the Beast seems to deserve his punishment for his selfishness, must all these people be condemned to lives of confinement as well? Consequently, when they remark, after first seeing Belle, that "Maybe, just maybe, the Beast could make Belle fall in love with him. And if he did the spell would finally be broken," audiences are to share these endearing and kind objects' dreams for a possible return to humanity (Singer 1992, 25).

There is another important change in the curse itself. While the older tales condemn the prince to live as a Beast until someone can see past his exterior ugliness to his interior beauty, the Disney curse is that the prince must also learn to love someone else. He must, in other words, learn to change if he wishes to live in human society again. This change in the curse reinforces the plot focus on the prince and away from Belle, since audiences

Susan Jeffords

are now anxiously awaiting his changes as well as her insights. Will he be able to overcome his beastly temper and terrorizing attitude in order to learn to love?

This focus on the Beast helps to construct one of the key emphases of this 1991 *Beauty*, and that is the Beast's victimization. In the earlier versions, for instance, the Beast is invariably in command of the enchanted powers of the castle, using them to gratify Beauty's desires and make her comfortable in the castle. In one version, for example, the Beast anticipates all of Beauty's wishes, supplying magical trunks laden with gifts for her family, as well as the books and musical instruments that she enjoys. But for the Disney writers, the Beast is as much a prisoner in his castle as is Belle. He has no special powers, and the only services he can provide for her are at the hands—or the teaspouts—of the equally enchanted and helpless servants who surround him.

While the earlier Beasts are men who were often good but unfairly cursed by an evil fairy, it would seem that this Beast might well deserve his punishment, and therefore be legitimately punished through the curse. But the wording of the opening description of the prince is important here: "He had grown up with everything he desired, yet his heart remained cold. He was selfish, spoiled, and unkind. Yet because he was the prince, no one dared say no to him. No one dared try to teach him a lesson" (Singer 1992, 1). As an anticipated character shift would require, the prince was not innately selfish, but had been made that way, audiences can only surmise, through bad parenting. The anonymous "no one" 's who failed to teach him any differently seem finally to be more at fault for his behavior than does the prince himself. In this scenario, he simply didn't know any better. And while a man might be blamed for being knowingly cruel, can audiences fault this young man for having "no one" to teach him anything different?

Again, enter Belle to solve the Beast's problem. She becomes that absent "some one" who could, and will now, save him from the curse, for she will teach him all he needs to know in order to return to—or perhaps enter for the first time—humanity. For another of the key differences between the earlier and the Disney tale is that Belle is consistently cast as the Beast's teacher, positioning him again as powerless, awaiting her decisions to accept and love him: "He didn't know how to eat with a fork and knife, so she taught him. He didn't know how to read, so she read to him. She taught him how to feed birds and how to play in the snow" (Singer 1992, 48). One of the key romantic scenes of the earlier tales is when the Beast finally feels comfortable enough with Beauty to ask her to dance. In this scene, she is impressed with his grace as a dancer and begins to forget about his beastliness and think of him as human:

> Firmly, lightly, the creature danced with her, gently guiding her across the balcony. Beauty was astonished at the skill of his movement, the strength of his grasp and tenderness of his touch. She closed her eyes and released herself. Her heart pounded, and she was filled with an inexpressible happiness. (Apy 1980, 44)

But in the Disney *Beauty*, the Beast took Belle in his arms and "whirled her into a dance position. He lifted his huge, hairy foot and took the first step—and practically mashed her toes." Belle's reaction to the "clumsy" Beast typifies the shifts in their relationship in this story: "She gave him a warm smile and did what she had been doing for the last few days—she taught him" (Singer 1992, 49).

Why does this matter? Because in contrast to the commanding, sophisticated, and intelligent Beasts that frequent the other tales and that finally make them so deserving of Beauty's love, this Beast seems childish, blustering, "clumsy," petulant, and untutored. As with his upbringing and his initial acquisition of his selfish personality, the Beast does not have to take responsibility for his behavior. It is the work of other people, especially women, to turn this childish Beast into a loving man. This message is clear: if the Beast has not changed before, it is not his fault, but that of those around him who failed to show him otherwise.

This less-than-attractive character of the Beast explains one of the other Disney changes to the tale—the addition of the arrogant and beautiful Gaston, Belle's suitor. While Beauty's beauty and goodness made her the object of other men's affections in the earlier tales, none played as prominent a role in the plot development as Gaston. From the second scene, where he declares that Belle "is the lucky girl I'm going to marry" (Singer 1992, 6), to the climactic scene where he stabs the Beast with what seems to be a death blow, Gaston figures throughout the film as an antagonist in the clearest sense of the term. He thwarts all of Belle's desires: he tries to force her to marry him, arranges to have her father locked away in an insane asylum, and rallies the village to kill the Beast. He is, clearly, the external social version of the prince's flaw. At large in the world, Gaston seeks to gratify only his own interests and epitomizes the quality of selfishness.

But unlike the Beast, he is beautiful, as Gaston is the first to inform the audience. Belle's credential as heroine is early logged in when she is the only one of the town's single women not to swoon over Gaston. With his cleft chin, broad shoulders, brawny chest, wavy hair, and towering height, Gaston fulfills the stereotyped image of male beauty, the hard body that populated 1980s films. And with his pastimes of hunting, drinking, and male bonding, he fulfills a stereotyped image of masculinity as well. Gaston does not simply look the part of the hyper-masculine male, he holds all the opinions that are supposed to go along with it. Not only does he decide to marry Belle without asking her opinion, he paints this picture of their wedded bliss: "A rustic hunting lodge. My latest kill roasting on the fire. And my little wife massaging my feet while her little ones play on the floor—six or seven of them" (Singer 1992, 19). He operates through terror and bullying, intimidating those who do not succumb to his beauty. And, in his condemning moment of the film, he tells Belle that "it's not right for a girl to read" (Singer 1992, 7). But while Gaston serves both as comic relief and plot motivator, he functions as well to contrast to the Beast. Only the purely and self-consciously self-centered Gaston could possibly make the petulant and childish Beast appear to be an appealing choice. Once the character of the dignified and worldly Beast was abandoned in favor of Disney's spoiled brat, Belle's choice to love the Beast could only be made reasonable and effective by visualizing a worse man she could have chosen.

The film admires Belle for refusing Gaston's offers and resisting his scenario. But she is, as the audience's introduction to her reveals, an exception in her town. In fact, in one of the longest production numbers of the film—requiring a cast of voices, elaborate animation, and complex movement—the townspeople call her "strange" and not "normal," principally because she spends all of her time reading. While the earlier Beautys were also avid readers, the Disney film marks Belle's interest as more of a social than a character feature, using it to distinguish Belle from the rest of the townspeople, marking her as better and less provincial than they.

And here's the clue that Disney's *Beauty and the Beast* is more than just the "don't judge a book by its cover" morality play that characterized so many of its predecessors. For Belle is, for all intents and purposes, a Disney Feminist. And Gaston is a Male Chauvinist Pig, the kind that would turn the women of any primetime talkshow audience into beasts themselves. And the Beast—well, where does this new gender scenario leave the Beast?

The Beast is The New Man, the one who can transform himself from the hardened, muscle-bound, domineering man of the '80s into the considerate, loving, and self-sacrificing man of the '90s. The Beast's external appearance is here more than a horrific guise that repels pretty women, but instead a *burden*, one that he must carry until he is set free, free to be the man he truly can be. The body that is strong (he fights off a dozen snarling wolves), protective (he shelters Belle from their attack), imposing (he frightens Belle's father), domineering (he growls every order he gives), and overpowering (he is even bigger than Gaston)—this body is not, as it was for Rambo, a gift but a curse. It is as if, the Beast's story might suggest, masculinity has been betrayed by its own cultural imagery: what men thought they were supposed to be—strong, protective, powerful, commanding—has somehow backfired and become their own evil curse.

But whose fault is this? Presumably, men brought this curse on themselves by acting so self-centeredly and deriving pleasure from the power it gave them. But those opening descriptions of the prince put a halt to such an easy interpretation. For men, like the prince, were only doing what they had been taught. If no one stopped them from terrorizing the household, how were they to know that they should act any differently? With the film's emphasis on teaching, it's clear that such ugly and repulsive men are not *really* to be shunned; they're to be nurtured until their "true" goodness arises. For as the ever-reliable servants tell Belle, "the master's really not so bad once you get to know him" (Singer 1992, 35); this, from the people he has probably been terrorizing during all those selfish years. To reinforce this nurturing theme, the Beast's curse ends at age twenty-one, implicitly apologizing for all men over twenty-one who have remained Beasts, because they simply were not educated properly in time.

And why should audiences care at all about this transformation? Because, like the helpless servants who are equally suffering from the enchantress's curse, audiences are to believe that they too are implicated in this burden of hyper-masculinity, captured, like it, in a false and confining objectification that can only be reversed when the *Beast* is released from his enchantment. In other words, this plot suggests, no one can be free until men are released from the curse of living under the burdens of traditional masculinities.

While *Kindergarten Cop* showed that men could change and that they were really loving and kind beneath those brutal exteriors, *Beauty and the Beast* offered the reasons for men's aggressive behaviors and suggested that they should not only be forgiven but helped along toward revealing their "true" inner selves. The Disney film, like so many of its 1991 companions, pinpointed men's problems in the very place that their successes had been located earlier—in the muscular bodies that made them heroes. But for the Beast and his friends, those bodies are not resources but burdens, the exterior images that they must overcome in order to be happy. And the weight of this task lies less with the men themselves than with those who must learn to look past the hard body to the loving interior (Robocop is more than a machine; John Kimball is not just a cop; the Terminator is not a killer; and

Susan Jeffords

so on) in order to achieve their own real happiness. Without changing direction, only course, these films continue to suggest, as did the films throughout the '80s, that the happiness and well-being of society as a whole depends upon the condition of these men, whether that happiness be defined as national security, social justice, or familial bliss. True to these earlier narratives of masculinity, the quality and continuity of *everyone's* life finally depends upon these white men.

Notes

1. As Donald Bogle states in his study of blacks in U.S. films (1990), the heyday of black male action-adventure heroes was in the early 1970s, with the appearance of films such as *Shaft* (Gordon Parks, Sr., 1971) and *Superfly* (Gordon Parks, Jr., 1972), films that were made largely for black audiences. A 1992 film, *Passenger 57*, starring Wesley Snipes, seems to be challenging the black/white buddy films in its presentation of a black male as a single action hero.

References

Beauty and the Beast. 1980. Retold by Deborah Apy. New York: Holt, Rinehart and Winston.

Beauty and the Beast. 1992. Adapted by A. L. Singer. New York: Disney Press.

Bogle, Donald. 1990. *Toms, Coons, Mulattoes, Mammies, and Bucks: An Interpretive History of Blacks in American Film.* New York: Continuum.

III.

Erasures/Disney Film
as Identity Politics

Eleven

"Where Do the Mermaids Stand?"
Voice and Body in *The Little Mermaid*

Laura Sells

Where to stand? Who to be?

—Cixous (1975) [1986], 75)

A young pastor, finding himself in charge of some very energetic children, hit upon a game called "Giants, Wizards and Dwarfs." "You have
to decide now," the pastor instructed the children, "Which you are . . . a
giant, a wizard or a dwarf?" At that, a small girl tugging on his pants
leg asked, "But where do the mermaids stand?" The pastor told her
there are *no* mermaids. "Oh yes there are," she said. "I am a mermaid."

—Barbara Bush (1990)

In spring 1990 Barbara Bush addressed the graduating class of Wellesley
College, facing a hostile crowd of young feminist women who challenged
her ability to represent the woman they all hoped to become as they entered
the "real world." Arguing that Bush was selected as the wife of an important
figure rather than as someone with accomplishments of her own, students
first circulated a petition that one-fourth of the class signed, and later wore
to the graduation ceremony purple armbands, which signified their protest,
their graduating class color, and their first-ranked choice of commencement
speaker, Alice Walker. The controversy received national media coverage,
which, incidentally, characterized the protesting students as hysterics.[1]

   In response to her audience's rejection, Bush gracefully defended her lifestyle, spoke about the need for women to have multiple choices, and implicitly criticized the limits placed on women by American feminism. After in-
directly exalting women's role as wife and mother in the heterosexual family,
she invoked the image of a mermaid as the master trope of her speech: "For
over 50 years, it was said that the winner of Wellesley's annual hoop race
would be the first to get married. Now they say the winner will be the first
to become C.E.O. Both of those stereotypes show too little tolerance for
those who want to know where the mermaids stand." The mermaid thus

became Bush's attempt to broaden the spectrum of representations of women while simultaneously invoking a cartoon-like, stay-at-home Mom as a viable option. Framed by this oxymoron, the mermaid is an ironic figure that critiques the narrowness of identity politics in contemporary feminism; yet it simultaneously valorizes an equally narrow and conservative image of acceptable positions for women in American culture. This speech marks an interesting moment in the struggle to invent appropriate and liberatory images for American women, a moment in which "woman" slides between the complicated terms of mother, citizen, and subject.

Earlier that school year, in November, the Walt Disney Corporation conjured another cartoon image of woman as mermaid in their animated feature *The Little Mermaid* (1989).[2] A hallmark Disney film, *The Little Mermaid* is their first commercially successful animated feature since Walt's death in 1966, and the first in a spate of new animated features that reaffirm Disney's position as one of the largest producers of "acceptable" role models for young girls. The film portrays the story of the teenage mermaid, Ariel, who first desires independence and entry into the human world, and who eventually desires the handsome Prince Eric. She trades her voice to the Sea Witch Ursula for a human body and for access to the Prince and his world. The narrative recounts the ritual slaughtering of the archetypal evil feminine character and the marital union of the girl and her prince. Embedded within this classic narrative about an adolescent girl's coming of age is a very contemporary story about the costs, pleasures, and dangers of women's access to the "human world."

Undoubtedly, feminists have criticized *The Little Mermaid*'s Ariel because she seems to have little ambition beyond getting her prince (Trites 1990). I find this criticism somewhat reductionist. The message of *The Little Mermaid* is more insidious and also more liberatory. On the one hand, with the traditional fairy-tale trappings of finding true princely love, the Disney rendition can be seen as more insidious because it sanitizes the costs of women's access to the "male sphere" by vilifying women's strength and by erasing the pain that so often accompanies "passing." On the other, I see *The Little Mermaid* as also more liberatory because it contains the means of its own undoing in the camp character of Ursula the Sea Witch, and in Disney's compulsory happy ending, which bestows the mermaid with both access *and* voice.

Clearly, both Bush's and Disney's versions of the mermaid can be read as conservative images. Yet both versions of the mermaid critique the narrow range of options that constrain women's lives, and both emphasize issues of choice and agency. This essay situates *The Little Mermaid* within the context of contemporary American feminism and the struggle over the cultural definitions of "woman." By reading against the backdrop of Bush's speech, and the media's representation of the Wellesley students, I find that *The Little Mermaid* reflects some of the tensions in American feminism between reformist demands for access, which leave in place the fixed and complementary definitions of masculine and feminine gender identities, and radical refigurings of gender that assert symbolic change as preliminary to social change. In this context, then, the mermaid figure becomes both an icon of bourgeois feminism and a sign of the stakes in reinventing the category of "woman," or reimagining women as speaking subjects.

Upward Mobility

"Bright young women, sick of swimmin', ready to stand. . . . "
—Ariel's song

In 1837, Hans Christian Andersen wrote the original literary fairy tale of "The Little Mermaid." Like most of Andersen's work, the tale is considered autobiographical, an expression of his lack of social acceptance in the aristocratic circles that offered him patronage, a personal narrative of the pleasures and dangers of "passing." Ever the outsider, Andersen "projects his nagging sense of deprivation" in his writings (Spink n.d.; Bredsdorff 1975; Zipes 1983).[3] If a fairy tale is chameleon-like, as Joseph Campbell suggests, putting on "the colors of its background," living and shaping itself to "the requirements of the moment" (1972, 850), then Disney's contemporary version has shifted colors from class to gender privilege. Given the autobiographical theme of "passing" in Andersen's literary version, the Disney version, along with its ritual affirmation of women's coming of age, invites a reading of this film as a parable of bourgeois feminism. Ariel's ascent to the "real world" easily becomes metonymic of women's access to the white male system.

The Little Mermaid establishes the world on land and the world under the sea as two contrasting spaces, one factual and one fictive, one real and the other imaginary. In this dualistic and hierarchical construction, the human world can be aligned with the white male system and the water world situated outside that system. In *Women's Reality* (1981), Ann Wilson Schaef uses the term "white male system" to characterize the dominant culture of American patriarchy. According to Schaef, the white male system operates on several contradictory myths, at least two of which are relevant to the complementary worlds of this film. First, nothing exists outside the white male system; and second, the white male system knows and understands everything (8–9). Those who are privileged by the white male system are oblivious to anything outside the system, while those outside the system know about the dominant culture as well as their own marginalized culture. These two contradictory myths speak to the relationship between the land and sea worlds: the sea world is rendered either invisible or mythic while the land world is endowed with cultural validity. As contradictory and complementary, the two-world motif creates permeable yet dangerous borders, furthers the plot, and establishes a hierarchy of desires.

As Pat Murphy convincingly argues in his ecofeminist critique of *The Little Mermaid*, the film firmly establishes a colonialist, first-world/third-world relationship between the human and sea worlds. The world under the sea, despite its aristocratic decor, is the colonized space of marginalized or muted cultures, often invisible to the inhabitants of the white male system. Sebastian, and many of the other sea creatures, have the facial features of people of color. When in their own world, the sea creatures spend their days singing and dancing to calypso music. When they venture across the boundary into the "real world," they risk being reduced to human food. (See chapter 7 in this volume.)

This human oblivion to other worlds becomes a major plot device in the film. In a characteristic Disney moment of ironic self-referentiality, Eric and his companions dismiss the undersea world and its inhabitants as mere "fairy tales." With the blinders of his world, Prince Eric believes that he is saved from drowning not by a mermaid but by a human girl, thus complicating Ariel's efforts to win his affection. Like real animals, Eric's dog cannot speak, and cannot tell Eric the truth about Ariel.

The repeated depictions of land and sea as complementary also create a hierarchical relationship in which Eric's human world on land is privileged as the real world. This is most frequently reinforced through the language and imagery of "up there" and "down here." One notable instance is during Ariel's song, "Part of Your World," in which she yearns to be "up there." Indeed, this Ashman-Menken musical formula is described in Disney production circles as the "I Want" number (Avins 1992, 70). During this "I Want" scene, the spatial imagery supports the hierarchy of dominant and muted cultures: the cartoon's simulation of camera shots either positions the audience as omniscient viewers looking downward on Ariel, or we see upward through Ariel's eyes. All of this is embedded in sweeping seascapes which resemble Georgia O'Keeffe paintings, rich with the female imagery of sea shells and cave openings.

"Where Do the Mermaids Stand?"

In these contrasting worlds of dominant and muted cultures, Ariel's song "Part of Your World" becomes more than an adolescent yearning for adulthood. As Ariel sings of access, autonomy and mobility, she yearns for subjecthood and for the ability to participate in public (human) life. She is figuratively and literally an upwardly mobile mermaid.[4] As the film opens, her adolescent curiosity and rebelliousness are both immediately apparent. She is late for her singing debut, a coming-of-age ritual ordained by her father, because she is out and about salvaging forbidden human objects from sunken ships.[5] Her curiosity about the human world, and her rebelliousness toward her father and his prohibitions against human contact, are particularly evident in her song. The song intones her desire to run, walk, and dance, all synonyms for mobility. While singing, she caresses a book that she cannot read, expressing her longing for knowledge. Her desire for access is characterized by her hunger and fascination with a different world in which she believes she can have autonomy and independence.

Autonomy and independence, as many feminists have recognized, is never easy; the cost for participating in the white male system can be quite dear. About to enter the real world, Ariel faces the pain of conforming to impossible ideals as she physically mutilates her own body by exchanging her fins for the mobility of human legs. Even more disheartening, she purchases this physical transformation with her voice. Like so many women who enter "the workforce" or any other "male sphere," Ariel wrestles with the double-binding cultural expectations of choosing between either voice or access, but never both. Our culture's continued difficulty with sexual difference is evident in the public persona of figures such as Geraldine Ferraro and Hillary Clinton. Ferraro failed in her 1984 vice-presidential bid in part because voters considered her too aggressive after hearing her forceful "masculine" speaking style (Jamieson 1988). Similarly, Hillary Clinton has been called the "Lady Macbeth of Little Rock," the "Evita Peron of America," and Bill's co-president. The Bush presidential campaign sought to discredit Hillary Clinton by suggesting she was "not a real woman" (qtd. in Wood 1994, 299–300). Women so often find themselves in a position much like Andersen's, a position in which access is really just a form of passing that compromises personal integrity and immolates voice.

Disney, however, obscures these costs through several related sanitizing maneuvers that contrive to create a bizarre erasure of "the feminine." Irigaray writes that Western patriarchy is constructed on a history of matricide, and on the expropriation of women from the mother's genealogy to the father's. As the film concludes with Ursula being impaled on a phallic mast from a ship and with Ariel being passed from her father to her prince, *The Little Mermaid* enacts this expropriation and makes Ariel's choices appear to be cost-free.

First, Ariel's fascination with the human world becomes transformed into love for Prince Eric. Through this sanitizing maneuver Disney obscures Ariel's interest in the human world as metonym for access to power. Once she meets the prince, her curiosity is minimized and her drive becomes externally motivated rather than self-directed. As Ariel passes from her father's hands to her husband's hands, the autonomy and willfulness that she enacted early in the film becomes subsumed by her father's "permission" to marry Eric. In other words, the marriage plot (Radner 1993) prevails as her interest in the role of citizen becomes supplanted by her interest in the role of wife.

Many feminists found objectionable this transformation from the Andersen version. In Andersen's tale the mermaid dies because she fails to earn the prince's love. Upon her death, the daughters of the air grant her the ability to earn an immortal soul through three hundred years of service. Trites argues that the Disney version subverts the mermaid's self-actualization process, and that Andersen wanted the mermaid to earn a soul on her own, not as an attachment of someone else: "Andersen offers women several paths toward self-realization, so the message to children is much more far-sighted than Disney's limited message that only through marriage can a woman be complete" (1990/91, 150). Andersen's version, however, is not quite that liberatory. As Zipes suggests, Andersen's reward was never power over one's own life, but security in adherence to power—in the little mermaid's case, the power of servitude to god (1983, 84).

Second, Disney erases the pain of access by sanitizing the physical, bodily pain of Ariel's self-mutilation when she trades her fins for feet. Within the context of the first sanitization, and of Ursula's song about beauty and looks ("poor unfortunate souls . . . this one longing to be thinner . . . "), the legs indicate Ariel's compliance with the beauty culture, rather than her desire for access, mobility, and independence. Ariel becomes "woman as man wants her to be" rather than "woman for herself." In Andersen's version, the mermaid feels incredible pain, as if a sword goes through her body and knives pierce her feet with each step; the pain is so deep that her feet bleed. For Andersen, the pain reflected his discomfort and the price of his own integrity as a peasant whose literary talents earned him entry into aristocratic circles (Zipes 1983). His story expressed his own discomfort and loss of voice as he attempted to "pass" in high society. Disney masks the pain of self-mutilation that often accompanies this access by excising the pain from Andersen's story. By eliminating this pain, however, Disney only enhances Andersen's original version. As Zipes puts it, "Ideologically speaking, Andersen furthered bourgeois notions of the self-made man or the Horatio Alger myth, which was becoming so popular in America and elsewhere, while reinforcing a belief in the existing power structure that meant domination and exploitation of the lower classes" (1983, 81). The Disney version thus becomes a bourgeois feminist success story in which access is achieved with minimal cost.[6]

Third, Ariel sacrifices her connection to the feminine in the matricide of Ursula, the only other strong female character in the film. Eventually, Ariel achieves access by participating with Eric in the slaughtering of Ursula, relegating her and that which she signifies to silence and absence. Ursula is reassigned to the position of the repressed that keeps the system functioning. Embedded in gynophobic imagery, Ursula is a revolting, grotesque image of the smothering maternal figure (Trites 1990/91). Of course, within Disney's patriarchal ideology, any woman with power has to be represented as a castrating bitch. Ariel's entry into the white male system is at the expense of her connection with the mother. The gynophobic imagery sanitizes this cost, making it more palatable. By vilifying feminine power in the figure of Ursula, Disney simplifies Ariel's choice: in the white male system it is much easier to be silent than to be seen as monstrous.

Admittedly, the film is a problematic text for a feminist resistant reading, because it teaches us that we can achieve access and mobility in the white male system if we remain silent, and if we sacrifice our connection to "the feminine." We all know the storyline about Ariel sacrificing her voice. Indeed, Ursula tells an ancient story when she convinces Ariel that her voice will be useless in the human world. Although Ariel severs her connection with the one strong female character of the film, Ursula, she ultimately retrieves her voice. This final sanitization is clearly the product of Disney's compulsion for rainbows, violins, and happy endings. If voice is a symbol of identity, then Ariel retains a measure of autonomy and subjecthood. Philosopher Margaret Whitford argues that women cannot be social subjects until they are subjects of language (1991, 43). In this final sanitization lies the film's undoing.

In the House of Divine

"This little girl knew what she was and she was not about to give up on either her identity *or* the game."

—Barbara Bush (1990)

Laura Sells

If the Little Mermaid is, indeed, a budding young woman severing her connection to the feminine symbolic, what possible sites of resistance and pleasure are available? Where do I find hope for Ariel as she enters the white male system, passed from the hands of her father to the hands of her husband? How can Ariel's compliance with the laws of the Father be recuperated? Much like Ariel, I find myself turning to Ursula for answers to these questions. Trites tells us that the wealth of gynophobic imagery precludes us from reading Ursula's wry comments ironically: "Although some viewers might perceive those of Ursula's statements that capitalize on Ariel's inexperience as ironic and as an intended tribute to feminism, these comments are voiced in the midst of too much gynophobic imagery to honestly promote feminism" (1990/91, 152, n7). But beyond the gynophobic imagery, the character of Ursula, who is unlike any other Disney villain, teaches a different lesson about access, mobility, and voice. Ursula can retrieve Ariel from her destined alliance with patriarchy. Not only does she give Ariel legs, she schools her in disruptive reconstructions of gender and harbors her voice in the feminine home of *jouissance*. Ursula teaches Ariel that performance and voice are manifestations and liberations of gender.

The lessons that Ursula gives Ariel about womanhood offer an important position from which to resist narrowly drawn patriarchal images of women, a position absent in Disney's previous fairy tales. During her song about body language, Ursula stages a camp drag show about being a woman in the white male system, beginning "backstage" with hair mousse and lipstick. She shimmies and wiggles in an exaggerated style while her eels swirl around her, forming a feather boa. This performance is a masquerade, a drag show starring Ursula as an ironic figure. According to the directing animator, Ruben Acquine, Ursula was modeled on the drag queen Divine, while the voice and ethos behind Ursula belong to Pat Carroll. Both of these character actors are known for their cross-dressing roles. Ursula's theatricality is undeniable; to prepare her voice for her role, Carroll envisioned Ursula as an aging Shakespearean actress because, as she says in *People* (11 December 1989), "only someone who has done the classics has that kind of arrogance." A composite of so many drag queens and camp icons—Joan Collins, Tallulah Bankhead, Norma Desmond, Divine—Ursula is a multiple cross-dresser; she destabilizes gender.

Reading Ursula as a drag queen is not implausible considering two important elements that contribute to shaping the Disney narrative. Smuggled into the Disney version are the multileveled tensions of Andersen's original tale. Given his sexual ambiguity (one historian suggests that his pining away for a number of lost loves was a performance to disguise his homosexual-

"Where Do the Mermaids Stand?"

ity—see Bredsdorff 1975), his own uncomfortable and self-policed passing in aristocratic circles, and the double-consciousness motif that informs the "original" tale, *The Little Mermaid* is storied as layers of conflicting desires and codes of performance. Additionally, the influence of songwriters Howard Ashman and Alan Menken, the creators of the camp *Little Shop of Horrors*, guided musical characterizations. Ashman and Menken were brought in as cocreators of the project, and the score was written before any animation began. Consequently, the plot and characters are substantially developed through the film's music (Grant 1993, 333–42). The influence of Ashman and Menken undermines Disney's sanitizations.

In Ursula's drag scene, Ariel learns that gender is performance; Ursula doesn't simply symbolize woman, she *performs* woman. Ursula uses a camp drag queen performance to teach Ariel to use makeup, to "never underestimate the importance of body language," to use the artifices and trappings of gendered behavior. Ariel learns gender, not as a natural category, but as a performed construct. As Ariel stumbles away from the shore into Eric's arms, she winks to her undersea companions, indicating that she is *playing*: "The game is dangerous, and has a compulsive quality, but it *is* play. We may hope that when this game isn't fun any more Ariel may use her stubbornness, if not her beauty, to play another, more interesting one" (White 1993, 191).

Drag performances such as Ursula's and Ariel's are spectacles that can teach us something important about gender. Gender is composed of repeated, publicly performed, regulated acts that are "dramatic" and therefore "contingent" embodiments of meaning. Drag denaturalizes gender by showing us its imitative structure; it operates on the contradiction between anatomical sex and gender identity, a contradiction that is interrupted by the performance itself. Defining gender as a performative production dismantles the illusion of a natural category (Butler 1990; Butler 1991; Capo and Hantzis 1991; Garber 1992). Mary Russo puts it more simply: "To put on femininity with a vengeance suggests the power of taking it off" (1986, 224). Butler, however, refutes this equation of gender with style, as something to be put on or taken off as a conscious choice: "Performativity has to do with repetition, very often with the repetition of oppressive and painful gender norms to force them to resignify. This is not freedom, but a question of how to work the trap that one is inevitably in" (1992, 84).

Andersen, who inhabited a position that was radically other than himself, struggled with working this trap. "Throughout his life Andersen was obliged to act as a dominated subject within the dominant culture despite his fame and recognition as a writer," as Zipes reminds us (1983, 77). Indeed a recurrent theme in many of Andersen's fairy tales is to dismantle what

Butler calls "zones of legitimacy": *pace* "The Emperor's New Clothes." Andersen's writing is often simply about passing, but passing in itself is not subversive. For drag to be subversive, it must go beyond exposing an ideal as uninhabitable. Drag becomes subversive when it "dissolves and rearticulates" ideals (Butler 1992, 89). The ideal woman represented by the mermaid image is immobile, her only power in her sexuality. As one journalist describes Bush's mermaid: "Those free-floating mermaids she mentioned are sheathed in glittering, confining, fantasy fins that really get the sailor going but leave the woman foundering if she tries to walk" (Johnson 1990). Ariel is a dissolution and rearticulation of this gender ideal: she is a mermaid passing as a human with both legs and voice, or mobility and subjecthood.

Just as Ursula's drag performance destabilizes and deconstructs gender, her excessive figure provides the site upon which we can reconstruct the image of the mermaid. It is no accident that Ursula is an octopus, an inverted Medusa figure. Very early in the film we learn that she is exiled by King Triton from the world of the merpeople. She represents that which is outside even the patriarchally domesticated outside, and hence, outside patriarchal language. Ariel's outside, the undersea world, is a colonized outside ruled by the patriarchal father, King Triton, who has the power to name his daughters. Ursula, who is banished from Triton's realm, is outside the outside. Ursula is a double-voiced, multiple character. The sprawling seascapes of Ursula's home are what Cixous calls "the dark continent" of the feminine body. To visit Ursula, Ariel must enter through the toothy jaws of a gigantic mouth, and swim through womb-like caves. Ursula is the female symbolic encoded in patriarchal language as grotesque and monstrous; she represents the monstrosity of feminine power. This is why Ariel trades her voice to the Sea Witch in the first place.

Feminist theories of women's *jouissance* help us to understand the metaphors of voice, body, and language as they create a force that displaces the dualistic order of the white male system. The multiplicity of women's *jouissance*, or women's bodily, sexual pleasure, cannot be represented dualistically. Although it means woman's pleasure, *jouissance* cannot simply be translated into bodily pleasure. It connotes sensual enjoyment, the enjoyment of rights, and the enjoyment of language. *Jouissance* implies "total access, total participation, as well as total ecstasy." The multiplicity of woman's sexuality indicates "she has the potential to attain something more than total, something extra—abundance and waste, Real and unrepresentable" (Wing 1986, 165–66). The language of women's bodies jams the machinery of phallocentric discourse that generates a dualistic world view, disrupting the symbolic system that demands the complementarity of gender and the dual world construction of land and sea. A voice that has spent time with Ursula, that has spoken in the language of *jouissance*, could never return to innocence.

The configuration of voice, bodily excess, rupture and the feminine is established by the visual alignment of images in the climax of the film. In the first wedding scene, Ursula wears Ariel's voice in a shell around her neck in her disguise as Vanessa, Ariel's evil double. The bird Scuttle swoops down and shatters the shell, freeing Ariel's voice. The metaphor of flying/stealing (*voler*) is central to Cixous's notion of *l'écriture féminine*, because "to fly/steal is a woman's gesture, to steal into language to make it fly . . . for all the centuries we have only had access to having by flying/stealing" (1986, 96). Ariel's voice literally becomes "the spoken word, exploded, blown to bits by suffering and anger, demolishing discourse. Broken from her body where it was shut up and forbidden" (94). The freeing of Ariel's voice literally interrupts the wedding, or the ritual enactment of patriarchal symbolic order.

This release of Ariel's voice also releases Ursula, who then seizes King Triton's crown and the phallic scepter. Just as Disney transforms Ariel's desire for autonomy and access into desire for a husband, Disney also warps Ursula's desire into a form of penis envy, or in this case, scepter envy. With the scepter in hand, Ursula swells into an enormous monster, exploding, diffusing, overflowing. Her growth is more rupturing than an erection. Eventually, Ursula dies as Eric pierces her with the phallic mast of a ship. This undeniable event makes a recuperation of *The Little Mermaid* rather questionable. As the film concludes with Ariel in Prince Eric's arms, the dangerous message about appropriation and the sanitized cost of access cannot be ignored. Yet, even though Ariel has been complicit in the death of Ursula, and the destined alliance with patriarchy is fulfilled, I remain hopeful. After all, Ariel enters the white male system with her voice—a stolen, flying voice that erupted amidst patriarchal language, a voice no longer innocent because it resided for a time in the dark continent that is the Medusa's home.

Conclusion

"Because for woman speaking—even just opening her mouth—in public is something rash, a transgression."
—Cixous (1986, 92)

Cixous reminds us of "the bond between woman's libidinal economy—her *jouissance*, the feminine Imaginary—and her way of self-constituting a subjectivity that splits apart without regret, and without this regretlessness being the equivalent of dying" (90). I argue that Ariel will not forget this bond so easily. I prefer to read Ursula's death without regret, for dominant representations of "woman" must be displaced in order to be replaced, dislocated to be relocated. The grotesque Sea Witch is slaughtered, and displaced, but what remains after Ursula's death is the image of a voiced, speaking subject who has been taught that gender is a performance. It is not simply that Ariel gives me hope, but that I have to find hope in her. As Rosi Braidotti puts it, the project of disengaging woman from "the trappings of a 'feminine' defined as dark continent, or of 'femininity' as eternal masquerade will take my life time, all the time I have" (1987, 239–40).

Perhaps I'm guilty of Tania Modleski's charge that feminist critics often label a text feminist simply because we enjoyed it. Maybe I am in

> danger of forgetting the crucial fact that like the rest of the world even the cultural analyst may sometimes be a cultural dupe—which is after all only an ugly way of saying that we exist inside ideology, that we are all victims down to the very depths of our psyches of political and cultural domination (even though we are never *only* victims). (Modleski 1991)

Butler puts it similarly when she writes, "It is important to realize that your own critical position may be an effect of the very power regime that you seek to criticize, without being fully coopted by it" (1992, 89). Yet maybe Modleski's implied charge of my own duplicity is, itself, a bit too easy. I am as much a product of the contradictions and tensions of contemporary feminism as I am a dupe of dominant culture.

To return to the other mermaid, the more material one: like Ariel, the mermaid of Bush's speech indicates the stakes in reimagining role models for women. Occasioned by the Wellesley students' graduation as a rite of passage, Bush's commencement address is an affirmation of the bourgeois fairy tale about ascent to the "real world." Like Ariel, the mermaid students of Wellesley must confront the questions of voice and access that attend the conflicting roles of woman and citizen. As Irigaray puts it, "Have fathers ever been asked to renounce being men? Citizens? We do not have to renounce being women in order to be mothers" (qtd. in Haas 1995; see chapter 12 in this volume). The double bind of our culture's inability to accept women as citizens is quite apparent in columnist Lewis Grizzard's efforts to desexualize the protesting Wellesley students:

> I wonder where these children will be 20 years from now. A lot of them will be extremely successful professionally, I'm sure. Perhaps there are future CEOs in the crowd. . . . But how many of them will also leave their

top floor office suites and go home to a cat? (*Atlanta Constitution*, 25 April 1990)

Indeed, the students' own ambivalence about sexual difference is registered in their close vote between Alice Walker and Barbara Bush. As feminist psychologist Phyllis Chesler remarks, the close contest suggests that there is "war raging in the hearts and minds of women. For so many students to have voted for Mrs. Bush suggests that many women still want to live in the castle and still believe in the myth of rescue by marriage and still believe in Prince Charming" (*New York Times*, 4 May 1990). Regardless of the fact that "choices" between wife and CEO are really available only for a very small group of people, women struggle under the *representation* of these roles as choices and the burden that these narrow images place on them.

The Wellesley students who signed the petition and wore the armbands resisted the complementarity of gender, and the retrograde image of women that Bush represented. After all, Barbara Bush dropped out of school to marry, and she publicly disclaims owning political views. As Eleanor Clift writes in *Newsweek*:

> The First Lady is known to have more liberal views than her husband on gun control and abortion rights. But she has always put her husband first, and she's proud of it. Asked which side of a controversy she is on, she replies "I'm on *his* side." (11 June 1990)[7]

The students rejected Bush's public submersion of her own identity into her husband's. As the students' petition states, inviting Bush would "honor a woman who has gained recognition through the achievements of her husband." The students were not concerned that Bush was "just a mother" instead of a "male-clone careerist," as one feminist columnist accused. Economic, social class, and race privilege carefully aside, the Wellesley women resisted the prevalent image of women as accessories to men rather than agents in their own right. Indeed, they were more concerned that, during this moment in which they marked their own entry to the "real world," their figurehead was a woman but not a citizen; or, perhaps in the metaphors of *The Little Mermaid*, they were concerned with their prospect of having access without voice or subjecthood.

While the students rejected Bush because she was chosen as an accessory to an important figure, the press construed this as a rejection of motherhood. What was for the students a statement about their possibilities, and a disavowal of narrow definitions of woman as attachment to man, became reframed as a controversy about devaluing motherhood in contemporary feminism. Although the Wellesley petition received a variety of responses in

Laura Sells

the media, two concern me most. First and most obvious is the conservative response, or the backlash response, indicating how much work lies ahead. The second response found established feminists yoked with conservatives: successful liberal feminists such as Pat Schroeder, Linda Ellerbee, Betty Friedan, and Ellen Goodman immediately accepted the conservative frame, and translated the students' petition into a rejection of motherhood. It is the response from those feminists who saw the students as "missing the point of feminism" that I am most uncomfortable with. Linda Ellerbee, for instance, chastised the Wellesley students in her column: "There's more to feminism than your individual career paths and/or rat races. There's more to feminism than leaving home. There's more to feminism than you" (*New York Post*, 3 May 1990). Arguing that a central goal of the women's movement is to value women's work, especially in the home, Ellerbee suggests that the Wellesley students missed the point in Women's Studies 101. While, indeed, feminism is a broad and multiple discourse and movement with a spectrum of adherents, Ellerbee's comments invite a dangerously narrow interpretation of feminism's agenda. Most disturbing, liberal responses such as Ellerbee's were complicit in seeking to silence these students, and in retrenching the incident into the same terms and its old double bind of *The Little Mermaid*. That is, access to the white male system is achieved at the cost of the feminine and defined in terms in which women are mothers or citizens, but never both.

The Wellesley controversy appeared in the media for two months before Bush's appearance on campus. With her life choices under scrutiny, Bush's ethos became the organizing principle of her speech as she responded to the crisis. The master trope of her response became the mermaid, an image that both aligns her with the women students in the audience and separates her from them as well. "Where do mermaids fit into the scheme of things," she said. "Where *do* mermaids stand . . . all of those who are different, those who do not fit the boxes and the pigeonholes?" In one sense Bush invites the women students in the audience to become the mermaid who resists squeezing herself into the boxes and pigeonholes that limit the cultural definitions of woman. This mermaid speaks the same language as the protesting students who, like the girl in Bush's narrative, are not about to give up on either their identity or the game. This mermaid affirms the students' discontent with their prospects. In another sense, however, Bush herself embodies the mermaid who doesn't fit the categories of "appropriate role model" or "citizen." In this sense, then, the mermaid trope critiques feminist derisions of her life choices, a critique that ultimately confirms woman's traditional role as wife and mother. The mermaid image allows Bush to create common substance with the students and to disarm them by simultaneously affirming and accusing.

Yet as the speech unfolds, Bush's ethos becomes infused in the mermaid, and she reaffirms traditional roles for women. For Bush, the mermaid stands at home. In the speech, she gives her audience three pieces of motherly advice (because in fairy tales wishes always come in threes). Bush outlines three apparently distinct choices for the graduates that collapse into a single moment: this moment explicitly valorizes the American family and implicitly glorifies wife and mother. She lists her choices as "believe in something larger than yourself," which for her is literacy; "enjoy life," which for her means marrying George Bush; and, "cherish human connections," which she translates into cherishing the family. The only choice in this list that is followed by an example other than the family is literacy. "Literacy" is an integral part of Bush's ethos and an important term in the speech. Bush's activities in the literacy "movement" were hailed by her supporters and by Wellesley's President Nan Koehane as Bush's premier accomplishment, one overlooked or ignored by the protesting students. Bush's work with literacy was upheld as her moment of autonomy and agency. In the speech, however, literacy becomes subsumed by the family, as Bush locates the practice of literacy within the home. She exhorts the students to teach their children to read, because "our success as a society depends *not* on what happens in the White House but on what happens inside your house." Bush's moment of autonomy and individual accomplishment becomes the act of a Republican Mother preparing her sons to be literate citizens. Despite her witty efforts at gender balance when she suggests that one of the women in the audience might become President someday, Bush's traditional values dominate the speech. Unlike a different mother, the drag queen Ursula, whose performance of femininity offers the possibility of undoing the double binds of sexual difference, Bush's own performance leaves her incorporated into the genealogy of the father, as Republican Mother raising citizen sons, a performance that interpolates women as *only* wives and mothers, having no other place than the home.

On a more positive note, the demands of the Wellesley students weren't so difficult to meet after all: the following year another mermaid and former Wellesley student, Hillary Clinton, returned to her *alma mater* to deliver the commencement address. Like Ariel, Hillary silenced herself—at the insistence of the Clinton campaign—in order to ensure her husband's presidential victory. But once Bill's victory was consummated in his inaugural ceremony, it didn't take Hillary long to transgress. This image gives me hope that, as Susan White predicts, when Ariel's game isn't fun anymore, she may indeed use her stubbornness to play a different, more interesting game.

> "But what if I'm a mermaid . . .
> hey but I don't care
> cause sometimes, I said, sometimes
> I hear my voice and it's been HERE
> silent all these years."
>
> —Tori Amos (1991)

Notes

The author would like the thank the women of the Pagoda at St. Augustine, Florida, for providing the space to draft this essay.

1. See, for instance, Mike Barnicle's *Boston Globe* column in which he describes Wellesley students as "a pack of whining, unshaved feminists" who cause the Boston College students to "appreciate the virtue of celibacy" (*Boston Globe*, 26 April 1990). The controversy provoked the production of T-shirts sporting the slogan: "Just a bunch of whiny unshaven radical spinster tartlets" ("The Wellesley Protest, Beyond Barbara Bush," *The Washington Post*, 29 May 1990).

2. *The Little Mermaid* is the first animated fairy tale released by Disney in thirty years. It broke national box office and video store records for "first release" animations, making it Disney's most successful feature-length animation (surpassed by *Beauty and the Beast* in 1991) (Thomas 1991). As Susan White points out in "Split Skins," mermaids have become a pervasive cinematic symbol of the girl's difficult rite of passage to womanhood (1993, 186): *Splash* (1984), a Disney/Touchstone film directed by Ron Howard; Richard Benjamin's *Mermaids* (1990); and of course, Madonna's music video "Cherish" (1991). Likewise, Tori Amos's song, "Silent All These Years" (1991), evokes the configuration of the mermaid and voice.

3. See Zipes for a brief discussion of the literary and folk origins of the tale, and for an insightful class analysis of Andersen's version (Zipes 1983, chapter 4).

4. Ann Wilson Schaef's (1981) terminology is particularly useful to discuss Ariel's desire to participate in the human world. Like many people who theorize about dominant and marginal cultures, Schaef agrees that marginalized people often experience a double consciousness, or an awareness both of dominant culture and of their own marginalized cultural systems (see also, for instance, Sandra Harding 1991). Unlike cultural critics who see this double consciousness as a product of political struggle, Schaef recognizes this double vision as simply the (frequently inchoate) recognition of being disenfranchised and disconfirmed as a member of a muted group. While Ariel certainly doesn't have a politicized consciousness, she is indeed aware of her own relative lack of power.

5. Ariel's desire to acquire human objects is interesting within the context of Hilary Radner's (1993) discussion of consumption as a way for women to negotiate the constraints placed on a sexual identity within the public sphere. *The Little Mermaid* can be seen as a variation on that theme. Indeed, a frenzy of consumption has sprung up around

the mermaid motif as young girls buy everything from Mermaid toothbrushes to Mermaid video games (White 1993). In addition, the obvious analogy between Ariel and Barbie suggests that Ariel teaches girls that adult female sexuality is inextricably linked to consumption (see Motz 1983).

6. By shifting the focus from class to gender, Disney creates what one reviewer calls "the fall of a fishy, feminist Horatio Alger" (Roberts 1992).

7. To be fair to Eleanor Clift, Ann McDaniel, and Clara Bingham, the authors of this article, they conclude with a more favorable (although questionable) assessment of Bush's character: "It is unlikely that Barbara Bush will change her style. It is equally unlikely that she will ever submerge her identity to that of her husband, even if he is the president."

References

Amos, Tori. 1991. "Silent All These Years." *Little Earthquakes*. Atlantic Recording Corporation.

Andersen, Hans Christian. (1837) 1974. "The Little Mermaid." *The Complete Fairy Tales and Stories*. Trans. Erik Christian Haugaard. Garden City, NY: Doubleday.

Avins, Mimi. 1992. "Aladdin." *Premiere*, December: 67–69, III.

Braidotti, Rosi. 1987. "Envy: Or, With My Brains and Your Looks." In *Men in Feminism*, ed. Alice Jardine and Paul Smith. New York: Methuen.

Bredsdorff, Elias. 1975. *Andersen, What Was He Like*. London: Phaidon.

Bush, Barbara. 1990. Remarks of Mrs. Bush at Wellesley College Commencement. Wellesley, MA: Wellesley College Office of Public Affairs.

Butler, Judith. 1990. *Gender Trouble*. New York: Routledge.

———. 1991. "Gender Trouble, Feminist Theory, and Psychoanalytic Discourse." In *Feminism/Postmodernism*, ed. Linda J. Nicholson. New York: Routledge.

———. 1992. "The Body You Want: Liz Kotz Interviews Judith Butler." *Artforum*, November: 82–89.

Campbell, Joseph. 1972. "Folkloristic Commentary." In *The Complete Grimm's Fairy Tales*. New York: Pantheon, Random House.

Capo, Kay Ellen, and Darlene M. Hantzis. 1991. "(En)Gendered (and Endangered) Subjects: Writing, Reading, Performing and Theorizing Feminist Criticism." *Text and Performance Quarterly* 11: 249–66.

Cixous, Hélène. (1975) 1986. "Sorties." In *The Newly Born Woman*. Trans. Betsy Wing. Minneapolis: University of Minnesota Press.

Garber, Marjorie. 1992. *Vested Interests: Cross-Dressing and Cultural Anxiety*. New York: Harper Perennial, Harper Collins.

Grant, John. 1993. *Encyclopedia of Walt Disney's Animated Characters*. New York: Hyperion.

Haas, Lynda. 1995. "Eighty-Six the Mother." In *From Mouse to Mermaid*, ed. Elizabeth Bell, Lynda Haas, Laura Sells. Bloomington: Indiana University Press.

Harding, Sandra. 1991. *Whose Science, Whose Knowledge?* Ithaca: Cornell University Press.

Jamieson, Kathleen Hall. 1988. *Eloquence in an Electronic Age: The Transformation of Political Speechmaking*. New York: Oxford University Press.

Johnson, Rheta Grimsley. 1990. "What Mrs. Bush Didn't Say." *Dallas Morning News*, 10 June.

Laura Sells

Modleski, Tania. 1991. *Feminism without Women*. New York: Routledge.

Motz, Marilyn Ferris. 1983. "I Want to Be a Barbie Doll When I Grow Up: The Cultural Significance of the Barbie Doll." In *The Popular Culture Reader*, ed. Christopher D. Geist and Jack Nachbar. Bowling Green: Bowling Green University Popular Press.

Murphy, Patrick. 1995. " 'The Whole Wide World Was Scrubbed Clean': The Androcentric Animation of Denatured Disney." In *From Mouse to Mermaid*, ed. Elizabeth Bell, Lynda Haas, and Laura Sells. Bloomington: Indiana University Press.

Radner, Hilary. 1993. "Pretty Is as Pretty Does." In *Film Theory Goes to the Movies*, ed. Jim Collins, Hilary Radner, and Ava Preacher Collins. New York: Routledge.

Roberts, Susan C. 1992. "Fractured Fairy Tales." *Common Boundary*, September/October: 17–21.

Russo, Mary. 1986. "Female Grotesques: Carnival and Theory." In *Feminist Studies/Critical Studies*, ed. Teresa de Lauretis. Bloomington: Indiana University Press.

Schaef, Anne Wilson. 1981. *Women's Reality*. San Francisco: Harper and Row.

Spink, Reginald. n.d. "Hans Christian Andersen: Fairy Tales in a Hundred Languages." *Fact Sheet/Denmark*. Copenhagen: Press and Cultural Relations Department of the Ministry of Foreign Affairs of Denmark.

Thomas, Bob. 1991. *Disney's Art of Animation: From Mickey Mouse to Beauty and the Beast*. New York: Hyperion.

Trites, Roberta. 1990/1991. "Disney's Sub/Version of *The Little Mermaid*." *Journal of Popular Television and Film* 18: 145–59.

White, Susan. 1993. "Split Skins." In *Film Theory Goes to the Movies*, ed. Jim Collins, Hilary Radner, and Ava Preacher Collins. New York: Routledge.

Whitford, Margaret. 1991. *Philosophy in the Feminine*. New York: Routledge.

Wing, Betsy. 1986. "Translator's Glossary." In *The Newly Born Woman*, by Hélène Cixous and Catherine Clément. Trans. Betsy Wing. Minneapolis: University of Minnesota Press.

Wood, Julia T. 1994. *Gendered Lives*. Belmont, CA: Wadsworth.

Zipes, Jack. 1983. *Fairy Tales and the Art of Subversion: The Classical Genre for Children and the Process of Civilization*. New York: Wildman Press.

Twelve

"Eighty-Six the Mother"
Murder, Matricide, and Good Mothers

Lynda Haas

> It is hard to speak precisely about mothering. Overwhelmed with greeting card sentiment, we have no realistic language in which to capture the ordinary/extraordinary pleasures and pains of maternal work. (Ruddick 1989, 29)

Phone conversations at my house are frequently the most trying moments of the day; regardless of what my children are involved in before I pick up the receiver, all three decide they need my immediate, undivided attention the moment I begin to talk. People without children, I'm sure, find the constant interference—"just a minute, no—no chocolate milk right now"—frustrating. I must admit, I too am usually frustrated; but, I have learned that motherhood means

> being constantly interruptible, responsive, responsible. Children need one *now*. . . . The very fact that these are real needs, that one feels them as one's own (love, not duty); *that there is no one else responsible for these needs*, gives them primacy. (Olsen 1978, 18–19)

When I happen to be talking with someone like my friend and coeditor, Elizabeth, she understands (because the same thing is happening on her end of the line). Our fragmented conversations suit our interruptible lives—we share secrets about theory, writing, good books, and potty training. In a way, those conversations teach us to shape and reshape our identities—as cultural workers, as women, and as mothers—by comparison and contrast.

In *Maternal Thinking*, Sara Ruddick suggests that because of their parental roles, women who are also mothers think and act from a particular (but not unified) maternal standpoint. Considering motherhood from a cultural perspective adds the complexity that a "mother" does not construct her identity in a vacuum, nor is she alone responsible for its construction. Cultural myths and everyday situations and associations become part of what it means to be a mother. As cultural critic Paul Willis suggests, the fundamental paradox of our social life is that when we are at our most natural, our most everyday, we are also at our most cultural: "When we are in roles that look the most obvious and given, we are actually in roles that are constructed, learned, and far from inevitable" (1979, 184). Focusing on the hope of changing the construction of a woman's identity fully appropriated by the maternal function—the overdetermination of woman via biological function and societal expectation—French feminist philosopher Luce Irigaray writes,

> As for us, it is a matter of urgency not to submit to a subjectivized social role, that of the other, governed by an order subordinated to a division of labour—man produces/woman reproduces—which confines us to a mere function. Have fathers ever been asked to renounce being men? Citizens? We do not have to renounce being women in order to be mothers. (1991, 42–43)

Irigaray argues that a woman whose identity is her motherhood is "the other of the same"—a woman drawn by the patriarchy who is ultimately a residual, a defective man, an object of exchange in a male market. If we wish to subvert this order, women must become self-defined in such a way that we are not satisfied with sameness, but instead construct an otherness and difference that finds a place in social *and* symbolic representation. Because the bodily encounter from and with the mother is the first link any one has to culture, how she is identified—and how her role has been naturalized—is of utmost importance in the first step of recreating the feminine.

Surpassing this masculine construction of feminine identity, finding ways to represent ourselves socially (to ourselves and to men)—identifications that work for us and among us—and learning to interpret our masculinely drawn identities resistantly—these are complex projects. This work has been undertaken by many feminist film critics, especially those who theorize from the standpoint of psychoanalysis and feminism's rereading of Lacan and Freud. It is not surprising that feminist film theorists would look to the philosophical work of Irigaray, because her emphasis on sexual difference and the representation of the feminine in the imaginary and the symbolic is easily recast for talking about cinematic representations of women.[1] In this essay, I address various constructions of the mother in the films of the Disney corporation, pointing out what is debilitating about representations of mothers and how mothers interpret those images, as well as some locations for possible resistance and reclamation.

The Cultural Imaginary: Murders and Mothers

> The culture, the language, the imaginary and the mythology in which we live at the moment . . . this edifice that looks so clean and subtle . . . let's

see what ground it is built on. Is it all that acceptable? The substratum is the woman who reproduces the social order, who is made this order's infrastructure: the whole of our western culture is based upon the murder of the mother. And isn't there a fluidity, some flood, that could shake this social order? And if we make the foundations of the social order shift, then everything will shift. That is why they are so careful to keep us on a leash. (Irigaray 1991, 47)

When Irigaray critiques current theory, looking for that which subsists below it, she looks to psychology, philosophy, and Greek literary constructs to find traces of the cultural imaginary—a collective register for cultural representations. As well as these sources interrogated by Irigaray, popular representations form the cultural imaginary—film and television reach far into our collective unconscious, setting the grounds for how we construct our identities, our politics, the personality of our culture and our location in it. Our vast exposure to these media is obviously important to cultural and personal identity politics. For instance, *TV Guide* recently reported that children in today's culture will see some 600,000 murders on screen before they reach adulthood; with a repetition rate so high, one must infer some influence from that exposure. I would like to suggest that the media's repeated erasure of the mother's place and her origins is a kind of ideological dominance accomplished on the unconscious (as well as the conscious) level, and that this symbolic murder is just as violent and even more frequently portrayed.

In *Totem and Taboo* (1919), Freud interprets Greek tragedy to hypothesize that Western culture is founded on patricide—the need to remove the father so the son can take his place. When Irigaray rereads Freud, she also looks back to Greek myth, finding other originary stories. In "The Bodily Encounter with the Mother" (1991), Irigaray analyzes how *The Orestia* unveils a story of the installation of the patriarchy, built over the sacrifice of the mother and her daughters.[2] Because the mother's place is silently elided in traditional readings of myth, a requisite cultural taboo has also been placed on the relationship with the mother. Cultural stories of maturation and family interaction preoccupied with the son's oedipal struggle, with castration, conceal another severance, the cutting of the umbilical cord to the mother. Not until this original erasure, this matricide, is brought to light, will the relationship with the mother be brought out of silence. The stakes in how to undo the erasure and how to reconstruct the cultural imaginary involve the very foundation of feminist hope for a better world:

If woman is not recognized by the cultural imaginary, theory, no matter how far-reaching and innovative, goes on perpetuating the founding obliteration. The absence of creative intercourse in the imaginary leads, eventually, to an impasse in thought; thought is condemned to go on repeat-

ing over and over again the same gesture of silencing and repression.
(Whitford 1991, 75)

The Missing Mother

Although the mother/woman is the mirror into which men look to find
their "other" and thus their identity, she has no identity of her own. As I've
argued, this lack of identity exists because the mother and the mother-
daughter relationship are, as yet, unsymbolized in our cultural imaginary.
There is no maternal genealogy, no importance attached to a mother's heritage. The available versions of the maternal afford women "too few figura-
tions, images, or representations by which to represent herself" (Irigaray
1985a, 71). This point is easily illustrated by the representations (and lack of
representations) of mothers and daughters in Disney films (and in most
films); the typical mother is absent, generously good, powerfully evil, or a
silent other, a mirror that confirms the child's identity without interference
from hers. In this way, mothers are either sentimentalized or disdained; in
either case, their identity and their work are simultaneously erased, naturalized, and devalued.

The motherless family instituted in Disney's first offering, *Snow White and
the Seven Dwarfs* (1937) (there is, however, an evil stepmother), is repeatedly
commemorated in films such as *Pinocchio* (1940), *Cinderella* (1950), *Alice in
Wonderland* (1951), *The Rescuers* (1977), *Tex* (1982), *Something Wicked This
Way Comes* (1983), *The Little Mermaid* (1989), *Beauty and the Beast* (1991),
Aladdin (1992), *Super Mario Brothers* (1993), and *Life with Mikey* (1993). In
these films, the mother of the represented "family" is either dead or totally
unaccounted for, never mentioned. In a few of these films, it was not Disney,
but the original text that forgot the mother. In many cases, however, a
mother appeared in the original text, but was excised by the Disney revision.[3]
In films such as *Lady and the Tramp* (1955), *Old Yeller* (1957), *101 Dalmatians*
(1961), *Freaky Friday* (1977), *Pete's Dragon* (1977), *Watcher in the Woods*
(1981), *Flight of the Navigator* (1986), *Honey I Shrunk the Kids* (1989), and
Hand that Rocks the Cradle (1992), mothers exist primarily to nurture and
encourage their children in benevolent ways, often sacrificing themselves to
do so. A variation on this theme is the mixture of the sentimentalized
mother with the coming-of-age theme in films such as *One Magic Christmas*
(1985), *Adventures in Babysitting* (1987), and *V. I. Warshawski* (1991), in which
the female lead needs to learn the benefits and rewards of becoming a good
mother.[4] These are the familiar representations of the woman's identity as
purely maternal; and although these parts cast mothers as residual, many
women have been encoded to aspire to this identity. It is hard to calculate

the extent of the damage of such sentimentalized versions of mothers, for each woman identifies with her on-screen other to a differing degree, and each feels guilt (perhaps even unconsciously) for not being society's picture perfect mother in different ways.

In many representations, the mother is nothing more than a society girl with children, an object of the gaze with appendages: *Song of the South* (1946), *Mary Poppins* (1964), *Down and Out in Beverly Hills* (1986), *Betsy's Wedding* (1990), *The Doctor* (1991), and *Father of the Bride* (1991). These women aren't really there to represent motherhood as much as they are there to fill in a necessary gap in Disney's representation of a conventional family unit. Those films that point most clearly to an installation of the patriarchy on the foundation of matricide excuse the mother figure in order to replace her with a kindly—and often more competent—patriarch: *Bambi* (1942),[5] *Pollyanna* (1960), and *Three Men and a Baby* (1987). Although this brief listing is by no means inclusive, it is enough to suggest that of the three hundred and some films Disney has produced in the last sixty years, mothers, when represented at all, are more stereotypically (and ideologically) drawn than any other character.

To her contention that mothers must be symbolized in ways that are "other of the other," Irigaray adds that "the relationship between mother/daughter, daughter/mother constitutes an extremely explosive kernel in our societies. To think it, to change it, amounts to undermining the patriarchal order" (Irigaray 1991, 86). It is not surprising, then, that Disney has made only three films that feature mother/daughter relationships: Touchstone's *The Good Mother* (1988) and *Stella* (1990), and Hollywood Pictures' *The Joy Luck Club* (1993). The sheer fact that the mother is in the spotlight contests filmic norms. *The Good Mother* and *Stella* offer the obligatory sentimentalized versions of motherhood; neither mother is able to self-define herself, and both films focus on the necessary sacrifice/punishment that culture dictates to mothers who would be subjects in their own right. However, from within the Disney house—the place where in an insidious and seemingly apolitical way, stereotypes are usually entrenched and reproduced—comes *The Joy Luck Club*, perhaps the best example produced thus far to show that mothers can be represented in such a way as to resist hegemonic expectations and reclaim a feminine standpoint.

"Every Passion Has Its Price"

So goes the ad-line on the video release of Touchstone's *The Good Mother*. Directed by Leonard Nimoy (hot after his recent success with *Three Men and a Baby*),[6] and starring Diane Keaton (Anna Dunlap), and Liam Neeson

(Leo Cutter), *The Good Mother* is an adaptation of Sue Miller's morally di-dactic novel bearing the same title.[7]

Many popular film critics agreed with David Ansen (*Newsweek*), who is quoted on the video cover—"It's one Hollywood movie that will genuinely provoke discussion." For others, however, the point was lost; Fuchs calls it a sappy film that "feels like *Stella Dallas* in 80s drag" (1988, 22). It is probable that Nimoy's audience was women—the film has many family resemblances to other "women's" texts. He told newspapers that "it's about motherhood and sexuality in the same individual and our society's discomfort with that" (Lambert 1988, 16).

The film opens with a voice-over by Anna, who is remembering her child-hood summers at her grandparents' lake home. Through Anna's memory, we meet her aunt Babe, who is only a few years older. Unlike Anna, who describes herself as shy and "already a conformist," Babe was glamorous and rebellious, sneaking out at night to meet boyfriends, stealing away to smoke, and defying the family's patriarchal grandfather. When Babe found out she was pregnant, she took Anna to a hideaway to show how her breasts and uterus were changing. A week later, Babe was sent to Europe to have her baby; a few years later, she drowned herself by jumping out of the rowboat on the lake late at night. Thus, Babe joins a host of other rebellious women who die in their attempts to defy cultural codes. Miller's novel is even more explicitly didactic about what happens to rebellious women: "I came to think of Babe as a cautionary tale."

Although this "cautionary tale" is not specifically mentioned in the film, the beginning story of Babe is used to foreshadow what will happen to Anna herself. At the end of the voice-off, Anna sums up her feelings about Babe:

> In the years after Babe's death, I often thought of what she offered me
> in the summers in her presence. It felt like anything was possible. I
> wanted to take risks. I wanted to be a passionate person. And now, in
> spite of everything that has happened, I feel I really had to try.

An opening voice-over by a woman is unusual in mainstream cinema, espe-cially when the woman is talking about subjects important to women—fam-ily, pregnancy, the body. However, in "Disembodying the Female Voice," Kaja Silverman suggests that while women's voices are an important part of how the feminine is inscribed on film, only men have been allowed the kind of voice-over that is not immediately connected to diegesis or the body; in other words, the male voice-over can transcend a connection to the filmic images, and thus the body, reaching a state of power. On the other hand,

> There are no instances within mainstream cinema where the female voice
> is not matched up in some way, even if only retrospectively, with the fe-
> male body. For the most part woman's speech is synchronized with her
> image, and even when it is transmitted as a voice-off the divorce is only
> temporary; the body connected to the female voice is . . . always fully re-
> coverable. (1990, 315)[8]

Although Anna's voice-overs at the beginning and end of the film seem to
be invested with authority and appeal to a personal knowledge, in the con-
curring images and dialogue, even in the words she speaks during the voice-
overs, she acts and speaks about herself in codified, acceptable ways. In fact,
to a large extent, what she learns during the narrative of the film is that she
must stay within prescribed boundaries.

The boundary that is tested in the film concerns the female body—not
whether it can be transcended by a woman—but whether the body can be
pleasurable for a woman who is also a mother. Let me make clear that I am
not creating a good/bad dichotomy between body as evil and transcendence
of body as good; quite the contrary, since much French feminist philosophy
begins with the feminine body and its capability for *jouissance*. But if women
are to enter into equalized cultural representation, men must sometimes be
shown as connected to the body and women must sometimes be shown as
being able to transcend it.[9]

In one of the positive moments in Miller's novel, Babe shows Anna what
it means to take pleasure in the body:

> Babe lifted her head and shivered. . . . Then she bent her head and gently
> kissed first one, then the other of her bare knees. She shuddered again
> and pulled her sweatshirt over them. Never, even later in her most overt
> wildness, did she seem more aberrant to me, more separated from what I
> understood my family to be, than in that moment of tenderness to her
> own body. (1986, 128)

Unlike Babe, Anna is even ashamed that she has flesh; her life has been one
of repression and silence. In the novel, two things help bring Anna out of
her shame: she learns to masturbate and she meets Leo. In Disney's version,
of course, the masturbation has to go, and thus only Leo is responsible for
Anna's sexual awakening.[10]

In this way, Anna is much like other fictional women such as Edna Pon-
tellier, Anna Karenina, and Emma Bovary, whose lovers open the possibility
of sexual enjoyment. Unlike these women, who either despised or were ambivalent about having to be mother-women, Anna's one great goal in life is
to attain the title of "good mother." Thus, when she has to make the choice

between a sexual life and a maternal life, she easily abandons herself (and Leo) and chooses Molly. In this crooked retelling of the feminine tragedy, therefore, Anna does not die—her life is not what's most dear to her. Instead, she loses her daughter. Her ex-husband, Brian, becomes aware that Molly has been exposed to a sexual relationship between Anna and Leo, and sues for custody; he wins.

Although the narrative encourages an identification with and sympathy for Anna, it is also embedded with reasons to judge her "mistake." In an interview Keaton gave upon the opening of the film, she judges Anna's position:

> She had this repressed family, and it took her all this time, until late in her life, to meet a man and fall deeply in love. But I think she fell too much in love in a way. She went too far. (qtd. in Lambert 1988, 16)

Since the actress playing the lead felt judgmental about the character's choices, it seems inevitable that the viewer would discern that attitude. Keaton also plays Anna as a totally passive woman who, although she would like to make her own choices, always does as she is told; Leo convinces her to let go of her inhibitions and enjoy sex, and she does; Brian decides she is unfit as a mother and so keeps Molly after a weekend visitation, and she lets him; her lawyer tells her to pretend it was all a mistake in judgment and that it was Leo's fault, and she does; the court says she lost the case, and so she leaves it at that. So, she may not choose what should happen in her life or even her daughter's—that would be to grant her a position of agency and power; and yet, even within the confines of the body, she is taught that she must not enjoy the flesh. Anna must trade passion for passivity, and by film's end, she is the obedient woman she is meant to be.

Silverman concludes that while the male subject finds his most ideal realization when he is heard but not seen, the female subject is usually represented as seen but not heard (or sometimes overseen and overheard). In *The Good Mother*, Anna is both overseen and overheard; her body and her sexual "awakening" become the spectacle upon which the narrative turns. She is under visual and auditory surveillance (by many men in the film—Leo, Brian, the male psychiatrist, her lawyer, and the court), and she always responds as expected. She is never, therefore, inaccessible to definitive male interpretation; she accepts the limitations of her place, her time, and her desires, and this constantly resecures her as a male construct.

Anna's appearance as "other of the same" is, in many ways, even more damaging than if she were totally absent. Silverman writes,

"Eighty-Six the Mother"

It is of course precisely what is invisible to a symbolic order which is organized around the phallus—that which the symbolic order can only perceive as an absence or lack—which threatens to escape its structuration, and to return as heterogeneity or a foreclosed real. Hence the fascination with the female body, the concern to construct it in ways which are accessible to the gaze and to hear it attest in a familiar language to dominant values. (1990, 322)

The Good Mother, then, establishes a semiotics of self-reference for Anna that requires her voice to signify her body; then, since her body (or pleasure in it) is inscribed as dangerous, even wicked, she is taught to signify passivity. This isolates her, as woman and as mother, from any effective action; prevents her representation from making any investments in a new social order; and in a familiar language, guarantees that women-mothers will remain in the same place.

"It's a Great Life if You Don't Weaken"

Both *The Good Mother* and *Stella* portray women who wish to be mothers and nothing more; after Leo criticizes Anna for not being passionate about anything (her music, her work), Anna screams that she is passionate for one thing—for Molly. The other things in her life are definitely secondary. Stella makes a similar comment to her coworker who has asked her why she doesn't date; Stella replies, "After Jenny, there's nothing left." Curiously though, each film emphasizes a different side of the joys and trials of caring for a child. In *The Good Mother*, the few scenes between Anna and Molly are highly sentimentalized. When we first see them together, Anna has just made pancakes in the shape of dinosaurs for breakfast. When Molly doesn't eat, but instead spills her milk, Anna laughs and happily cleans it up. Throughout the film, we see only happy moments between mother and child—they read together (a book about human anatomy), they go to the park, they have a great time. None of the difficulties of maternal love are present—only the difficulty of losing its object.[11]

In *Stella*, directed by John Erman, written by Academy Award-nominated Robert Getchell from Olive Higgins Prouty's 1923 novel, *Stella Dallas* (and the 1937 Barbara Stanwyck film directed by King Vidor), and starring Bette Midler (Stella), Trini Alvarado (Jenny), John Goodman (Ed Munn), and Stephen Collins (Steven Dallas), we see only a few happy moments between mother and child when Jenny is young. In one of these, Stella pretends to be "cousin It" and chases Jenny around the house. Generally, however, as Gaylen Studlar notes,

> *Stella* delays and downplays the special bonding between mother and daughter that formed the heart-tugging emotional core to the Stanwyck/Shirley version. Instead, the mother/daughter relationship appears characterized as much by conflict as by loving commitment. The conflict increases as Jenny reaches college age. In the presence of her father, Jenny is polite, content, and happy. With her mother, she is sullen and judgmental. (1980, 341)

Actually, we don't even really see Jenny grow up in Stella's care; we see a few shots of Stella and Jenny before her third birthday. Until this time, Steven had not seen his daughter. After he visits, however, we only see the young girl become a teenager through her visits with him. We see father and daughter in the park, and then her growth is narrated by several scenes with father and daughter in a New York restaurant, with each scene portraying an older version of Jenny, until she is a teenager. Evidently whatever bond that formed between mother and daughter in those ensuing years was unimportant to the filmmakers' (and society's) agenda.

There are, however, many points early in *Stella* that could make it a more resistant film than *The Good Mother*, and if it ended after its first hour, it could even be seen as a feminist statement of sorts. One is in the lead actress herself; Bette Midler, as a text, has much more capacity to resist cultural norms, in both appearance and attitude, than Diane Keaton. And in many ways, she does successfully contest cultural norms. At the opening of the narrative, we find that she is a woman bartender in 1969 who doesn't take mouth from anybody. When she chooses to make a spectacle of herself, as she climbs up on the bar and performs a mock striptease for her admiring male patrons, she could very much be seen as mimicking female excess. She seems in charge of the situation, and in charge of her relationship with Steven. When he first approaches her for a date, we see a certain self-assurance and maybe even a moment of self-definition as she tells him, "You're too fancy for me." When she does date him, we see, for the most part, her antics as the center of their enjoyment. In fact, Stella's ability to enjoy herself is one of her most remarkable features. Unlike Anna, Stella is not ashamed that she has flesh, or that she is what she is—a lower-class working woman. She refuses to be pitied for who she is by the wealthy people in the film; the upper-crust mother who tries to humiliate Stella by remarking on how it's too bad Jenny didn't get Stella's lovely color of hair is rejoined by Stella's ironic backhand—"Oh you like it? I liked it too when I first saw it on the grocery shelf."

Touchstone updates Stella by having her reject Steven's offer of marriage. Although she discovers she is pregnant, Stella refuses to fulfill the marriage plot, thus finding her subjectivity as a rich man's wife. She frequently says things like "It's a great life if you don't weaken," and "I have two hands, I can do it myself." She also refuses any offers of money from Steven to help her provide for Jenny.[12]

Unfortunately, in the second half of the film, Stella does "weaken": the marks of her strength all but disappear. Her ability to make comment on her own power by making a spectacle of herself is reinterpreted by her excessive performance in Boca Raton, where she embarrasses Jenny. Her performance does not have the same tone of self-awareness, and under the gaze of this wealthy audience, the irony of her performance is turned back on her. She is now a spectacle without the weapon of self-critique, and by film's end is reduced to being an outsider, a spectator at her daughter's wedding. The control she enjoyed in her relationship with Steven and with other men, such as Ed Munn, is frequently undercut later in the film. Stella's inability to continue her own self-definition is like the limited subjectivity conferred upon the roles of many women in classical cinema; and like those women, her identity becomes the effect of a masochistic misrecognition, propelling the female viewer into a negative narcissism (Silverman 1990, 322).

I have found myself very interested in how *Stella* is received by the working-class mothers who populate many of my classes at the community college; I ask them to view the film to provoke discussion for a paper on film criticism. When I ask what part of the movie they like best, I most often receive the answer: "the ending." That *Stella* is an obvious manipulation to effect sentimental emotion (it is classified as a "tear-jerker" at video rental stores such as Blockbuster), or that Stella has sacrificed her daughter for nothing more than money, does not seem to diminish my students' "enjoyment" of the film. They have told me that Stella exemplifies "true mother-love"—caring more what happens to the daughter than to herself. They are not surprised or upset by the image of the silent and suffering mother—Stella joyously looking on, knowing that her sacrifice made possible Jenny's marriage into the upper class. Their response illustrates Tania Modleski's (1991) suggestion that filmic texts often provide a very limited number of viewing positions for an audience to occupy, corresponding to a narrow range of ideological effects. Even though each mother in my class who watched the film was a different person with a separate identity, and probably a slightly different philosophy of how to do the work of mothering, the ideology they espouse based on their social reality—as working-class mothers, like Stella, who believe it is only "natural" to give up whatever is necessary in order that their children more fully realize the American Dream—causes them to respond to the invitation of the film without much negotiation, allowing their interpretation and even their pleasure to be colonized.

As Stella maschochistically smiles through her tears in this hyperbolic last scene complete with a swelling orchestra of stringed instruments, the mother-viewer's identification is structured and taught. Stella's inadequacy—except through erasure—is relayed to the mother who watches. Our inability to be "good mothers" unless we masochistically accept our place seals the closed theater of female subjectivity. It is difficult to look "inside" to find other options, or to turn away, since a mother's identity is relational. Her inability to approximate or transcend the mirror in which she sees herself as the dim reflection of the "good mother" locks her into a deadly narcissism more conducive of self-hatred than self-love. As *Stella* glamorizes pain and renunciation as a mother's duty, it reflects how films can "overdetermine the production of a docile and suffering female subject" (Silverman 1990, 322).

"Feathers from a Thousand Li Away"

We must reappropriate this maternal dimension that belongs to us as women. . . . We must refuse to let her desire be annihilated by the law of the Father. We must give her the right to pleasure, to *jouissance*, to passion, restore her right to speech, and sometimes to cries and anger. We must also find, find anew, invent the words, the sentences that speak the most archaic and most contemporary relationship with the body of the mother, with our bodies, the sentences that translate the bond between her body, ours, and that of our daughters. (Irigaray 1991, 43)

The Joy Luck Club, released by Hollywood Pictures, was a surprise "hit"—a film that grossed much more than expected and that stayed at box offices for extended showing. The film is based on Amy Tan's first novel (she also contributed to the screenplay), directed by Wayne Wang, and stars an outstanding ensemble of eight actresses. A few years ago, it would have been a strange movie to have come from Disney, but now with their recent buy-out of studios like Miramax and Merchant/Ivory, *The Joy Luck Club* fits in with the new face of Disney—the one that will make serious, artsy films as long as they watch the bottom line.

The film opens resistantly: a disembodied female voice-over tells the story of a Chinese woman who buys a special swan; it was once a duck, but "stretched its neck in hopes of becoming a goose, and now look—it is too beautiful to eat." Then the woman travels across an ocean many *li* wide, to America, where she hopes to have a daughter who will "be too full to swallow any sorrow. She will know my meaning, because I will give her this swan—a creature that became more than what was hoped for." However, when she arrives, the customs officials take her swan and she is left with only a feather. She keeps it until the day when she can tell her daughter, in perfect American English, "This feather may look worthless, but it comes from afar and carries with it all my good intentions."

The nontraditional opening signals the possibilities inaugurated by this film for contestation and reclamation of the mother/daughter relationship. As the circular, multivoiced narrative retraces the lives, hopes, and good intentions of four mothers and daughters, new representations of mothers appear—mothers who, yes, must sacrifice, but who resist any definition for themselves and their daughters that is not self-described. In a Chinese society where they must perform as expected, they nevertheless find a way to know themselves and to rewrite the boundaries. Because that is such a struggle, they refuse to forget who they are, turning from a masochistic acceptance of their place and offering their daughters, instead, a maternal heritage and a fighting spirit. Perhaps because *The Joy Luck Club* illustrates a culture so different from ours, an Eastern culture where we expect oppression of the feminine, the codes dictating a woman's place that usually present themselves as so profoundly naturalized become open to question, especially as we watch these mothers resist and escape societal expectations. Thus, instead of showing women interpellated by the patriarchal system, *The Joy Luck Club* shows how the ideologies of a film sometimes fail to determine, and also fail to dictate, preferred readings to the viewer.

In *The Practice of Everyday Life* (1984), Michel de Certeau suggests that oppressed groups often find ways to win small victories over larger, more powerful systems; emphasizing the creative power of popular culture, he argues that subordinated people often serve their own interests while appearing to acknowledge the interests of the dominant group. He provides the example of *la perruque*, which means "the wig," where an employee may use the employer's time to make a phone call, or the office stationery to write a letter, while appearing at all times, on the surface, to be an obedient employee. Something like this tactic of subversion in everyday life is apparent in *Stella*, although any possible change as a result of her resistance is undercut by her reification as "other of the same." Irigaray offers a stronger version of *la perruque*, a strategy that looks not only to subvert, but to transform: because one cannot simply step outside of phallocentrism, or simply reverse it, Irigaray suggests the performance of mimesis or mimicry:

> One must assume the feminine role deliberately. Which means already to convert a form of subordination into an affirmation, and thus begin to thwart it. . . . To play with mimesis is thus, for a woman, to try to locate the place of her exploitation by discourse, without allowing herself to be simply reduced to it . . . [Mimesis makes] "visible," by an effect of playful repetition, what was supposed to remain invisible. (1985b, 76)

Irigaray's mimetic performance, making visible the naturalized codes for women while still appearing subordinate to the system, resonates in *The Joy Luck Club*. The best example is the story of Lindo Jong, a woman who averts her oppressive societal role by subversively performing what is expected. Betrothed by the village matchmaker to Huang Taitai's son, Tyan-yu, when she is only two, Lindo begins life with no choices. As Lindo narrates the story of her early life, we see the matchmaker convince Huang Taitai that Lindo has a good face. "She will be a strong horse. She will grow up to be a hard worker who serves you well in your old age." On her wedding night, Lindo's adult voice-over tells us her thoughts:

> I saw the curtains blowing wildly, and outside rain was falling harder, causing everyone to scurry and shout. I smiled. And then I realized it was the first time I could see the power of the wind. I couldn't see the wind itself, but I could see that it carried the water that filled the rivers and shaped the countryside. It caused men to yelp and dance. I wiped my eyes and looked in the mirror. I was surprised at what I saw. . . . I was strong. I was pure. I had genuine thoughts inside that no one could see, that no one could ever take away from me. I was like the wind. . . . I made a promise to myself; I would always remember my parents' wishes, but I would never forget myself. (Tan 1989, 58)

She makes a promise to herself to find a way out of her arranged life without bringing shame on her mother and family; "It was really quite simple. I made the Huangs think it was their idea to get rid of me." She practices mimesis in the most subversive of ways: on a festival day for thinking pure thoughts about the ancestors, she cuts her clothes and screams in agony. When Huang Taitai arrives to stop the commotion, Lindo tells of a dream in which she was visited by the family's patriarchal ancestor. He has told her that the marriage is not ordained by the ancestors and that Tyan-yu will die if he keeps her. She provides three "signs": a black mark on Tyan-yu's back that will grow and eat away his skin (a mole she has looked at every night as she stares at his back), a tooth that has fallen out because the ancestors touched her mouth (she shows the cavity where a tooth fell out years before), and a servant girl who is carrying Tyan-yu's spiritual child (she has watched this servant girl and her lover from the window and knows she is pregnant out of wedlock). Lindo's performance is convincing—it speaks with the authority of the patriarchal ancestral gods—and the Huangs send her on her way to America.

Along with the strategy of mimesis, Irigaray argues that women need to resist their commodification, relate woman-to-woman, and invent a new symbolic register. In Ying-Ying's story, some new images for women's strength are drawn, a step toward reclaiming the feminine imaginary. She tells the story of the bad man she married who, after they had a son, began bringing lovers home with him: In the film's most heart-wrenching scene, we watch Ying-Ying's resistance as she allows her infant son to drown in his bath water.[13] She is only partially conscious of what she is doing—taking the only thing that matters away from her husband. But after, and because of, this act, she loses her strength: "I did not lose myself all at once. I rubbed out my face over the years washing away my pain, the same way carvings on stone are worn down by water."

Years later, Ying-Ying lives in America and is remarried. Upon seeing that her daughter, Lena, is repeating her mistakes, she makes a decision to gather her strength, to reclaim her identity, and to save her daughter by drawing alternative images of what can be. Ying-Ying sees what An-Mei, another mother in the film, sees:

> I was raised the Chinese way. I was taught to desire nothing, to swallow other people's misery, to eat my own bitterness. And even though I taught my daughter the opposite, still she came out the same way. Maybe it is because she was born to me and she was born a girl. And I was born to my mother and I was born a girl. All of us are like stairs, one step after another, going up and down, but all going the same way.

Ying-ying's narrative and her intervention in her daughter's intertwining story illustrate that a mother can break this pattern. Lena and her husband, Harold, "share" their marriage and their finances by keeping track of every penny spent and paying each other back as "equals," even though she works at his architectural firm where he makes seven times her salary. That they are not equals when it comes to decisions is very clear. As Ying-Ying looks at the list hanging on the refrigerator, she sees "ice cream" as something Lena must pay for. "This you do not share. Lena cannot eat ice cream." Although Harold does not understand, Lena knows the implications. Later, as she shows her mother to the guest room, Ying-Ying puts her bag down on an unbalanced table designed by Harold in his college days. "What use for? You put something else on top, everything fall down." The table becomes a metaphor of Lena's marriage; she listens as her mother tells her to "leave this lopsided house," that she will not be losing her marriage, she will be finding herself. As Lena returns downstairs and attempts to talk to Harold, the narrative flow changes to Ying-Ying, who has relocated her spirit in order to give it to her daughter: "All around this house I see the signs. My daughter looks but does not see. This is a house that will break into pieces."

In Tan's novel, Ying-Ying's story focuses on a more detailed account of a story her mother told, of why the tiger is gold and black, and how it has two different ways: "The gold side leaps with its fierce heart. The black side stands still with cunning, hiding its gold between trees, seeing and not being seen, waiting patiently for things to come" (Tan 1989, p. 248). In the film, as Ying-Ying narrates her story, we learn she was born in the year of the tiger. As she sits in her daughter's lopsided house, she tells herself that she has been a ghost for too long—she has seen and not been seen since the loss of her infant son. Now she must tell Lena everything:

> How can I leave this world without leaving my spirit? So this is what I will do. I will gather together my past and look. I will see a thing that has already happened. The pain that cut my spirit loose. I will hold that pain in my hand until it becomes hard and shiny, more clear. And then my fierceness can come back, my golden side, my black side. I will use this sharp pain to penetrate my daughter's tough skin and cut her tiger spirit loose. She will fight me because this is the nature of two tigers. But I will win and give her my spirit, because this is the way a mother loves her daughter. . . . She will hear the vase and table crashing to the floor. She will come up the stairs and into my room. Her eyes will see nothing in the darkness, where I am waiting between the trees. (Tan 1989, p. 248)

As Ying-Ying waits in the darkened room, the sun filtering through venetian blinds and striping her shadow, a new symbol for mother's work is created. The tiger, the gift of spirit, is the kind of image necessary in the cultural register before mothers can reconstruct their identities.

As the film ends, June, the daughter whose mother has died at the beginning of the story, travels to China to find her two lost sisters. When they meet, they form a bond of sisterhood based on the heritage of their mother. The last two images of the film show a photograph taken before June's trip of the "Joy Luck Club," the four daughters and the three living mothers. As the screen fades, another photograph appears, with June's mother included. The spirit of the absent mother is reclaimed. I hope more mothers in our culture will be reclaimed—that they will feel their strength, like the wind's—and that their daughters will inherit the spirit of tigers.

Notes

1. Film critics such as Linda Williams (1989), Mary Ann Doane (1988) and Kaja Silverman (1990) all refer (sometimes not agreeably) to the work of Irigaray.

2. Irigaray, in *Sexes et Parentes*, defines patriarchy as "an exclusive respect for the genealogy of sons and fathers, and the competition between brothers" (in Irigaray 1991, 202). When she calls for the institution of matriarchal respect, she does not want to overturn, to replace, but to place a second genealogy alongside—two represented genders, respect for both.

3. In *Aladdin*, for instance, after the film had been drafted with the mother as a central character and a song written by Howard Ashman and Alan Menken about her, Katzenberg is reported to have said, "Eighty-six the mother. The mom's a zero" (Avins 1992, 111).

4. The "learning-to-be-a-good-mother" film is a weaker version of the prevalent "father-learning-the-benefits-of-being-a-good-family-man" theme ubiquitous in Disney films such as *Father of the Bride* (1992), *Cocktail* (1988), *FatherHood* (1993), and *Three Men and a Baby* (1987). 1993's most notable entry in this genre was not Disney's, but rather, Spielberg's *Jurassic Park*. Thanks to Mary Pharr for pointing this out to me.

5. An interesting alter-Bambi is the Don Bluth (once a Disney animator) film, *Land Before Time*, in which the mother is killed early in the narrative; unlike Bambi, Littlefoot (the "star" of *Land Before Time*) survives by remembering his mother's voice and learning to negotiate relationships with other little dinosaurs. For more insight on the animated mothers, see chapter 7 in this volume.

6. Industry magazines like *Premiere* and *Variety* hinted that Michael Eisner was, at first, not thrilled about Disney doing *The Good Mother*. It's probable that *The Good Mother* was a "vanity" flick for Nimoy; frequently when a director produces a box office hit, the studio allows that director's next film to be his choice. Since Nimoy doesn't seem like a natural pick for a film like *The Good Mother*, it's likely he chose this project.

7. The novel's didactic qualities are not accidental: "[The novel] is informed, she observes, by her moral perspective. Miller is influenced by her ecclesiastical family—her father is an ordained minister and both her grandfathers were Protestant clergymen. Several reviewers note the novel's moral viewpoint. 'It *is* a didactic book and finally that's the kind of person I am and that's the kind of writer I am,' Miller explains" (Wilson 1986, 4D).

8. A notable exception to Silverman's thesis is Martin Scorsese's *The Age of Innocence*, in which Joanne Woodward's authoritative, documentary-like voice-over is not connected to the film's diegesis or to a character's body.

9. Some films do seem to bring the male closer to the body; I am thinking in particular of David Cronenberg's films, in which the male protagonists—scientists, doctors, creators—always come into some conflict as a result of trying to separate their minds from their bodies.

10. In fact, everything Anna gains in the film (unlike the novel) is the result of a gift from a man—and the site of pleasure is moved from Anna's body to Leo's and to being

able to care for Molly; these changes make it hard for me to be much more than ambivalent about Anna's final tragedy.

11. In the novel, we are exposed to a more ordinary life between mother and daughter; Molly is not always perfect, Anna is not always perfect. At one point early in the book, Anna leaves Molly, who is about seven, asleep in the car, thinking she will only be gone for a moment. Molly wakes up crying and screaming, which Anna doesn't know until she gets back.

12. This could be seen as an "improvement" on the novel and the 1937 film version, in which Stella sets her sights on the rich Stephen Dallas and marries him to move out of her working-class life. Her working-class desires, attitudes and behaviors, however, still remain.

13. In the novel, Ying-Ying is pregnant with his son and performs an abortion on herself. I am unsure as to why the filmmakers chose to sensationalize this story; however, what is important here is Ying-Ying's struggle to live beyond her past and help her daughter.

References

Avins, Mimi. 1992. "Aladdin." *Premiere*, December: 67–69, 111.

Certeau, Michel de. 1984. *The Practice of Everyday Life*. Trans. Steven Rendell. Berkeley: University of California Press.

Doane, Mary Ann. 1988. "Woman's Stake: Filming the Female Body." In *Feminism and Film Theory*, ed. Constance Penley. New York: Routledge.

Freud, Sigmund. 1919. *Totem and Taboo*. Trans. A. A. Brill. London: Routledge.

Fuchs, Cindy. 1988. "Annie Hall Meets Stella Dallas." *Philadelphia City Paper*, 4–11 November: 22.

Irigaray, Luce. 1985a. *Speculum of the Other Woman*. Trans. Gillian C. Gill. Ithaca: Cornell University Press.

———. 1985b. *This Sex Which Is Not One*. Trans. Catherine Porter with Carolyn Burke. Ithaca: Cornell University Press.

———. 1991. *The Irigaray Reader*. Ed. Margaret Whitford. Oxford: Basil Blackwell.

Kurtz, Debra. 1988. "Roll 'Em: *The Good Mother* Asks Tough Questions." *Des Moines Skywalker*, 7 November.

Lambert, Brian. 1988. "Mothers Are Still Women." *Twin Cities Reader*, 2 November: 16.

Miller, Susan. 1986. *The Good Mother*. New York: Harper and Row.

Modleski, Tania. 1991. *Feminism without Women*. New York: Routledge.

Murphy, Patrick. 1995. " 'The Whole Wide World Was Scrubbed Clean': The Androcentric Animation of Denatured Disney." In *From Mouse to Mermaid: The Politics of Film, Gender, and Culture*, ed. Elizabeth Bell, Lynda Haas, and Laura Sells. Bloomington: Indiana University Press.

Olsen, Tillie. 1978. *Silences*. New York: Delacorte Press.

Ruddick, Sara. 1989. *Maternal Thinking: Towards a Politics of Peace*. Boston: Beacon Press.

Silverman, Kaja. 1990. "(Dis)embodying the Female Voice." In *Issues in Feminist Film Criticism*, ed. Patricia Erens. Bloomington: Indiana University Press.

Studlar, Gaylen. 1980. "Stella." In *Magills Survey of Cinema: Volume 4*. Englewood Cliffs: Salem.

Tan, Amy. 1989. *The Joy Luck Club*. New York: Putnam.

Whitford, Margaret. 1991. *Luce Irigaray: Philosophy in the Feminine*. London: Routledge.

Williams, Linda. 1989. *Hardcore: Power, Pleasure, and the "Frenzy of the Visible."* Berkeley: University of California Press.

Willis, Paul. 1979. "Shop Floor Culture, Masculinity and the Wage Form." In *Working Class Culture: Studies in History and Theory*, ed. John Clarke, Chas Critcher, and Richard Johnson. London: Hutchinson.

Wilson, Robert. 1986. "*The Good Mother* Who Loved Too Well." *USA Today*, 4 April: 4D.

Thirteen

Spinsters in Sensible Shoes
Mary Poppins and *Bedknobs and Broomsticks*

Chris Cuomo

When Mary Poppins, who is "practically perfect in every way," floats down onto the Banks family doorstep, Jane Banks sizes her up immediately. "Perhaps it's a witch," Jane wonders aloud, and though young Michael Banks reminds us that witches have brooms, the question remains—indeed, it is answered affirmatively throughout the events that follow. Walt Disney's 1964 film is based on the P. L. Travers children's classic *Mary Poppins*, published in 1934. Travers's book, and the series of Mary Poppins novels that followed it, tells the story of the nanny extraordinaire who cares for Jane and Michael Banks and the baby twins in their Victorian nursery. In the book, Poppins is curt, unsentimental, perfunctory even while creating magical realities. Disney's Poppins is sweeter (after all, she's Julie Andrews), spunkier, and not a bit maternal. Disney even gets rid of the twins in order to avoid the image of this independent nanny pushing a tram. But the fantastic tales of an amazing nanny spun by Travers become a social parable in the hands of Disney. The celluloid Poppins is on a moral mission to save a family run by a failed patriarch and an inattentive suffragette. Disney, through song and sketch, sets the story of the magical nanny in the context of English society in 1910, with its class struggles, its imperialist and racist assumptions, and its equation of British nationalism with morality, and tells us—the Disney audience—how to rise above those nasty social concerns and get back to what really matters in life: family and home.

Disney's *Bedknobs and Broomsticks* (1971) is based more loosely on two novels for children, *The Magic Bed-Knob* and *Bonfires and Broomsticks*, written by Mary Norton and first published in 1943 and 1957, respectively. In the film, which takes place during World War II, we have another story of a magical nanny, albeit a reluctant one. Eglantine Price, forced to take in three children evacuated from London, is a witch-in-training who does ride a broom (and a motorcycle), dislikes children, and lives in a huge house with her cat Cosmic Creepers. Secretly studying witchcraft through a correspondence school, Price hopes to use her mystical powers for the good of the

Crown, and has a plan to foil the Nazis with a spell for which she lacks a few magic words. Rather than interfere with her plan, as she fears they will, the children become enthusiastic accomplices. After making contact with Professor Emelius Browne, a counterfeit magician who eventually becomes the group's symbolic leader and Price's romantic interest, the group locates the requisite incantation and defends their village.

Since 1937, the Disney Studio has created immensely powerful cultural icons ranging from the innocent Snow White to the vengeful Wicked Witch. Not surprisingly, the attraction and meaningfulness of these icons often rest on the moral positions that they occupy, and some of the most central and popular Disney symbols are represented as embodying good and evil. The meanings of such cultural representations and symbols are identifiable only in terms of the manifold contexts in which they are created and received. I come to this interpretive project curious about how the moral and sexual positioning of two Disney spinsters are central to their functioning as cultural symbols. Though I believe it possible that these characters could be simply described as strong, independent women of good moral standing, these Disney spinster-witches also play out and subvert social roles and norms concerning the meanings of woman and caretaker. Here I am most interested in the kinds of moral agency represented in Mary Poppins and Eglantine Price, how the values they embody both undercut and strengthen the traditions in which they sit, and how the very fact of their spinsterhood fuels the narratives.

Both Poppins and Price are witches; they are also autonomous females who care for children while resisting becoming mothers, at least initially, and whose magic opens up new worlds of possibility. But though Disney remains faithful to Travers's ferociously independent nanny and Norton's quirkily intellectual old maid, these witches are effective not at disrupting social order but reestablishing it. Here I will explore the ways in which Disney's representations of decidedly unwomanly women serve as vehicles for the validation of traditional values and images of woman and family and how, in the end, being a strong and independent female is not tantamount to subverting the sexual status quo.

Mary Poppins: Rebel Nanny without a Feminist Cause

The film *Mary Poppins* opens with an image of a young, prim and proper Poppins sitting on a cloud, powdering her nose. In the streets below, Bert, a street performer, senses a change in the wind, and Admiral Boom, the local meteorological expert, warns of heavy weather and storms brewing at the

Banks domicile. We enter the house to find that the current nanny, Katie Nana, in her mannish dress and brusque manner, is notifying the other domestic workers of her resignation. Through the front door waltzes Winifred Banks, singing "Sister Suffragettes." This song, the first production number of the film, helps set up an underlying, fundamental tension in the story. Winifred is caught up in the excitement of the fight for women's suffrage, and her song is a nineteenth-century liberal feminist anthem. She marches about the house along with the maid and the cook, who join her song about the fight for women's votes and agree that men, on the whole, "are rather stupid."

Despite their apparent political fervor, the women of the household scramble to reestablish order before the arrival of George ("You know how The Cause infuriates Mr. Banks"), who enters his castle singing of the joys of his scheduled, orderly, consistent life. He feels like "a king astride his noble steed," returning to his "hearth and wife" where "the heirs to his dominion are bathed and fed." But it is already obvious that he is full of hot air. In actuality George Banks is a failed patriarch. His wife is a suffragette, gallivanting around the town, throwing rotten eggs at the Prime Minister, singing to Mrs. Pankhurst in prison. His children are out of control, misbehaved monsters who have driven six nannies away. Despite his assertion that his home is governed by consistency and order, the Banks household has no rule of law. This British family is on the verge of collapse. Mother is preoccupied, father is absent, and the bedrock of the Empire is in danger.

Enter Mary Poppins, whose function is to bring this household under order. The subsequent story—the success of Mary Poppins as savior of the Banks family—is predicated on the social issues of the day: feminism and the fight for women's suffrage, global British imperialism, class struggle. Mary Poppins ends up creating local order by agitating but never truly upsetting prescribed gender roles and social configurations. She is not a traditional English lady, she hangs out with the street people, she helps save an Irish fox from the redcoats, and she randomly breaks the laws of society and science. Yet she brings reconciliation rather than revolution to the Banks household. The protagonist of this moral tale erases the tension between the "modern woman" and the ideal of the stable home through both feminist and conventional values.

Disney's Mary Poppins exemplifies a kind of feminist hero who lives out ideals of women's equality by being completely assertive and autonomous—a full moral agent. She is not a stereotypically nurturant caregiver, and she attends to the needs of the Banks children without becoming a sacrificial, self-deprecating mother. Mary Poppins values herself and is not male-defined. She does not compromise her needs to her charges' desires, and instead cultivates their independence. Her femininity is easily abandoned for comfort or fun, and her affiliations are not constrained by class or even species distinctions. One could say that she embodies certain liberal feminist egalitarian values and even some radical feminist critiques of femininity.

Mary Poppins's assertive manner and morally superior attitude demand the attention of the family patriarch. She cannot be ignored. However, rather than really serving even liberal feminist goals of equality, her actions glorify the father and mark the family as the ultimate location of existential meaning. Without a radical questioning of the patriarchal family, these so-called feminist values actually serve to strengthen the father's position of power and undermine the potential for transformation symbolized by the white, upper-class British suffragette mother. (In 1910, the Pankhurst camp of the English feminist movement, the Women's Social and Political Union, had split from Millicent Garrett Fawcett's National Union of Women's Suffrage Societies because Fawcett frowned upon the violent tactics of Pankhurst, who said, "The argument of the broken pane of glass is the most valuable argument in modern politics" [Anderson and Zinsser 1988, 364]. Perhaps Winifred Banks is a closet terrorist.)

Mary Poppins does not berate Winifred for neglecting her maternal duties, but her silence on the matter does not suggest feminist solidarity. The focus of Mary Poppins's efforts is to show the father, by example and by trickery, that he is neglectful of his children, overly serious, and too caught up in the meaningless activities of capitalism and preservation of the Empire. She establishes George as the loving patriarch without directly implicating the mother, though this failure to blame is not an endorsement of Winifred's activities and neglect of family. Despite the fact that George's work is portrayed as boring and in some ultimate sense meaningless, it is necessary, and in the end his revaluing of his children is rewarded with a partnership in the bank. In the final telling, Winifred's activism warrants hardly a comment: it is portrayed as somewhat silly and ineffectual. In fact, it's not regarded as a serious threat to the family, the children, or the Crown. It can be ignored. Though Winifred is overtly feminist, and Mary Poppins embodies and enacts certain feminist ideals, no exchange occurs between them in the entire film. Poppins's only interactions with adults other than Bert, who is a pseudo-adult, are with George. The patriarch is the linchpin in the family; *his* moral reformation is what's needed to save it.

The ethical message of Mary Poppins is clear. In the face of the disintegrating family, men have an opportunity to regain control. This opportunity, however, won't be met in the bank or boardroom—it must be met in the home (though not, of course, in the nursery: that's nanny's work). The father can save the family through involvement with children and a reorganization of priorities. Mother's marching is of no significance if Father capitalizes on his rightful position as king of the castle. In fact, her "votes for women" sash is used for a kite's tail at the end of the film. What is so interesting about Disney's construction of the tale is the effectiveness of Mary Poppins as the catalyst to the process. This good witch is effective because she is so feminist—because she is such a spinster, even. She does not blame, interfere with, or attempt to change or replace Winifred. Rather than aim to please the patriarch, she tricks him by turning his own arrogance around on him. There is absolutely no sexual tension between Mary Poppins and George. She is schoolmarmish. She wears sensible shoes.

This character evokes questions about resistance to heterosexuality not only in the context of 1970s or 1990s sexual discourse in the U.S., but also in the context of Victorian feminism and its movement of politically motivated spinsters. Mary Poppins is assisted in her program by Bert, the street musician cum sidewalk scrivener cum chimney sweep. Her relationship with Bert is flirtatious, but innocent even for a Disney movie. While taking the children on an outing into a sidewalk painting, she says to him: "You never think of pressing your advantage. . . . A lady needn't fear when you are near." Bert serves as her accomplice and exonerates the spinster in the eyes of the Disney audience (some of her best friends are men), but he is not at all effective as a romantic interest for Poppins. He is merely one of the beings that worship her, along with the penguins, the pigs, and the turtles. Her returned affections are gracious; yet she is merely entertained by him.

At one point in the film, George attempts to question Mary Poppins's morality by criticizing her lack of respect for "tradition, discipline, and rules," which he fears will lead to moral disintegration. Poppins responds, in appropriate feminist fashion, by taking the moral high ground and showing him that his worship of superficial traditions will undermine what he so longs to preserve. The disintegration of what is traditionally valued, family and Empire, is avoided not by the glorification of traditional rules, but by a minor reorientation of gender roles. Specifically, given the changing roles of women, men must reorient themselves to what is rightfully theirs in order to maintain control.

A constant theme in *Mary Poppins*, and generally in the Wonderful World of Disney, is the sense of a need to return to what supposedly gives meaning to life: the warm fuzzies of family life, of flying kites, of filial affection, laughter, and merry-go-rounds, of national pride and the triumph of justice. The message of *Mary Poppins* is that *fathers* can spearhead the campaign to return to "what really matters." The film serves as a reminder of the role of patriarchal responsibility and power in the face of paranoia over the supposed demise of the family and moral disintegration. Its placement in American popular culture in 1965 is almost too perfect. Smack in the middle of what Barbara Ehrenreich (1983) has called "the collapse of the male breadwinner ethic," in the midst of the fallout from publication of *The Feminine Mystique* (Friedan 1963), Disney redirects men to their responsibilities. Not merely economic, not merely nationalistic, those responsibilities are also personal, familial, paternal. Men can have it all, and if they choose to, they can save the family—the bedrock of the Empire. Women's participation or lack of participation in "what really matters" is inconsequential.

Mary Poppins functions not as woman, but as a relatively anti-feminine conscience and guide to George Banks. She is unsentimental, remarking, "What would happen to me, may I ask, if I loved all the children I said goodbye to?" and "Practically perfect people never allow sentiment to muddle their thinking." As spinster occupying the moral high ground, as magical being exempt from the laws of science, as witch kept aloft above the sexual order of the Banks household by her black umbrella, she establishes the patriarch by unsettling him just enough to make him take notice of the shifting social scene and readjust accordingly.

The Spinster Witch in *Bedknobs and Broomsticks*

Disney female protagonists typically embody an array of feminine ideals and warnings. Counterposed against the bright faces, adoring glances, and micro-waists of Cinderella, Snow White, Belle, and Ariel the Mermaid stands a lineup of ugly, evil, female characters: the witches. Though the witch is a powerful symbol in *Mary Poppins*, the roles and meanings of the witch there are a departure from cultural stereotypes and the standard Disney formula. In *Poppins* we see a queue of stereotypical broom-riders, ugly, crotchety old white nannies dressed in black, blown away from the Banks house in a scene reminiscent of the flight of the Wicked Witch of the West, and replaced by a pretty young witch with rosy cheeks and a flower in her hat. This good witch, who arrives on the East wind, becomes the purveyor both of moral code and magical occurrences.[1]

Though the witchy Mary Poppins flies in the face of common constructions of the hag, in *Bedknobs and Broomsticks* Eglantine Price embodies both traditional and contemporary clichés regarding the witch and also the spinster. Like "that Poppins woman," Price is definitively independent, an assertive and unattached spinster. The audience is made to sense she has a secret, and this turns out (ostensibly) to be her study of witchcraft. But Price is also presented as self-made intellectual, devoted to studies that include learning to use her new flying broomstick. Having discovered the clues for a spell that will enable her to move inanimate objects, her primary goals are to complete her studies and to use magic to defend her quiet coastal village. Price does not hesitate to make clear that the presence of children will interfere with these goals.

Bedknobs and Broomsticks opens with the Soldiers of the Old Old Guard, veterans of World War I, marching into the scene singing about their reliability and courage, and asking the musical question, "Who will defend England?" They are confident in their military abilities, in their belief that only they can keep their shores safe and protected. But they are seemingly inadequate to the task, their boasting betrayed by their dated weapons. Rather, the answer to their question rides up on her sulphur-fueled motorcycle. Who is this woman who can defend the Crown, given the impotence of the Old Guard, and what are her weapons? Eglantine Price, a prim and (mostly) proper loner, intends to defend England with magic. Her persona and behavior flaunt certain norms of social order, yet she possesses her own uncompromising loyalty to tradition. Coupled with this traditionalism, Price's quirky, feminist, witchy qualities, like Poppins's, effectively maintain rather than disrupt social order.

Eglantine Price is presented as suspiciously unconventional from the start. Hinting at her own rejection of both canonical Christianity and male attention, she tells the local pastor that a visit to attend the spiritual needs of the children, Charles, Carrie, and Paul Rollins, will not be necessary. In her passionate frenzy to open a package from Professor Emelius Browne, we find revealed an excited apprentice witch lovingly embracing her first broom. Attempting a side-saddled mount of her broom, she notes that "Technically a witch is a lady, except when circumstances dictate otherwise." Failing at the more delicate mount, she ends up astride her broom.

Price is not Mother. Initially, she makes it clear that she has no desire to care for children; she does not dote and coo when presented with her temporary charges. "Children and I don't get on. Besides, I have work to do," she tells the postmistress, adding that hers is not a suitable home for children. Her manner with the children is sharp and utilitarian—she is not comfortable in their presence. When she needs to negotiate with the children, she gives them a traveling spell in exchange for their cooperation and secrecy. This spell enables Eglantine and her wards to travel via her bed, gather Emelius Browne into it, and fly to the Island of Naboombu. Here they locate a missing spell that ultimately enables military victory over the Nazis and moral victory over spinsterhood.

When he first witnesses Eglantine's proficiency in the lessons from his own bogus school of witchcraft, Browne is surprised that the spells, jazzed-up "nonsense words out of an old book," really work for her. The implication is that she is a real witch, perhaps with some sort of natural ability, and that he is incapable of truly working magic. He initially reacts to the traveling bed with disbelief, but even after witnessing its authenticity remains hesitant and fearful. Of course the power of the imagery should not be lost here: Eglantine's bed is the most dramatic and stark representation of her magical power, and hence her witchy, spinsterly identity. Emelius's hesitation and fear are logical—his role is to subvert that power and Price's identity.

During her early interactions with Emelius, Eglantine stands firm in her independence, her professional self-assuredness, her refusal to take up his amorous attention. Though Browne flirts with her immediately upon meeting her—this appears to be his standard *modus operandi*—she shows no interest, and comes off as humorless and asexual. Price's initial lack of heterosexual response is logically interwoven with the seriousness with which she attends her work.

But things change between Price and Browne, and her increased intimacy with him causes her power to fade as his swells. Her independence, her magical abilities, and her resistance to heterosexuality are reduced as her relationship with the children develops, and they further decompose when she allows the magician's collaboration in her plan. Soon after their initial encounter he sings "I'm your man" to an aloof Eglantine (as she pores over shelves of texts). Then, during the trip to Naboombu, complete with exotic encounters and prefaced by a foray into the sea, significant shifting occurs. Ultimately it is in the water that the two vital transformations begin for Price: she gets distracted from her mission for the very first time, and concurrently, she begins to get romantically attached to Browne. They are aware that the fantasy and emotive space of the water enables this. They sing that in the water "they get along swimmingly" and "could even fall in love." On the island, Browne continues the transformation that began in the water. He becomes a hero, takes control of the search for the spell, and acquires a more masculine self-assurance.

After the trip to Naboombu, as Browne wins Eglantine over, her magical ability wanes. Though they successfully acquire the spell for substantiary locomotion, granting Price the ability to give inanimate objects "a life force of their own," she is unable to make the spell work herself. Earlier it seemed that Price was the true possessor of magical power, but now Browne tells her that her approach is too "old fashioned," and she is only able to implement the spell with his assistance. The children are impressed with his ability to make this humorless woman laugh and grateful for his sausage and mash. When the postmistress unexpectedly returns to retrieve the children, they say they want to stay because they "have a dad now." Their naming of Browne as father articulates the shift in the sexual order and the domestication of Price.

Finally, Browne becomes the possessor of full magical ability and masculine power. In the midst of the Nazi raid and after finding within himself both virility and belief in magic, he is able at last to turn himself into a rabbit. His encouragement motivates Price actually to use the substantiary locomotion spell against the German soldiers. And though the spell is successful and she leads a troop of ghosts into battle, it is clear that her success now depends on his assistance. By the end of the story, the Eglantine we met earlier has all but vanished. When her magic broom gets bombed in battle, she falls from her broom and is no longer able to fly. When pulled from a bush by Browne she gratefully exclaims, "Dear Mr. Browne!" She realizes she cannot work magic but is glad that she was able to perform some small service and then admits to having known some time ago that she "could never be a proper witch." He asks if she knew "that first magic moment when you first laid eyes on me?" in bald admission of the connection between her magic and her previous resistance to heterosexuality. Eglantine now succumbs to the romantic advances of the Professor and gazes lovingly at the children, but she has done what really matters, having fought the forces of evil on the battlefield and also within herself. She is now coupled with a man and firmly positioned as Mother.

As in *Mary Poppins*, both family and Empire are saved concurrently, and like Mary Poppins, Eglantine Price is cast as a spinsterly savior in this children's story. Her dedication to the Craft is inextricably linked to her loyalty to the British Crown, her single-mindedness a result of her feeling that she is on a mission to help save England. But unlike Poppins, Price ultimately cannot accomplish her goals single-handedly. The aid of the Rollins children, and even more important, Emelius Browne, are necessary for her success. Her "success"—her loyalty to the Crown and to traditional order—depends, in the end, on this group becoming a family. In the final scene Eglantine kisses Emelius good-bye as he goes off to fight with the Old Guard. So despite the fact that the members of the Old Guard are fakes who mistakenly believe they have defeated the Germans, they represent a traditional order that nonetheless endures. Browne's enlistment is a reminder of the impenetrability of that tradition. Eglantine Price, a woman, can defend England, but only clandestinely, as a member of a family.

But Price's witchiness—her ability to change boys and men into rabbits and to fly, the strange items in her basement, and her stereotypical old maidliness—her seeming inability to be distracted by fun and frolic, her preference for healthy, vegetarian foods, her solitude—enable her effectiveness as the protagonist of this Disney tale. It is Price's independence, her commitment, her quirkiness, that motivate the plot. Her desire to learn witchcraft and to help in the war effort actually fuels the story and the unlikely adventures; her desire opens up the possibility of adventure, extraordinary occurrences, and the break from the horrors of war and the norms of class. Her pseudo-feminist sensibilities, reminiscent of Mary Poppins's, drive her and ensure the success of the story. She is given these children merely because she is a woman, but she defies so many norms of motherhood that the children get to escape the mundane. In fact, Price's independence and commitment are so realistic and strong that she must be undermined by the end of the story if she is to be an appropriate Disney model of femininity. The family must be the end product for this story to work as a Disney fantasy: Family created, Empire saved, Gender order reestablished.

Lesbian Subtexts: The Opaque Spinster

In *The Spinster and Her Enemies*, Sheila Jeffries argues that "any attack on the spinster is inevitably an attack on the lesbian" (1985, 100). Could it be argued that any representation of the spinster is an implicit representation of the lesbian? While I do not want to conflate meanings embedded in representations of spinsters and of lesbians, the concept of the spinster has historically enabled the invisibility of lesbians and lesbian sexuality. This fact, coupled with the significant overlap in stereotypic conceptions of spinsters and lesbians, makes it worthwhile to ask how representations of the spinster point to lesbian possibilities.

To a contemporary dyke audience (whatever on earth *that* might be), Eglantine Price is strongly coded as a stereotypical white middle- or upper-class lesbian. Like Katie Nana, Price has a classic lesbian look and no feminine fluff, and is tailored, direct in manner, and stiff in posture. Villagers are wondering whether she'll ever have a (male) romantic interest. Her manner with the children is direct, unsentimental. In may ways Eglantine embodies negative Western cultural stereotypes of the lesbian: drab, humorless, willing to sacrifice pleasure for the greater good, obsessively intellectual, private, and asexual. Even her diet, which includes cabbage buds, rose hips, glyssop seed, elm bark, and stewed nettles and bran porridge, fits the contemporary and historical constructions of the puritanical, health-obsessed or vegetarian lesbian-feminist. Beyond her desire to foil the Nazis and complete her lessons, she seems passionless. Most significantly, she is confident in the fact that she does not need a man and is uninterested in male attention. Her initial response upon actually meeting Browne is condescending: she has no patience for the fake magician and sees through his charade.

A central aspect of the narrative foundation of *Bedknobs and Broomsticks* is the fact that Eglantine Price has a secret. But is her study of witchcraft all there is to this secret? Price's lack of heterosexual interest is highlighted at the very beginning of the film and remains centrally important throughout. She tells the children, "I live alone. It suits my purpose." And when young Charles says, "Game's up, Miss Price. We know what you are," the implications loom large and stay present in the background. What is she, anyway? Certainly she is not a "normal" woman.

Both Price and Poppins participate in the supernatural. They fly, work magic, and bring others to strange and wonderful places. Each film contains a central scene in which objects are made to move as if occupied by ghosts. In fact, Eglantine Price leads an entire army of ghosts into battle. Terry Castle, in *The Apparitional Lesbian* (1993), argues that the lesbian has been characterized as or associated with the ghost in modern and contemporary Western culture. Her analysis of portrayals of lesbians suggests that there are ways in which the characterizations of both Mary Poppins and Eglantine Price resonate with both homophobic and friendly representations of ghostly and witchy lesbians in the history of Western literature and film.

The spinster-witch of *Bedknobs and Broomsticks* appears within a more realistic framework than Mary Poppins. She doesn't float down from a cloud, and her magic is anything but seamless. She is a woman and a citizen. Her magic is pedestrian, not very mysterious, and requires a book of spells. Because of this realistic context, and her near-perfect fit into lesbian stereotypes, her transformation is necessary for a satisfactory Disney ending. Eglantine is coded so strongly as a real lesbian, that her heterosexuality must eventually be firmly established. Unlike Poppins, who remains unbound by sentiment and familial roles and is able to disappear by floating up and away from the Banks household, Price is from and will remain in the real world. She cannot remain there as spinster-witch; she must be changed into mother-wife. Eglantine Price, the dykey witch, is finally reduced to Mother, while the spinsterly Mary Poppins flies away in avoidance of the trappings of maternal love.

Notes

The author offers spoons full of sugar in thanks for the helpful comments of Karla Goldman and other participants in the Women's Studies Mini-Conference on Popular Culture, University of Cincinnati, April 1993.

1. The symbolic and cinematic connections between *Mary Poppins* and *The Wizard of Oz* (1939) are many, and their careful consideration would produce a fascinating essay.

References

Anderson, Bonnie S., and Judith P. Zinsser. 1988. *A History of Their Own: Women in Europe*. New York: Harper and Row.

Castle, Terry. 1993. *The Apparitional Lesbian: Female Homosexuality and Modern Culture*. New York: Columbia University Press.

Ehrenreich, Barbara. 1983. *The Hearts of Men: American Dreams and the Flight from Commitment*. Garden City, NY: Anchor Press.

Faderman, Lillian. 1981. *Surpassing the Love of Men: Romantic Friendship and Love between Women from the Renaissance to the Present*. New York: Morrow.

Friedan, Betty. 1963. *The Feminine Mystique*. New York: Norton.

Fuss, Diana, ed. 1991. *Inside/Out: Lesbian Theories, Gay Theories*. New York: Routledge.

Jeffries, Sheila. 1985. *The Spinster and Her Enemies: Feminism and Sexuality 1880–1930*. London: Pandora Press.

Norton, Mary. 1943. *The Magic Bed-Knob*. New York: Harcourt, Brace and World.

———. 1957. *Bonfires and Broomsticks*. New York: Harcourt, Brace and World.

Travers, P. L. (1934) 1981. *Mary Poppins*. New York: Dell Publishing.

Fourteen

Pretty Woman through the Triple Lens of Black Feminist Spectatorship

D. Soyini Madison

Africanism is the vehicle by which the American self knows itself as not enslaved, but free; not repulsive, but desirable; not helpless, but licensed and powerful; not a blind accident of evolution, but a progressive fulfillment of destiny.

—Toni Morrison

Black women are employed, if not sacrificed, to humanize their white superordinates, to teach them something about the content of their own subject positions.

—Valerie Smith

In viewing a film, the black feminist spectator gazes at the images, plot, and meanings unfolding before her through a lens formed out of an awareness that race, gender, and class are inextricable as sites of struggle in the world and that they operate variously in all symbolic acts. As a spectator she sits before the screen, all the while reading what she watches through a consciousness of the profound confluence of what it means to be underclass, to be woman, and to be black. Whether she is witness to cultural representations wherein these factors are prominently manifest or deliberately made to appear nonexistent, the black feminist spectator carries her ideology with her and is focused on the interworkings of these "isms"—projected or masked—on all human representation and action. Black feminist critics are in a kind of "third wave" of analysis that is focused, not so much on the invisibility or the silencing of the black female voice, as on the ways specific conceptualizations of literary and cultural study are fostered and institutionalized and how the effects of race, class, and gender operate on the practice of criticism.

Valerie Smith discusses the methods entailed in this black feminist perspective:

These methods are necessarily flexible, holding in balance the three variables of race, gender, and class and destabilizing the centrality of any one. More generally, they call into question a variety of standards of valu-

Pretty Woman and Black Feminist Spectatorship

ation that mainstream feminist and androcentric Afro-American theory might naturalize. (1991, 47)

Black feminist spectatorship proceeds by illuminating certain rhetorical and aesthetic elements of a film by underscoring how these elements engage, enlighten, and serve specific populations and communities. This perspective also interrogates certain presumptions reflected in popular culture and the power of its icons, messages, and popularity "to do violence to people" on the interpenetrating levels of race, class, and gender (hooks 1992, 117). The black feminist critic and spectator grounds her critical and theoretical work in contributing to the material struggles of communities and populations whose identities and self-determination are under threat.[1] The charge of black feminist spectatorship, then, is to help "recreate the bonds between the text and the world" (Said 1983, 175). Proceeding from this charge, what better place is there to begin than with the recycled fairy tales of Hollywood where millions find refuge, inspiration, and new identities beyond that of "real" time and space.[2]

Touchstone Pictures' *Pretty Woman* (1990), with its fairy tale–princess plot of a very attractive street hooker rescued by a handsome corporate raider, evokes important questions for black feminist spectatorship. On the one hand, the film reflects aspects of society's changing attitudes and ambivalence concerning women's autonomy and sexuality, as well as values associated with class differences; on the other hand, it takes these same issues and resolves them by ultimately upholding traditional, hegemonic conceptions and practices regarding marriage, chivalry, and consumer capitalism. The film relies on chauvinistic fairy tales of romance, alienation, masculinity, femininity, and wealth, while presenting these ideas in a pseudo-feminist package that says "up in your face" to female chastity. The initial motto of the film's heroine expresses a pseudo-feminist sentiment of sexual self-reliance and control: "We say who. We say when. We say how much." Willful, smart, independent, sexually uninhibited, and self-employed, Vivian's portrayal is glossed to appeal to "today's woman," but she is still a hooker and a member of the underclass. Therefore, it is through Edward, the prince, that Vivian must be transformed. She becomes a proper lady, gains higher ambitions, and, presumably, becomes his wife. But in this post-feminist era, since today's female audiences must witness some semblance of reciprocity for the contemporary fairy tale to be successful, Vivian in turn transforms Edward into a more sensitive human being (she "rescues him right back"), thereby making him a more humane capitalist.

The ways in which feminist agendas are easily appropriated and class issues

D. Soyini Madison

easily elided in this contemporary tale suggest that the politics of race are not absent in Touchstone's *Pretty Woman*. According to Toni Morrison, "even, and especially, when American texts are not 'about' Africanist presences or character or narrative or idiom, the shadow hovers in implication, in sign, in line or demarcation" (1992, 46). For the black feminist spectator, when Edward meets Vivian, a Pandora's box of gender, racial, and economic implications relative to power issues is opened, exposing Hollywood's glittery facade of myth and fantasy. The triple lens of black feminist spectatorship, a way of looking at *Pretty Woman*, denaturalizes the universality of the marriage plot and creates a place for critical intervention in the myths of beauty that disempower all women.

The First Lens: Transcendence

Feminists of color view white women as heroines or fairy-tale princesses through a kind of triple lens that develops as part of our survival and adaptability to dominant culture's myths and norms. At one level, we temporarily suspend or displace a very real awareness of racial difference for a universal consciousness of sorts in order at least to have the experience. We know these characters don't look like us; we may even know that if they did, the story could not exist. But we are engaged, because there are moments when passion and yearnings transcend race distinctions, and we empathize with those human feelings.

Pretty Woman, in its contemporary Hollywood packaging, mirrors certain basic myths few American girls—"colored" or white, rich or poor—can escape: a beautiful girl, stigmatized in some way, is rescued and thereby actualized by a handsome, rich, adoring man; the Pygmalion transformation of a downtrodden, unpolished, poor girl into a refined, elegant, and glamorous lady; and the lauded prince—the "good catch"—finally made truly happy by attaining the beautiful damsel he so gallantly rescues. Although the boy-meets-girl plot is an old one, it seems never to lose its appeal, whether we experience it in the "high" culture of opera or in the "low" culture of soap opera. Beginning with Snow White who sings "Some day my prince will come," the theme has been quintessential Disney. The theme prevails with *Pretty Woman* credited as one of the highest grossing movies ever made (Radner 1993).

Since cultural symbols serve as mediators and reservoirs of meaning (see, e.g., Geertz [1973], Rosaldo [1989], Turner [1982]), they affirm and help us understand our place in the "real" world, along with contributing to the formulations of our dreams and imaginings. As one of the largest commercial producers of cultural symbols, Disney film obviously has the potential to reflect, enhance, and subvert our understandings of our real lifeworlds as well as our fantasies. Given Disney's stronghold on fairy tale–princess plots, it should be no surprise that Touchstone's first release, *Splash* (1984), is a live-action adult version of the fairy tale, *The Little Mermaid* (1989). With its second release, *Pretty Woman*, Disney's Touchstone established itself as a financially successful production company. With its modern, fairy tale–princess storehouse of symbols and meanings, *Pretty Woman* discloses a possible world that continues to celebrate and reinscribe the dominant American narrative of marriage and romance. American women grew up with the marriage-plot fairy tale, and for some more than others, to be beautiful, to be adored by a special man, and to live with him happily ever after is a fairy tale turned life goal. *Pretty Woman* reinscribes in live action the Cinderella fairy tale of heterosexual love and marriage as the ultimate resolution for a fulfilled life, particularly for women. Although these fairy-tale motifs are charmingly played out on the silver screen, underneath all the glamour and hype linger serious questions regarding value, identity, and power. *Pretty Woman* evokes a discussion of these larger issues because when the rich, corporate-raider prince meets the poor, underclass prostitute, two worldviews collide, opening a dialectic of competing and contrasting values. The added twist for black feminist spectatorship, however, is that beyond the harm of the ubiquity and regression of this master narrative in limiting the aspirations, life goals, and imaginations of all women, it insidiously categorizes and isolates women (and men) to specific character types. The prince and princess also "look" and "act" and "desire" according to specific norms— they are always white or nubile or beautiful (most often all three); one or the other or both are aristocrats or transformed into aristocrats; and, they are always heterosexual.

Since this master narrative does not represent everyone, it would follow that men and women who do not fit these norms should then be exempt from the influences of the traditional marriage-plot ethic with its culmination of heterosexual love through marriage as the ultimate happy ending in both life and fantasy. But ironically they are not. Rather they are marked twofold by its effects. Those outside the norm internalize the myth of the happy endings, as well as the stigma that, while they must live the myth to be happy and fulfilled, they do not meet criteria of the myth—the glamour, elegance, sexuality, beauty, and drama of its characters. They are instead shadow characters or marginal substitutes. Though they may consciously or unconsciously aspire to live the prince and princess myth, even in their fantasies they are only too conscious that they do not fit the description of the

D. Soyini Madison

true hero and heroine. The possibilities for transcending racial difference in the first, empathetic lens of black feminist spectatorship are cut short. The pleasures of experiencing *Pretty Woman* are in constant tension with the realities of normative categories and characters, especially for women of color.

The Second Lens: Metacriticism

At another level, while racial difference is suspended—though obviously never completely obliterated despite universal commonalities—we are criticizing meanings and symbols from our historical subject positions of race and class. We can be drawn into a fictive world while simultaneously criticizing how our identities, traditions, and experiences are masked and misrepresented inside that world. Living the polarities of inclusion and exclusion, seeing ourselves exoticized and vilified, and having to reside within the symbols and codes of both dominant and disenfranchised communities, evokes a "double consciousness" that reflects critiques of intervention that can examine a text or film from an insider/outsider perspective, but more important, is always turning the critique upon itself in a form of metacriticism. The assumptions made by the insider perspective are always under watch by the presence of the outsider perspective and vice versa. Black feminist spectatorship, then, offers a double-edged critique that by its nature is always asking questions from its position of inside/outside and then questioning the questions from its position of outside/inside. Black feminist criticism does not separate from its analysis implications of race and race privilege regardless of whether the texts under examination are explicitly racial or not. It is understood that whether one is white, yellow, red, or black, race is never erased in social interaction and cultural identity. Although the significance of race is a factor in analysis, the black feminist critic cannot focus on race absent class and gender issues. Since gender and race influence how one's meanings and interpretations are formed, the structures, implications, and productions arising from the political economy that undergird many of the inequities surrounding race and gender must be understood through a recognition of class differences.

As we look at *Pretty Woman*, we see that for the sake of romantic comedy, the film reflects relatively clear demarcations of classes and races only to trivialize them—the "haves" with their opportunities and opulence and the "have-nots" with their murdered prostitutes thrown in dumpsters, their night life, and their drugs, are elements juxtaposed for the purpose of unfolding the fairy-tale romance. The film gives us a few quick glimpses into the dark "bad" world of prostitution as the detective inquires about the dead crack addict, Skinny Marie. But the realities of drugs, murdered prostitutes, and the exploitation on Hollywood Boulevard are not the purpose of the film; fantasy is. Any hints of underclass grime or crime are glossed over as the film quickly shifts to the glitter and glamour of the "haves." The spectator is then brought into bourgeois affinities for appearances, "high" culture, luxury, and power. Although this glamour world is on display with its own bad guys, it is still the world that reforms our pretty princess and the world in which our prince reigns supreme. Through the world of rich men, opera, and big deals, the film tells us "dreams come true," suggesting that a little mixing up of the classes can be a good thing, especially if the people are "pretty." So as the film attempts to counter the prince/princess myth with a few popular feminist clichés, it also attempts to give a "nod at realities of social difference," but ultimately goes on to obfuscate them (DeMott 1991). Benjamin DeMott observes: "This country has an ignoble tradition of evading social facts—pretending that individual episodes of upward mobility obviate grappling with the hardening of socio-economic differences in our midst" (1).

Class privilege is best illustrated in the central "Pretty Woman" scene in the film, in which Edward defends Vivian against snobbish elites who shamelessly insult her for looking "low class." After learning that an exclusive shop on Rodeo Drive refused to serve Vivian and asked her to leave because "we cannot help you here," the outraged Edward returns in person with her. Coolly announcing to a shop manager who he is, Edward asks whether the manager has anything in the shop as beautiful as Vivian. The manager, frightened and intimidated by Edward, says no. Edward announces he will spend a "vulgar" amount of money for anything she fancies and demands that the salespeople attend to her every wish and whim. They do. The camera flashes on Vivian trying on various outfits to the tune of "Pretty Woman" while the salespeople scurry to serve her. This is sweet retribution on Vivian's behalf all due to Edward's money and class privilege.

Shouldn't the audience gain some pleasure and satisfaction in seeing the Rodeo Drive snobs squirm? Or should they be repelled by the chauvinistic paternalism and material ostentatiousness of Edward's wealth? Either attitudinal choice is grounded in the surety that Vivian's pivotal transformation from low-class whore to high-class mistress takes place when she goes shopping with Edward's money. Hilary Radner observes that, "In *Pretty Woman*, the new heterosexual contract is not, then, based on female chastity. Rather it is based on the 'world's oldest profession,' on the exchange of female sex for male property" (1993, 62). Radner goes on to make the point that through Edward's money, Vivian's "transformation from prostitute to a

D. Soyini Madison

woman of privilege is effected solely through her ability to purchase and wear fashionable garments" (67).[3]

What Radner fails to consider in her analysis of gender and class issues in this economic exchange is the implicit impact of race. Vivian's being stared at in an exclusive hotel and being asked to leave a boutique seem contrived and a little silly to black women who experience this kind of humiliation constantly in various forms no matter *how* they are dressed. For Vivian, class discrimination is turned to wonder and glowing admiration by merely changing her style and fashion. Money and clothes mark the beginning of Vivian as a seriously desirable princess, reinforcing the idea that "little girls learn to desire by being desired" (Wolf 1991, 157). Vivian's race is not a subject of explicit significance in the film; however, it *is* fundamentally significant that only because she is a white woman, a "pretty" white woman, can the plot unfold in the manner that it does.

In *Pretty Woman*, race seems erased or displaced. The black characters in total—a party guest, a prostitute, a pimp, a chauffeur, and the street talker—all play minimal roles, and all effectively reflect the peripheral importance of black people in white people's stories and lives. One need only mentally substitute a beautiful black woman in Vivian's role to understand how thoroughly racial difference and its absence informs this contemporary fairy tale as an important commentary on sexual, economic, and political constructions of difference. The second lens of black feminist spectatorship is a critical act that both interrogates the misrepresentations and erasures as it imagines the possibilities, and violence, of other constructions.

The Third Lens: Oppositional Gaze

This brings us to the third level. While black feminist spectatorship holds in tension an empathetic perspective, a critical perspective *and* a self-critical perspective, this means that as we look with an oppositional gaze at the way patriarchy and racism operate against women of color, we can point to the way patriarchy has also simultaneously denigrated *and* pedestaled white women. Black feminist criticism acknowledges that white women are victims of similar yet different polarities in a sexist and racist society as "objects" of both glorification and dishonor—sanction and censure—in being of the same race as but of a different sex from the men who construct and enforce dominating rules and discourses. Because of the analysis and insights black women can bring to the discussion of patriarchy, particularly in the manner it is further reinforced by racism, it is unfortunate that many popular feminist critiques still do not acknowledge black women's spectatorship or seem to take seriously black feminist criticism. bell hook states:

> Mainstream feminist film criticism in no way acknowledges black female spectatorship. It does not even consider the possibility that women can construct an oppositional gaze via an understanding and awareness of the politics of race and racism. Feminist film theory rooted in an ahistorical psychoanalytic framework that privileges sexual difference actively suppresses recognition of race, reenacting and mirroring the erasure of black womanhood that occurs in films, silencing any discussion of racial difference. . . . Many feminist film critics continue to structure their discourse as though it speaks about "women" when in actuality it speaks only about white women. (1992, 123)

The problem with such an erasure of black women's perspectives is that important insights and intellectual assessments that could extend and deepen white women's understanding of their own behaviors and cultural productions are cut short. The critical black feminist spectator then looks through what may appear to be paradoxical lenses: the humanist lens as she empathizes with universal human conditions unfolding before her; the lens of race and class consciousness, as a person of color, aware of the political economy and its impact upon race; the lens of feminism, understanding that patriarchy constrains and misrepresents white women and women of color the same and variously. As a result, these lenses function to critique and interrogate, as hooks further explains:

> the existence of black women within white supremacist culture problematizes and makes more complex, the overall issues of female identity, representation, and spectatorship. . . . Identifying with neither the phallocentric gaze nor the construction of white womanhood as lack, critical black female spectators construct a theory of looking where cinematic visual delight is the pleasure of interrogation. (1992, p. 126)

This "pleasure of interrogation" means that the pleasure of looking is inseparable from critical judgment, and that the symbols and messages being disclosed when we look critically are under the scrutiny of our judgments as women, as people of color, and as humanists.

The ways in which Vivian's character is disclosed—a pretty, white woman who just happens to earn her living as a prostitute—are carefully choreographed to distance her from grime and crime. At first glance, it would seem that a bold, unchaste, street hooker would disqualify as princess, but she becomes an acceptable princess heroine because, after all, she is beautiful and white and *clean*: she flosses her teeth, she doesn't kiss on the mouth, she doesn't use drugs, and she uses color-coded condoms. She is also pure at heart, whimsical, and although sassy, she is sweetly spirited and can appreciate both the low farce of *I Love Lucy* and the high art of opera. Vivian's persona is constructed to counter our notions of the "bad" girl as whore. She may be a bad girl, but she is a "good" bad girl. Real bad girls are generally understood as lewd, lecherous, and lascivious. The whore and the bad girl have conventionally been outcasts, their very presence allowing the civility and chastity that characterizes good girls. Nonetheless, the bad girl has always been a bit of an enigma in patriarchal societies, for although she may be a formal outcast to some, she is exciting and intriguing to others. Vivian's bad girl sexuality is a point of scorn, resentment, and dismissal for some characters in the film, but at the same time compelling for Edward and several others. With its characteristic sanitizing gesture, however, Disney desexualizes Vivian's bad girl occupation: She is never shown engaging in sex with another man or soliciting customers on the street. When she refuses Edward's money, she breaks the explicit economic contract of their initial relationship. The film is careful to distance Vivian from the serious, bad girl hooker, because, after all, real street hookers are "soiled" women—equated with uncleanliness, disease, and drugs. Her monogamous relationship with Edward and her staunch defense of that loyalty in her confrontation with Edward's attorney further distance Vivian from the licensed promiscuity of prostitution.

So in the fashion of the romantic comedy, Vivian provides the titillation of a bad girl, but none of the grime. Black feminist spectatorship, however, can inform cultural, racial, gender, and class issues in the definition of "pretty." Vivian can only be a pretty woman because she is white; she can only be a pretty woman because of the benefit of class; she can only be a pretty woman because she is desired by a rich, white male. So, the film moves to the opulence of Edward's Beverly Hills suite where our heroine, Vivian, the clean, safe, drug-free, happy hooker, will be transformed into a princess by her prince, never to return to the world of bad girls again.

This confluence of race, gender, and class brings us to another set of symbols and messages intervening on women's identity and culture—the myth of female beauty. Through a black feminist lens, we may look at what writer Naomi Wolf calls the "beauty myth":

> This is not a conspiracy theory; it doesn't have to be. A backlash against
> women's advancement does not originate in a smoke-filled room; it is
> often unconscious and reflexive, like racism. A backlash against feminism
> that uses an ideology about beauty to keep women down is not an organ-

Pretty Woman and Black Feminist Spectatorship

ized conspiracy with maps and pins, but a generalized atmosphere in which men's fears and women's guilt are addressed and elaborated through the culture's images of women, and its messages to women about their relationship between their value and their bodies. . . . The beauty myth tells a story: the quality called "beauty" objectively and universally exists. Women must want to embody it and men must want to possess women who embody it. This embodiment is an imperative for women and not for men. (Wolf 1991, 3–12)

As women gain in economic and political status, we are beginning to displace the feminine mystique of the "happy housewife," and in the case of *Pretty Woman*, "the happy hooker," yet we continue to be confronted with standards of beauty and appearance more oppressive than the generations that preceded us. Naomi Wolf states, "The more legal and material hindrances women have broken through, the more strictly and heavily and cruelly images of female beauty have come to weigh upon us" (10). While popular films may be telling stories about self-possessed women, they must generally meet certain standards of beauty; since as little girls "we understood that stories whether interesting or not only happen to beautiful women" (61).

Vivian may gain ambition and decide to go back to school to make a better life for herself, but all the while gestures, innuendoes, and declarations of her beauty are ever present, even to the very end. Wolf uses John Berger's well-known quotation to remind us that, "Men look at women. Women watch themselves being looked at. This determines not only the relations of men to women, but the relation of women to themselves" (quoted in Wolf 1988, 58). When Vivian returns to the hotel with Edward's purchases, the looking and watching are central to the film's transformation of Vivian in the eyes of others and in her own self-appraisal. This "looking," however, takes still another form when women of color watch white women being looked at. Women of color are not always required to succumb to the same beauty myth that constrains white women, yet, ironically, we are further marginalized by media and society because we are, for the most part, outside the myth. The beauty myth is centered on white women and is therefore a standard of beauty only achievable by and awardable to them.

Since femininity and womanhood are too often valued by the myth's white standards of beauty, women of color who come closest to the standard are more admired for having those qualities. The insidiousness of the myth is that it is oppressive for the women it targets as well as those it ignores. In each case, womanhood is valued or devalued by shutting out virtuality and personhood.

D. Soyini Madison

Conclusion

This modern day fairy tale certainly celebrates traditional notions of romance and marriage, and Edward's capacity for opulence makes it all the more classic and appealing; however, in the 1990s and against the backdrop of feminism and a heightened sensitivity around issues of difference, it is no longer easy for the majority of audiences to accept wholesale images of the damsel rescued by her prince. As a result, films are attempting to interject hints of women's independence and reciprocity. The fact that Vivian doesn't have a pimp, drives a Lotus like a pro, mocks genteel pretentiousness, transforms Edward into more of a human being, and says that she is rescuing him "right back" are all efforts to bring this fairy tale into the '90s. Nonetheless, Vivian remains, as film critic John Koch states, "Man's creation, shaped and endowed with value by him and his bottomless bank account" (1991, 107). For the purpose of this essay, we might amend Koch's statement to claim that Vivian is very much a *Disney* creation. As in other Disney films, race, gender, and class issues are constantly obviated in the universalities of romantic fairy tales turned upward mobility success stories.

The triple lens of black feminist spectatorship is a critical perspective that simultaneously transcends, critiques, and teaches how the intersections of race, class, and gender are inescapable, especially in boy-meets-girl plots of the '90s. This is a lens of ambivalence and outsiderhood that understands the insidiousness of exclusionary "happily ever afters" and the absences of voices and lives of color in those scenarios. This is a lens that knows that the cultural adoration for the beauty, femininity, and sensuality displayed on film for white women is an adoration reserved for them, but at the same time aware that it disempowers the very women it props on its precarious pedestal.

Notes

1. The black feminist critic, therefore, works within the tradition of the organic intellectual: "by closely aligning [her] theoretical work with [her] identified social group's internal struggles for self-empowerment and local sovereignty, [the organic intellectual] can ideally generate counter-theories of social and cultural processes" (Strine 1991, 193). Strine further states that organic intellectuals provide "explanations that are at once historically grounded, contextually nuanced, and politically emancipating" (193).

2. The term "recycled fairy tales" is from Bremner (1991).

3. Radner argues that Vivian's ability to "look good" in expensive clothing "takes the

place of the glass slipper . . . the capacity to wear the glass slipper has been transformed into the capacity to wear fashionable clothing" (67).

References

Berger, John. 1988. *Ways of Seeing*. London: Penguin Books.

Bremner, Charles. 1991. "Looking towards Bette Davis Size." *New York Times*, 25 May.

DeMott, Benjamin. 1991. "In Hollywood, Class Doesn't Put Up Much of a Struggle." *New York Times*, 20 January.

Geertz, Clifford. 1973. *The Interpretation of Cultures*. New York: Basic Books.

hooks, bell. 1992. *Black Looks: Race and Representation*. Boston: South End Press.

Koch, John. 1991. "Films' Fatal Attraction to Pretty Women." *The Boston Globe*, 14 February.

Morrison, Toni. 1992. *Playing in the Dark*. Cambridge: Harvard University Press.

Radner, Hilary. 1993. "Pretty Is as Pretty Does: Free Enterprise and the Marriage Plot." In *Film Theory Goes to the Movies*, ed. Jim Collins, Hilary Radner, and Ava Preacher Collins. New York: Routledge.

Rosaldo, Renato. 1989. *Culture and Truth: The Remaking of Social Analysis*. Boston: Beacon.

Said, Edward. 1983. *The World, the Text, and the Critic*. Cambridge: Harvard University Press.

Smith, Valerie. 1991. "Black Feminist Theory and the Representation of the 'Other.' " In *Changing Our Own Words: Essays on Criticism, Theory, and Writing by Black Women*, ed. Cheryl A. Wall. New Brunswick: Rutgers University Press.

Strine, Mary. 1991. "Critical Theory and 'Organic' Intellectuals: Reframing the Work of Cultural Critique." *Communication Monographs* 58 (2): 195–201.

Turner, Victor. 1982. *From Ritual to Theatre: The Human Seriousness of Play*. New York: Performing Arts Journal Publications.

Wall, Cheryl A., ed. 1991. *Changing Our Own Words*. New Brunswick: Rutgers University Press.

Wolf, Naomi. 1991. *The Beauty Myth: How Images of Beauty Are Used against Women*. New York: Doubleday.

Fifteen

Pachuco Mickey

Ramona Fernandez

There is a place where for an admission fee of about thirty-five dollars at an average cost of two-fifty per hour for up to fourteen hours a day, the spectator can choke down as much as fourteen miles[1] of film image projected on screens of unimaginable diversity, employing every means available for display. The films are rarely delivered in a standard 35mm or 70mm format. Instead, the spectator's visual field is filled by 120°, 180°, 360° screens, by screens that rotate in complex patterns, by collections of screens uniquely arranged and constructed, by screens appearing in odd and unexpected places, of all shapes and sizes, in tunnels, in waiting rooms, in the midst of dioramas. In this place, films are delivered via interactive computer networks, videotape and videodisc; they are displayed in 3D and embedded in nonfilm displays of extreme complexity. In this place, the spectator can saturate herself, welcome disorientation, and willingly dissolve into a meticulously constructed environment. This place is EPCOT Center at Walt Disney World, a theme park cum world exposition, a kind of world's fair that allows for a continual Disneyesque rewriting of history, a Distory, as Stephen Fjellman has called it. Disney World offers its guests multiple pleasures within the context of Disneyesque representations of race and gender. Distory is presented in a framework of disorientation; indeed, its dominant mode is disorientation. Hence this essay's conscious anarchy.

Although WDW is unlike any other topos on the planet, it reflects an image of what we arrogantly call America. Despite Disney's explicit fakery and its implicit message that it is constructing a place apart, Disney World is a distillation of postmodern everyday reality with the horror excised. Disney attempts to create a world where we feel safe and completely unthreatened. Any fright here is fright for fun. Except for this caveat, Disney and the postmodern American landscape are coextensive. Purposely exporting itself far and wide, its success at this has created a Disney shopping mall reality. Disney "reality" has permeated our cultural aesthetic—or perhaps it is more accurate to say that Disney reflects our aesthetic back to us. Disney's many mutilations of history and body are coextensive with the world out-

Pachuco Mickey

side. EPCOT is a dream of the postmodern, a late twentieth-century chronotope. EPCOT is a giant library, a mnemonic device, a topos for the memorization of "facts" and a site for a kind of inductive association that threatens to run away with itself.[2]

Walt Disney's favorite project, EPCOT, the Experimental Prototype Community of Tomorrow, was envisioned to be a continually evolving paean to "the ingenuity and imagination of American free enterprise" and was "to take its cue from the new ideas and new technologies that are now emerging from the creative centers of American industry" (Birnbaum 1986, 101). Walt fantasized a precisely controlled city filled with carefully selected residents; instead, his heirs created an exposition that fills with approximately 60,000 "guests" for up to fourteen hours a day, a teaching machine for corporate capitalism. Shaped like a giant hourglass, EPCOT is a scientific origin story that ends in a techno-capital utopia at Future World and what Robert Sanchez has come to call a culti-multural[3] collage at World Showcase. In World Showcase, France, China, and Canada's Circle Vision-360 travelogues equate countries with landscape while the American Adventure presentation constructs an "American history" as metanarrative for the whole of EPCOT.

Although Walt Disney's vision for EPCOT was something far different from its reality, its heart is a Disney heart, seductive, exhilarating and deeply problematic.

EPCOT delivers a body blow, a somatic experience. Disney's currency at EPCOT is the simulacrum;[4] its integrating medium is film and its pleasure is sensory.[5] Film is folded into every experience at EPCOT, but the simulacrum is the ground of this experience, and our bodies traverse this ground again and again. EPCOT taxes physical resources as it tugs at associations and remembrances. Simultaneously exhausted by the sheer size of the space and the complexity of the display, her senses disoriented and intellect massaged, Disney's guest surrenders. The doors of perception are a prime target for Disney. Through these doors, EPCOT pleasures and pains the body.[6] Delivering soma without sex, Disney has created a library that deploys simulacra in the service of a culti-multural, technocratic, utopian landscape.[7] We are all bound in some way to the field of pleasure exploited at Disney World. This is a library that relies on simulacra to create its narratives and soma to capture its audience while rigorously suppressing race, gender, and class.[8]

While Disney ideology permeates everything it produces and is especially obvious at its parks, making money at Disney is predicated on delivering pleasure, not ideology. And while pleasure and ideology cannot be centrifuged apart at present, the Disney corporation would dump its cultural ideology tomorrow if it thought that ideology was reducing profit. Both its simulacra and guests are configured and refigured according to its ideology, but it is a mistake to assume that Disney's ideology represents a radical departure from the American norm. Its appeal is based on careful attention to centrist values.[9]

The library of the future will take on a profoundly different materiality, appearing more and more like EPCOT.[10] The shelf as a method of storage is *passe*. Film becomes potent in an electronic archive in a way it could not have been earlier. Individuals enter a virtual network of film in a kind of electronic mediation of experience; EPCOT provides a literalization of this process. Film and body are caught together in this virtual reality.

The bodies presented here (usually as part of numerous overlapping origin stories) are beautifully crafted fictions. Disney's narratives are, like all, ideological constructs and so too are its bodies. Ironically, while the human body is absent from most of EPCOT's didactic films—natural force, landscape and edifice standing in for human agents, simulacra for human actors—the spectator's body is engaged as often as possible. If the body is intrinsic to semiosis, EPCOT is a sophisticated engine for furthering a complex set of messages aimed at pleasuring the guest's body while representing a configured and idealized male body. The bodies of people of color and women, and therefore the narratives surrounding them, are largely absent in EPCOT's displays.[11] When they are included as tokens, their agency is bleached away. They are deleted even when the narrative positively demands their participation. Disney, as the master trickster on the scene, has taken control of bodies, mutated and mutilated them without mercy in the service of his narrative. Three of EPCOT's presentations are particularly interesting in this regard: the CircleVision 360 *Wonders of China* film, the multimedia presentation *The American Adventure*,[12] and Michael Jackson's 3D film, *Captain E/O*.

WDW does not just suppress people of color and women, as does the larger world; it has a tendency to suppress anything problematic, no matter how central to European American history. This suppression is part of its pleasure contract. People spend a great deal of money in Disney parks in order to forget everyday unpleasantness and participate in a certain set of remembrances. EPCOT, produced as it was after many social changes (it opened in 1982), is more likely to acknowledge problems because history had already undergone tremendous revision in the '60s and '70s. Instead of obliterating all things negative, "The American Adventure" depicts the Great Depression as a healthy obstacle and World War II as a positively charged transformation (Fjellman 1992, 99–107).

WDW's film cannot be described with traditional vocabulary. Part of its somatic contract is to appeal to more than the visual; movement and smell are especially important. While the parks are giant technologies for the re-inscription of multiple ideological agendas, they are also sensory training grounds where millions, eventually billions of humans are being trained in an environment of sensory overload to adjust to new technologies of representation. Theme parks *à la* Disney may find a place alongside virtual reality technologies in a continuum of replicated experience in postmodern life.

WDW's intense sensory overload is preparing us for virtual reality entertainments that are already in existence but are not yet commercially available for mass consumption. These new entertainments will offer increasingly addictive bodily pleasures. WDW's 180- and 360-degree travelogues are sensory delights during which flight over a mountain, a valley, a castle, a river, or some other geographical feature or built structure in France, Canada, China, or the U.S. is replicated with enough visual cues to stimulate the sexy illusion of free flight. This sensory overload counterpoints ordinary film experience to which the postmodern audience has become somewhat immune. Disney's 360-degree, 3D and multiple screen theatres combined with sensarama and smellarama go beyond the average person's everyday film experience. The split-second timing of multiple images and sensations in many analogous mediums is intoxicating.

This mode of representation calls upon reading skills that extend beyond the visual. How is reading done at the somatic level? Disney has found the answer. It involves sound, motion, touch, and smell. Disney's outdoor sound systems are probably the best in the world; the air is filled with alternately soothing and stimulating music.

Disney uses multiple screens and multiple visual media to create displays of enormous complexity, integrating film seamlessly into other displays. Newer exhibits use off-screen space even more effectively than earlier ones. By definition, 3D film breaks the frame, but *Captain E/O* does so before the film begins by sprinkling the borders of the screen with stars that enhance the illusion of depth as the film progresses; the Muppets 3D film is preceded by a multiple video pre-show, which suggests the Muppets are moving into an "off-stage" "real" space. Inside the 3D theatre, Audio-Animatronic[13] Muppets in box seats to the right of the screen banter with the film's stars. All of this helps to wrap the spectator's body in a carefully constructed envelope of experience. This body becomes part of the narrative and is redrawn according to its dictates.

Other symbolic methodologies for breaking the frame result in complicated inclusions of the viewer/voyeur at Disney parks. At points, the spectator's body and/or representation is included in the scene, presented as part of the show, recruited as an actor or even referenced by the show, e.g., when the Muppets ironically point to each audience member in 3D and say, "All these other people think I'm talking to them but I'm really just talking to you."[14] Who is synopticoning whom at Disney?

While the "guest" gazes, s/he is under surveillance. At EPCOT, the Worldwide Information Service attendants can be summoned via a touch screen computer; while they speak directly to you, at first you do not realize that they can see you. These confusions add to the disorientation and serve to further envelop the spectator.

Another methodology for enveloping the body is CircleVision-360. These 360° travelogues become a sensory trope for freedom and pleasure that is echoed in Disney's use of water throughout the parks. Water is visual stimulus in the form of lakes, fountains, canals, pools, ponds, and even at the extraordinary water displays at "Journey to the Imagination." But water also stimulates through movement, as guests are conveyed over it in any number of vehicles; through smell, as aromas are pumped into displays; and through touch, as it contacts your skin. The sensation triggered by floating on water is a distinct pleasure Disney has not forgotten, and water scenes are key to many films, especially in CircleVision-360. Thus liquid simulacra in the form of artificial lagoons, ponds, lakes, rivers, etc., are echoes of the representations of water inside the theatres, working together to envelop the spectator.

The visitor to WDW encounters water directly. Damp air is created to enhance presentations like the "Universe of Energy"'s primeval dinosaur forest and "The Lands"'s boat ride through a hot, damp rain forest; conversely, it is withdrawn during "The Land"'s desert diorama. The Muppets' 3D film sprinkles you lightly; the "Backstage Studio Tour" at MGM includes an earthquake that causes a broken dam carefully to dampen those seated on the left side of the tram. There is so much water-based simulation at WDW that an employee was heard to announce to visitors who were being pelted by an all too frequent Florida rainstorm, "This isn't real rain. It's Disney rain" (qtd. in Fjellman 1992, 217).

From the center of EPCOT's hourglass, at the spot where Future World meets World Showcase, "China" is a quarter-mile walk[15] past "Mexico" and "Norway." "China"'s attractions are arranged in a rough circle. Passing under an ornate ceremonial gate, the pedestrian is attracted by a small footbridge just ahead and slightly to the right. It showcases a pond to the left and right of it and leads to the entrance to China's main attraction, one of two CircleVision-360° theatres at EPCOT. Housed in a building based on a section of Beijing's Temple of Heaven, the anteroom to this theatre is one of the few at EPCOT that provide seating. While guests wait for the film to begin, they can visit the museum to the left, the "House of Whispering Willows." In 1993, it was filled with a beautiful display of dragon iconography. Titled "Dragon: Ruler of the Wind and Waves," its figures have been contextualized within a stereotypical Disney narrative. An Orientalist paragraph on the center wall presents dragons as fairy tale with no hint that the dragon calls upon a spiritual tradition as subtle as the Christian Trinity.

Inside, the nineteen-minute travelogue, *Wonders of China: Land of Beauty, Land of Time*, is one of Disney's finest. Made in partnership with the China Film Co-Production Company (a subsidiary of the PRC's Ministry of Culture) and filmed in 1981–1982 during Deng Xaioping's "opening to the West," some of its aerial scenes were shot by Chinese crews while the Disney people were kept on the ground (Fjellman 1992, 238).

Uncharacteristically narrated by a guide, the eighth-century, Tang Dynasty poet Li Bai, played by actor Shich Kuan, it is much less Orientalist than it might have been. And it is stunningly beautiful. The audience is told to lean, not sit, on the supportive railings and is assured that the theatre does not move despite the distinct somatic feedback cued by the visual images. CircleVision-360 provides one of the most intense somatic effects at WDW, delivering its wallop during aerial scenes, summoning autonomic physical sensations. In this film, Chinese landscape painting is effectively juxtaposed with filmed footage of "actual" landscape. China's art and geography are one, we are told. Geographical touring via body sensation is a major methodology in CircleVision-360 and its close technological cousins.

Water is figured in this presentation not just as soothing and exciting entertainment but as a historical actor. Li Bai intones,

> It may be said that the history of the Chinese people is not written in ink but with water. Water, at times too much and sometimes not enough, it has been China's sorrow for ages. Along the 3,000 miles of the Yangtze river live and work one tenth of the population of the world; they are no longer the servants of water, but its master.

The Yangtze becomes a stand-in for thousands of years of exploitation and oppression by unnamed political actors. Dangerous water can bring us more than sensual delight, but we can contain it. This message is intrinsic to the rest of EPCOT; humans are willfully mastering the environment with the help of science and technology. It is interesting to note that water is a central trope in Chinese culture and is configured as an immense force. For once, Disney's ideological goals dovetail nicely with key elements in a cultural narrative. Nowhere else in Disney World does water threaten danger.

Ramona Fernandez

Ordinarily, Disney grossly distorts culture differences, homogenizing them into a happy culti-multural mix from which every alien element emerges Mickey-clean and ready for shopping mall consumption. It has at its disposal a vast array of techniques that neatly reinscribe difference, writing over bland diversity. From the Gobi desert, to Tibet, to Inner Mongolia, to the Forbidden City of Beijing, to Suzhou, Shanghai, Harbin, Guilin, the Yangtze, it is no accident that China's culti-multural travelogue reinscribes the east/west vocabulary of North America on the Asian continent. On the eastern coast, "Shanghai, the city of cosmopolitan delight" is presented as European and sophisticated. On the other hand, even in modern times western China is represented as filled with "traditional" Mongolian horsemen. And "the world's most inland city," Urumqi, is located in the "wilderness" of the Xinjiang Province despite the wrap-around view filled with the smoke of industrialism. Disney has managed to inscribe onto the vast Asian topos a classic North American dualism: the east signifies culture, the west, primitive nature. This beautiful film delights our senses and is more informative than the average, all the while containing China's powerful dragon, white tiger and monkey spirits in mythological discourse and understated visuals. This film suggests that China's human bodies have never suffered, and though we are told the continent has a long history, we are never introduced to it. This is not the case at EPCOT's centerpiece, "The American Adventure."

A long walk from China past Germany and Italy, "The American Adventure" is unlike any other presentation in the park or anywhere else for that matter. It combines film with Audio-Animatronic figures in one of the few traditionally styled theatres in the park. Most major attractions include a "ride-through" presentation, but in this centerpiece pavilion, the audience remains stationary while the figures and stage move. Housed in a Georgian colonial edifice built with hand-made pink clay bricks, it combines thirty-five Audio-Animatronics figures with the world's largest rear-projection screen (72 feet wide) and ten sets that rise and rotate from below (Birnbaum 1986, 93, 150–51).

The uncharacteristically "live" pre-show is delivered by the vocal group, "The Voices of Liberty," inside the rotunda. Presented by Coca-Cola and American Express, this twenty-nine–minute pageant begins with John Steinbeck's words delivered by Ben Franklin to Thomas Jefferson, "America did not exist. . . . We built America and the process made us Americans." America the topos, the chronotope, did not exist, but America the continent most certainly did. "The American Adventure" spans four centuries and begins with this erasure of Native American peoples and culture.

Pachuco Mickey

Disney takes great pains to advertise the authenticity of its simulations. The voices of many of the figures of *The American Adventure* were reproduced with painstaking attention to detail. For example, Will Rogers's actual recorded voice was used, his words edited and reedited from published quotations. Nevertheless, Disney has no qualms about writing an entire speech for Chief Joseph, the only Native American represented in this program; his lines are pure Disney except for the very famous sentence, "I will fight no more, forever!" (Fjellman 1992, 104).

The Distory includes only three African American men and three women, all Anglo, in its Audio-Animatronic narrative. No other people of color are represented during this expensive segment. Chief Joseph's sequence segues into Susan B. Anthony delivering a bland speech. She is held in check by simulacra of Alexander Graham Bell and Andrew Carnegie at the 1876 Pennsylvania Centennial Exposition. Similarly, Frederick Douglass is depicted poling through a Mississippi swamp instead of delivering speeches and meeting with political leaders in Washington. Locating him in a wilderness setting strips him of his intellectual and political persona. Later, two Audio-Animatronic African Americans share a Depression-era rural gas station porch and an unrealistically relaxed and equal dialogue with the only anonymous European American Audio-Animatronic figures in this sequence. The final segment in the main portion of the show features two Rosie-the-Riveters bemoaning the absence of men during World War II after which the penultimate "The Golden Dream" sequence begins. Thus two of the three African American men are anonymous, exactly paralleling the anonymous Rosies and European American men. This is equal opportunity simulation. Its mechanistic notion of balance only underscores the narrative's shortcomings.

Less than five minutes out of the twenty-nine, "The Golden Dream"'s series of images forgoes the expensive Audio-Animatronics simulacrum for still photos and film portraits from the twentieth century. Iconic figures and symbols fill the screen at dizzying speed while a sentimental and stirring melody once again reinforces the illusion of flying and freedom. The song's lyrics supply the only dialogue for this sequence of images. "Flying high. . . . " The viewer's associations with these familiar images supply the narrative content.

"The American Adventure" provides some evidence that Disney is sometimes forced to respond to the increasing sophistication and diversity of its audiences while remaining within the enforced limits of that same audience's literacy and cultural exposure. Because Disney's research revealed Will Rogers was not recognized by today's high school students, plans to make him the central narrator were canceled (Fjellman 1992, 105). And the recently revised "Golden Dream" sequence, which includes European American women and men of color, tries to undo some of the objectionable omissions and distortions of the earlier Audio-Animatronic segment, which could not have been reconfigured without great expense.

Unfortunately, it falls far short, reinscribing some of its earlier sins. The Vietnam War is represented by six photos that disappear so quickly they are barely registered. Forty-six individuals appear in this segment, including six African Americans, twelve women, and the only two Latinos and single Asian American to appear in the entire program. Of the twelve women, only two can be said to have had any agency, Eleanor Roosevelt and Gloria Steinem.

Because the male gaze dominates at Disney, with these two exceptions, the women represented in the American Adventure have been influential because their bodies have entertained. Even the female athletes portrayed here are representatives of sports that lend themselves to the male gaze: tennis, gymnastics, and figure skating are represented by Billie Jean King, Mary Lou Retton, and Kristi Yamaguchi. Except for Yamaguchi and the Spirit of Heritage statue (an iconic "Indian Maiden") at the right side of the stage, women of color are entirely absent from "The American Adventure" presentation. In this aspect, Distory is no different from canonized history.

Other problematic bodies are also represented so as to repress their potential political force. The heterosexuals Ryan White and Magic Johnson iconically recall AIDS, while Rock Hudson's homosexuality is diffused by Elizabeth Taylor's presence in the same frame. The juxtaposition of Walt Disney, Tinker Bell, and Albert Einstein forms a fascinating triptych of creator, invisible body and brain.[16]

This impressive and entertaining production ends with EPCOT's theme song. An omnipresent sensual pleasure at Disney World, song envelops the body and the library. Song is precisely the point.

Music "authenticates" much of the experience at EPCOT. If African American intellectualism cannot be represented here, the black minstrel can. For the only African American of any prominence at EPCOT is Michael Jackson. Another long walk around the lagoon and past Japan, Morocco, France, the United Kingdom, and Canada returns us to "Future Showcase" and the "Journey into Imagination" pavilion. Inside its Magic Eye Theatre, the fifteen-minute, 3D production, *Captain E/O*, is distinctive for several reasons. This science fiction short is the only film at WDW not produced by Disney. Created by Jackson, George Lucas, and Francis Ford Coppola, its entirely fictional nature contrasts with the didactic narrative that is standard everywhere else at EPCOT; *Captain E/O*'s purpose is ostensibly pure entertainment.[17] Jackson's affinity for Disney and his parallel ability to layer childhood onto his own adult body make him particularly suited to this scene.[18] That Jackson tropes his body constantly only adds to the complexity of his art and the thesis of this essay. In this film, Jackson is both Mickey[19] and a postmodern Peter Pan accompanied by bodies created by Lucas.

At EPCOT, exclusion is balanced by a curious choice of inclusion. When Disney decided to incorporate rival popular contemporary entertainment icons, it admitted into its domain competition for Walt's alter-ego trickster figure, Mickey (Brockway 1989). These alien figures present interesting challenges to the Disney ideology. It is no accident that the Muppets show at MGM-Disney Studios is one of the few that parodies Disney and comments on the viewer as mutual participant in a negotiation of meaning. Similarly, *Captain E/O* presents explicit challenges to the Disney monolith. While it is one thing for Disney to encase Frederick Douglass in a simulacrum in the service of Distory, it is another to admit a figure of Jackson's considerable cultural capital into its empire. This capital trails into EPCOT with his 3D image.

While Jackson's public persona deconstructs age, gender and race, the pre-show for *Captain E/O*, a filmed slide presentation, is an extended advertisement for heterosexual reproduction. Produced by Kodak, it manages to trace a male child from infancy through marriage and fatherhood without picturing a single female who has or is about to reproduce.[20] Females are babies, children, teenagers and brides, but apparently, they are not photogenic after that, despite the fact that female guests roam EPCOT in enormous numbers. Perhaps this does not so much contrast Jackson's androgyny as prepare us for it. If Michael can be so pretty, women are entirely unnecessary.

Any review of Michael Jackson's public self over more than twenty years confirms that he was always a beautiful and compelling being. Despite this, Jackson's confessed dissatisfaction with his appearance mirrors modern preoccupations with the body as perfect commodity and obviously reflects the damage heaped upon him as an abused child in a racist society.

To his ambiguously coded gender, plastic surgery and his bleached skin have now added ambiguous race. As one African American television commentator remarked, "It is almost as if racism has caused Michael Jackson to want to jump out of his skin." His transmuting body enacts and reenacts the multiple problematics of race, generation and gender. This multiply coded and unstable identity presents a problem for some of his audience. In a vigorously racist and sexist society, a shifting identity on those two axes presents dangers because it is an explicit challenge to those ideologies and the ideology of identity construction.

While Jackson's skin disease is a genetic accident, his manipulation of gender is entirely deliberate, clearly a part of his long-term artistic agenda. In his videos, Jackson has taken his own body and others' bodies through successive transmogrifications with costume and computer. Many of these mutations systematically blur boundaries between human and other species and between animal and machine. He has remade himself into Cleopatra and panther, ghoul and super-hero. The boundary confusion is well within a long tradition of African American tricksterism. Undoubtedly a conscious methodology, the cover art for his *Dangerous* album places the well-recognized trickster figure, a monkey king, over Jackson's portrait. Enacting the trickster role is a dangerous but powerful option. Michael Jackson is body and being, persona and construct. These multiple selves and conjoined aspects can be and are caught in a complex web of semiosis that disturbs some in his audience and rebounds on his material and psychic self.

Despite appearances, Jackson's metamorphosis from child to adolescent to adult was not produced by Disney or computer. A physical presence, his material body can be beaten and burned, remade under the surgeon's knife; it can succumb to disease. And at the end of 1993, can be photographed nude under the auspices of legal inquiry.[21]

But Jackson's body is also a virtual body turned into commodity and corporation. Perhaps influenced by Jackson's experience of his own fading skin, his video "Black and White" uses advanced computer techniques to seamlessly mutate a series of human faces into one another, producing a visual deconstruction of the physiognomy of race and gender. The earlier *Moonwalker* is an explicit biographical record of Jackson's public transmogrifications. Submitting numerous simulacra to increasingly extreme transmutation in this video, he becomes child again, animated cartoon, fantasmic supermobile, pachuco dance man, robot and spaceship. These cyborg selves strike back at evil and defend Michael himself against rational and irrational fans.[22] All this is strong stuff, too strong for Disney.

Nevertheless, the theme of *Captain E/O* is precisely this: transmutation. A classic David and Goliath story, it attempts magical mutation of the face of evil. *Captain E/O* does not take Jackson's methodology as far as his other productions, but it does contain identical key elements. Greek for light, E/O, in his white spacesuit with traditional Jackson military flourishes, cape and white gloves, appropriates Mickey's persona in "The Sorcerer's Apprentice" segment of *Fantasia* (1940) and, by extension, appropriates the persona of Walt himself. In *Fantasia*, a caped Mickey makes music and magic with his hands, and current depictions of Mickey in Disneyland's "Fantasmic" show depict his white gloved hands emitting magical light. Similarly, Captain E/O possesses the sorcerer-like ability to make magic from the ends of his gloved fingers, which emit laser-like energy.[23]

Jackson and Mickey intersect on other unexpected axes, which help to create other iconic similarities. Jackson has paid subtle homage to famous film dancers Fred Astaire and Gene Kelly and to the pachuco[24] style in his videos. His white suit, hat and spats in numerous scenes in *Moonwalker* are clearly influenced by his '40s Chicano style, which itself represents a complex mixed cultural interplay between African American, Hollywood, and perhaps even global fashions of the period. The white zoot suit of Jackson's *Moonwalker* video becomes a white space suit in *Captain E/O*. The "Smooth Criminal" segment of *Moonwalker* is the centerpiece of this video, clearly drawing much of its referential power from Jackson's sexual presence wrapped in an envelope of contained violence. The pachuco's sometimes feminine flourishes in a macho context, a particular sensibility, neatly describe Jackson's eclectic costumes and persona.

Although Mickey's sexuality is normally repressed, one of Mickey's costumes in the late '40s and '50s was also reminiscent of the pachuco costume. He wore spats and donned an overly large straw hat. Rather than evoking a traditional turn-of-the-century gentleman, the style is cartoonishly extreme. Disney was producing Mickey in the Los Angeles area from 1928 on. The exaggerated pachuco style had to be familiar to him. Although the 1928 sound cartoon, *Steamboat Willy*, is acknowledged to be Mickey's first public appearance, two earlier silent films, later remade with sound, had been previously rejected by distributors (Brockway 1989, 26). One of these, *The Gallopin' Gaucho*, appropriated a Latino style. And in the '90s, Mickey has donned the oversized clothing of the younger generation associated with juvenile gangs, a '90s style that itself echoes the pachuco. Mickey's persona reverberates in Captain E/O. Even Jackson's high-pitched voice recalls the mouse.

Captain E/O's crew is composed of an Ewok-like Tinker Bell named Fuzzball, a creature called Hooter appropriating Dumbo's persona in the chronotope of outer space, a two-headed furry creature named Geex whose heads are called Idy and Ody, an animated robot called Major Domo who turns into a drummer, and a Minor Domo who becomes an electronic synthesizer. Fuzzball plays the string base while Hooter plays the synthesizer, and Captain E/O turns into a song-and-dance man. The pleasure of this presentation largely rests on the titillation of 3D and the enjoyable confusion of ambiguously coded bodies. These creatures and machines are "humanoids" who blur the boundaries between animal and machine. They represent intertextual references to Disney, Lucas and Jackson productions. The signifyin' monkey is alive and well within Jackson's work, and Jackson is completely within the tradition Henry Louis Gates has documented.

Mapping is central to our experience at Disney World, so it is consistent that sensaround travelogues provide a set of geographic maps. When our maps are very tentative as in "The Wonders of China," Disney has thoughtfully provided a guide. "The American Adventure" and its Audio-Animatronics provide another set of maps of American history carefully calculated to remain within Disney ideological outlines. But Michael Jackson in *Captain E/O* provides us with an alternate map, one that makes the semiotics of the body explicit while simultaneously deconstructing and pleasuring through transmogrification.

Is it coincidence that as the film begins Hooter has eaten the map provided by Central Command? Like the map provided to Captain E/O by Central Command, Disney enforces a map, but both are myopically unaware that a trickster like Michael can do without one in a pinch. Indeed, Captain E/O arrives at his destinations sans the ingested map. Tricksters have the ability to chart their own trajectory. One of the pleasures at Disney is precisely this: the spectator's ability to make an original map. Because Disney has affected everyday reality to an astonishing degree and has meticulously tailored its product to appeal to those who accept a normalized American version of culture, those who are experienced negotiators of that everyday map have attained some degree of power to enjoy Disney while they subvert its meanings for themselves.

Those who are excluded for any reason must regularly draw alternative maps, rewrite narratives to move from a place of invisibility to imaginative inclusion. This is precisely what they do everyday: live lives of complex negotiation within a simulated and distorted landscape. All of us have the potential to make another fruitful map. Disney cannot stop this. The ability to read critically is hardwired into the human organism. Jackson, as an alternate trickster on the scene, has created a countertext to Disney's master narrative. In *Captain E/O* and his other productions, Michael Jackson's musical talents are equated with his magic and are key to his alternate readings and writings. The film portrays E/O as possessing the power to transform the dystopian, Dark Star genre planet into a colorful, sylvan landscape through music and dance. E/O's mission is to find the Supreme Leader and present her with a gift that turns out to be music and dance. These talents amount to the magical ability to transform her and her minions from colorless cyborgs[25] into a racially mixed cadre. It is certainly no accident that Michael Jackson as Captain E/O sings, "We are here to change the world" in a presentation in the techno-capitalist utopian heart of Disney World. Neither is it an accident that the viewer, who is largely white and middle class, hears as one of the few intelligible, oft repeated and last lines of this ear-splitting film, "You are just another part of me."

Jackson is singing to the Supreme Leader, played by Angelica Huston, who is costumed as a white-faced, medusan postmodern cyborg, a machine encased in a body, one of the few female figures of prominence in the entire park. The transformation of her guards and soldiers from "Borg"-like minions into dancers, many of whom are regulars in Jackson's videos, precedes the Supreme Leader's unexpected mutation into a darkly tanned woman in a rainbow-colored gown. The figures before us become people of color wrapped in rainbows. Even Jackson's costume and the background color scheme recall Jesse Jackson's rainbow coalition. Whatever the liberal tendencies of Michael Jackson's ideology, these depictions represent a radical departure from the rest of the narrative in the park. And whatever the problematics of his inclusion as a "pure" entertainer at didactic EPCOT, his interventions are not unconscious. Whether they amount to an effective counterpoint is another question.

It would be unwise to rail against Disney for creating this simulated experience as if he and his corporation invented the human propensity to enjoy replication. Representation is a pre-historic activity and pleasure. The pleasure of representation seems to stitch together the somatic and the intellectual. As our technologies for representation evolve, the complexities of the issues concerning them seem to evolve. It may be that our understanding of these issues is still rudimentary. Analyses that mark an irremediable distinction between pre- and post-technological representation name profound changes, but they characteristically are not helpful when it comes to discussing lineage.

It might be argued that the "Age of Mechanical Reproduction" has produced powerful images precisely because humans have long been prepared to accept representations as pleasurable and useful. Leslie Marmon Silko's Native American storyteller, in her short story of the same name, whose narrative occupies many times the "real" time the action would presumably take, and the virtual display that attempts to simulate experience in "real" time with "real" bodily experience, are mirror images of one another. Both Silko's storyteller and the virtual reality display are utilizing representational techniques aimed at "transporting" us somewhere else. Disney delights us for ancient reasons while its ideology and corporate structure propagandize our social selves, educate our imaginations, and appropriate our bodies. May Pachuco Mickey strike back soon.

Notes

1. Two hundred eighty-four miles of raw footage have been edited to fourteen. To see all the film in one day would require viewing a mile of film an hour.

2. If you have not visited central Florida, it is crucial to realize that this state has ceded forty-three square miles to the Disney Corporation. Within the Disney zone, Florida's Orange County does not have the legal right to challenge land use or to set fees for increased water, sewer or other services. Disney advertising points out that WDW, which is four miles wide and eleven miles long, is roughly the size of San Francisco or twice the size of Manhattan Island. A more interesting comparison might be to seven-mile-wide and ten-mile-long Washington, D.C., which covers sixty-nine square miles. D.C. and Disney are America's major pilgrimage sites. The developed portion of WDW covers eight square miles and includes EPCOT (at 232 acres more than twice the size of California's Disneyland); the Magic Kingdom (98 acres); the Disney-MGM Studios (135 acres); numerous resort complexes, including Contemporary Resort, a fifteen-story hotel that admits the monorail into its lobby; Polynesian village resort; the Grand Floridian Resort; the postmodern Dolphin and Swan hotels; three golf resorts; a campground resort, Fort Wilderness; six major hotels not owned by Disney; two water games resorts, River Country and Typhoon Lagoon; an endangered species reserve, 11-1/2-acre Discovery Island; a 7,500-acre nature preserve; facilities for boating, fishing, and horseback riding; a conference center; six lakes; a shopping center; a night club complex, "Pleasure Island"; and more. Thirty-five square miles of WDW are undeveloped and valued at six hundred fifty million dollars.

Shaped like a giant hourglass, EPCOT is divided into Future World and World Showcase. Guests enter through the lower half of the hourglass at a spot coded "Spaceship Earth," EPCOT's trademark geosphere, named for Buckminster Fuller's concept. "Future World" is comprised of seven major pavilions; each is an arcade composed of dozens of dioramas arranged in every conceivable manner. All are underwritten by major corporations and dedicated to purveying overlapping corporate-technological origin stories directed toward fostering an acceptance of a bureaucratized, capitalistic utopia. Each of these arcades offers a unique "ride" through a main exhibit. Often the main exhibit is a film, followed by any number of dioramas, organic and inorganic. When one of these "attractions" ends, the "guest" is ejected into a simulated landscape that iconically echoes the main presentation.

The "upper" half of the hourglass, World Showcase, is composed of more modest arcades arranged around a forty-acre lagoon. Meant to "capture" Mexico, Norway, China, Germany, Italy, "America," Japan, Morocco, France, the United Kingdom, and Canada, these too are underwritten by corporations from the countries involved. Each exists as a travelogue and a major corporate advertisement. Significantly, no country south of twenty degrees north latitude is represented.

Disney World is growing constantly, all the while increasing its revenues proportionately. Since I first visited the "park" in 1987, it has made additions totaling at least 1.4 billion dollars. A partial list of plans for the near future includes a new Tomorrowland (1996) in the Magic Kingdom, a new 3D movie (1994), a "Journeys in Space," a Russian and a Switzerland showcase in EPCOT, three new attractions at Disney-MGM Studios, four major new resorts, a Disney Institute, a wedding chapel, and a residential town named "Celebration." Any analysis of Disney World is hampered by the need to describe this immensity at least in outline.

The roots of Disneyland and Disney World lie in Walt's fascination for railroads. After building a steam engine and half-mile track in his yard and after the Disney Studio property proved too small to accommodate engines from San Francisco's 1915 Pan American Fair, he turned his attention to the creation of Disneyland. Thus, the Disney park connection to expositions begins here at the foundation of his parks and is echoed in his contributions to the 1964 New York World's Fair. The first fully realized Audio-Animatronics figures were produced for four displays at that fair, Ford Motor Company's "Magic Skyway," General Electric's "Progressland," Pepsi Cola's "It's a Small World," and "Great Moments with Mr. Lincoln" for the Illinois pavilion. Versions of these last three are still on display at Disneyland and Walt Disney World (Finch 1975, 145).

3. The term "culti-mutural" is a coinage of "robo-raza II" Robert Sanchez put into wide circulation by Guillermo Gomez-Pena. It attempts to name the problematics of multicultural discourses that seek to encapsulate issues of race and ethnicity in sanitized and static narratives of liberalism (e.g. Gomez-Pena 1992). In the New World (B)order, all traditional borders and categories have been destroyed. "Culti-mutural" is what came before.

4. By simulacrum/simulacra, I mean to conjure both the simple denotation of an image or representation of something and also the postmodern connotation of a representation that has been split from its original and has attained the status of "real" in and of itself. My use of this term follows Baudrillard. "Simulation is no longer that of a territory, a referential being or substance. It is the generation, by models, of a real without origin or reality: a hyperreal" (1988, 166). For Baudrillard, "No longer does the code take priority over or even precede the consumer object. The distinction between object and representation, thing and idea are no longer valid" (5–6). In their place, Baudrillard fathoms a strange new world constructed out of models or simulacra that have no referent or ground in any "reality" except their own. I am not, however, as cynical about this phenomenon as is Baudrillard.

5. The hands-on exhibits at the "Wonders of Life" pavilion are labeled a "Sensory Funhouse."

6. The film *Jurassic Park* makes the connections between theme parks and bodies all the more explicit. While the body is pleasured at Disney World, it is ravaged at Jurassic Park. This is not as clear in the novel as it is in the film, largely because the bodies on the screen partake of virtuality. One subtext of this essay is the violence of exclusion. A favorite line from *Jurassic Park* illustrates this dichotomy, "When the 'Pirates of the Caribbean' breaks down, the pirates don't eat the guests." Perhaps more eating occurs at Disney than this essay makes explicit.

7. Disney was the son of a turn-of-the-century socialist. Utopian socialist sentiments in books like Edward Bellamy's *Looking Backward* undoubtably influenced Disney's father. Interestingly, Michael Harrington has pointed out that such books not only contained notions about the underdog and social justice, they also contained a kind of "warm-hearted, futurist authoritarianism" (Harrington 1979; Fjellman 1992, 115–16). This is replicated in the Disney parks.

8. I agree with Cornel West that this phrase has become monotonous. It is, however, useful as a shorthand. Class, by the way, is entirely invisible at Disney World. Everyone, but everyone, is middle class in this universe. Somehow, even the third world is represented

as middle class. The problem of representing nonindustrialized countries and cultures is not just a problem of race, because for Disney the only imaginable life is a middle-class one punctuated by geniuses who make millions because they create valuable commodities.

9. Those who feel that Disney's ideology is unacceptably right wing might note that Christian Fundamentalists find it objectionable. It depicts reproduction, evolution, science, and a secular lifestyle as "good" and "true." There is evidence that Jim and Tammy Baker's Christian theme park was constructed as an alternative to Disney parks.

10. Stephen Fjellman has said, "I hope WDW becomes the important museum representing the historical period when commodification ruled. People can bring their children to see what life was like in those dangerous days" (1992, 17). He continues, "The Critics Have Only Interpreted Walt Disney World, in Various Ways; the Point, However, Is to Make It into a Museum" (403). Disney paid Neil Postman and twenty-nine other consultants to make recommendations regarding improvements at EPCOT. Postman found the task hopeless but observed that EPCOT is perhaps America's most popular museum. The subtext of this essay is: What does it teach and how can we read it?

11. Disney has taken special pains to attract African Americans in recent years. Special advertising in publications like *Ebony* has paid off. My last visit confirmed that African Americans are visiting EPCOT in greater numbers. They seem to enjoy it as much as anyone else. So too do the vastly underrepresented people of color and females who visit EPCOT. These groups have been trained to accept underrepresentation in their entertainments and educational materials. Disney is careful not to offend African Americans by releasing *Song of the South* in the U.S., but that does not prevent it from releasing it in Japan where it fosters American-style racism abroad.

12. "The American Adventure" is the only pavilion that does not in its nomenclature metonymically confuse pavilion with country. Thus, we do not visit the Canadian pavilion, we visit Canada.

13. "Audio-Animatronic" is one of the neologisms coined by the Disney organization. It names Disney's own brand of "robotic" figure. These simulacra are not robots; they are "lifelike" simulations that are part of numerous theatrical presentations at his parks. Most Americans have seen these figures even if they have not been to the parks.

14. Thanks to Ivan Karp for drawing my attention to the Muppets' self-referential criticality and Disney parody.

15. "The World Showcase" promenade is about 1.3 miles around its forty-acre lagoon.

16. A portrait of Einstein is on display in the pavilion's Heritage Manor gift store. Labeled "America's greatest scientist," his outrageous appropriation is embarrassingly counterpointed just three feet away by a racist display of knickknacks trivializing slavery.

17. It is due for replacement in 1994. This decision was made before any legal action and the ensuing media spectacle concerning Jackson's alleged child molestation. It replaces an earlier 3D film, *Magic Journeys*, which is now shown in The Magic Kingdom and is itself due for replacement in 1994.

18. Jackson's personal obsession with the Disney parks is well known. He keeps a suite filled with his Disney memorabilia at Walt Disney World (Fjellman 1992, 442).

19. The parallels between Michael Jackson and Mickey are substantial and are worthy of a separate essay. No doubt the Disney Corporation is aware of these parallels. These include the white gloves, the benign tricksterism, the constant transformation of form (Mickey's physical appearance has been constantly updated in subtle reconfigurations). Susan Willis (1991) has pointed out that Jackson moves like Mickey, that both are rubbery and seemingly without skeleton. And while Michael is a bad boy trickster gone cyborg in many of his video productions, Captain E/O is introduced to the audience as simultane-

ously infamous and inept: "The Command considers us a band of losers. We're gonna show them we're the best. If we don't, we'll be drummed out of the corps." Shades of Mickey's understated and underrecognized competence.

Jackson's affection for and identification with mice dates to his childhood when he turned a household rodent into a pet. Disney is said to have tamed a field mouse when he lived in Kansas City (Brockway 26).

20. Thanks to Lynda Haas for cuing me in to this while we watched it together.

21. It is not appropriate or even relevant to question Jackson's veracity regarding his descriptions of his illness. Neither is Jackson's guilt or innocence regarding these legal matters relevant. While important moral questions are at issue here and should not be minimized, what counts on the ground at EPCOT is Michael Jackson's cultural capital. As that changes, so do the meanings guests make out of his figure.

22. In "Speed Demon," a particularly funny claymation sequence, Jackson is pursued by two nerdy and obese teenagers who ask him to autograph their tummies. An animated Statue of Liberty provides the commentary, "America, land of the brave, home of the weird."

23. One of the most popular new attractions at Anaheim's Disneyland is "Fantasmic," which presents "Sorcerer Mickey's" powers as emanating from his light-filled gloves.

24. Most famous for the zoot-suit riots of 1943 in Los Angeles, the pachuco was a distinctly American type that has been portrayed in Luis Valdez's *Zoot Suit* and Edward Olmos's *American Me* and surfaces again in Spike Lee's *Malcolm X*. The pachuco adopted a dandified and exaggerated style of dress centered around his dramatic suit. The origin of the style is uncertain, but it may have been invented at the close of the nineteenth century. Some believe it derived from Clark Gable's dress in *Gone with the Wind* (see Mazon 1984, 1–7).

25. They are very similar in appearance to the Borgs in *Star Trek: The Next Generation*.

References

Baudrillard, Jean. 1988. *Jean Baudrillard*. Stanford: Stanford University Press.

Birnbaum, Steve. 1986. *Steve Birnbaum Brings You the Best of Walt Disney World*. New York: Houghton Mifflin Company.

Brockway, Robert W. 1989. "The Masks of Mickey Mouse: Symbol of a Generation." *Journal of Popular Culture* 22(4): 24–34.

Finch, Christopher. 1975. *The Art of Walt Disney: From Mickey Mouse to the Magic Kingdom*. New York: Abrams.

Fjellman, Stephen M. 1992. *Vinyl Leaves: Walt Disney World and America*. Boulder: Westview Press.

Gomez-Pena, Guillermo. 1992. "The New World (B)order." *High Performance*, Fall: 59–65.

Harrington, Michael. 1979. "To the Disney Station: Corporate Socialism in the Magic Kingdom." *Harpers*, January.

Mazon, Maurice. 1984. *The Zoot-Suit Riots: The Psychology of Symbolic Annihilation*. Austin: University of Texas Press.

Silko, Leslie Marmon. 1981. *The Storyteller*. New York: Seaver Books.

Willis, Susan. 1991. *A Primer for Daily Life*. New York: Routledge.

Contributors

BRIAN ATTEBERY has written two books and many articles about science fiction and fantasy, and is editor, along with Ursula K. LeGuin, of *The Norton Book of Science Fiction*. He directs the American Studies Program at Idaho State University, where he is a Professor of English. His book *Strategies of Fantasy* received awards from the Mythopoeic Society and the International Association for the Fantastic in the Arts.

ELIZABETH BELL, performer, director, and Assistant Professor of Communication at the University of South Florida, teaches courses in performance of literature, oral tradition, and women and communication. She has published articles on feminism and performance theory and on organizational folklore in *Text and Performance Quarterly*.

CLAUDIA CARD is a Professor in the Department of Philosophy at the University of Wisconsin and Faculty Affiliate in Women's Studies and Environmental Studies. She is the author of *Lesbian Choices* and editor of *Feminist Ethics* and *Adventures in Lesbian Philosophy*. She has published more than fifty articles and reviews and serves on the editorial boards of several journals. Her research interests include ethics, social and political philosophy, feminist philosophy, and lesbian culture.

CHRIS CUOMO is an Assistant Professor of Philosophy and Women's Studies at the University of Cincinnati and is currently a Rockefeller Postdoctoral Associate in the Department of Science and Technology Studies at Cornell University. Unlike many of her friends, as a young girl she did not have a crush on Julie Andrews.

RAMONA FERNANDEZ completed her doctorate in History of Consciousness at University of California Santa Cruz and is Professor of English at Sacramento City College. One chapter of her soon to be published dissertation, *Imagining Literacy*, focuses on the cultural literacy enforced by EPCOT Center at Disney World; another chapter focuses on The Smithsonian Institution as a material encyclopedia of culture.

HENRY A. GIROUX is the Waterbury Chair Professor in Education at Penn State University. He is the author of numerous books and articles. His most recent books include *Border Crossings* and *Disturbing Pleasures*.

LYNDA HAAS is an Assistant Professor in the Writing Program at Ithaca College. She is book review editor of *Journal of Advanced Composition* and is currently working on a book-length study on feminism, cultural studies, and writing theory.

ROBERT HAAS is the guest editor of a special edition of the journal *Post Script*, dedicated to the films of David Cronenberg. He is co-editor of the forthcoming book *The Haunted Mind: The Supernatural in Victorian Literature*. He currently serves on the Board of the International Association for the Fantastic in the Arts.

SUSAN JEFFORDS is Chair of Women's Studies and Professor of English at the University of Washington. She is author of *Hard Bodies: Hollywood Masculinity in the Reagan Era* and *The Remasculinization of America: Gender and the Vietnam War*, and co-editor of *Seeing Through the Media: The Persian Gulf War*.

D. SOYINI MADISON is an Assistant Professor of Communication Studies at the University of North Carolina at Chapel Hill. She holds a doctorate from Northwestern University and served as academic director of the 1990–91 joint Duke–UNC Center for Research on Women Project, "integrating women of color into the curriculum." She teaches classes in the literature and culture of women of color. She has edited *The Woman That I Am: The Literature and Culture of Contemporary Women of Color*, and has written several journal articles and book chapters.

SUSAN MILLER is Professor of English and of Writing at the University of Utah. She teaches rhetorical and composition theory, cultural studies, and writing. Her books include *Rescuing the Subject* and *Textual Carnivals: The Politics of Composition*, which won both the MLA/Mina Shaughnessey prize and the NCTE/College Communication and Composition prizes for best book in composition theory.

PATRICK D. MURPHY, Professor of English, teaches graduate courses in critical theory, multicultural literature, and environmental literature. He is also author of *Understanding Gary Snyder* and *Literature, Nature, and Other*, and is editor and co-editor of seven other books, including *Essentials of the Theory of Fiction* and *Critical Essays on American Modernism*. He edits the journal *ISLE: Interdisciplinary Studies in Literature and Environment*.

DAVID PAYNE is Associate Professor of Communication at the University of South Florida. He is author of *Coping with Failure: The Therapeutic Uses of Rhetoric*, and has published monographs and book chapters dealing with rhetorical analysis of popular film and media culture.

GREG RODE is a Ph.D. candidate in Rhetoric and Composition in the University of Utah Writing Program's interdisciplinary graduate program.

LAURA SELLS teaches communication and women's studies at the University of South Florida. She is currently managing editor of *Hypatia: A Journal of Feminist Philosophy*. She has published in *Hypatia* and *Text and Performance Quarterly*, and is finishing her dissertation on a feminist critical rhetoric of the body.

JACK ZIPES is Professor of German at the University of Minnesota and has previously held professorships at New York University, the University of Munich, the University of Wisconsin, and the University of Florida. In addition to his scholarly work, he is an active storyteller in public schools and has worked with children's theaters in France, Germany, Canada, and the United States. His major publications include *The Great Refusal: Studies of the Romantic Hero in German and American Literature, Political Plays for Children, Breaking the Magic Spell: Radical Theories of Folk and Fairy Tales, Fairy Tales and the Art of Subversion, The Trials and Tribulations of Little Red Riding Hood, Don't Bet on the Prince: Contemporary Feminist Fairy Tales in North America and England, The Brothers Grimm: From Enchanted Forests to the Modern World*, and *Fairy Tale as Myth/Myth as Fairy Tale*. He has also translated *Beauties, Beasts and Enchantments: French Classical Fairy Tales* and *The Complete Fairy Tales of the Brothers Grimm*, and edited *Spells of Enchantment: The Wondrous Fairy Tales of Western Culture* and *The Outspoken Princess and the Gentle Knight*. He co-edits *New German Critique*, a journal of interdisciplinary studies, and *The Lion and the Unicorn*, a journal dealing with children's literature, and has written numerous articles for various journals in the United States, Great Britain, Germany, Canada, and France.

Index